T0329891

Understanding Systemic Risk in Global Financial Markets

The Wiley Finance series contains books written specifically for finance and investment professionals as well as sophisticated individual investors and their financial advisors. Book topics range from portfolio management to e-commerce, risk management, financial engineering, valuation and financial instrument analysis, as well as much more. For a list of available titles, visit our website at www.WileyFinance.com.

Founded in 1807, John Wiley & Sons is the oldest independent publishing company in the United States. With offices in North America, Europe, Australia and Asia, Wiley is globally committed to developing and marketing print and electronic products and services for our customers' professional knowledge and understanding.

Understanding Systemic Risk in Global Financial Markets

ARON GOTTESMAN
MICHAEL LEIBROCK

WILEY

Published by John Wiley & Sons, Inc., Hoboken, New Jersey.
Published simultaneously in Canada.

For general information on our other products and services or for technical support, please contact our Customer Care Department within the United States at (800) 762–2974, outside the United States at (317) 572–3993, or fax (317) 572–4002.

Wiley publishes in a variety of print and electronic formats and by print-on-demand. Some material included with standard print versions of this book may not be included in e-books or in print-on-demand. If this book refers to media such as a CD or DVD that is not included in the version you purchased, you may download this material at http://booksupport.wiley.com. For more information about Wiley products, visit www.wiley.com.

Library of Congress Cataloging-in-Publication Data:

Names: Gottesman, Aron, 1970– author. | Leibrock, Michael, 1966– author.
Title: Understanding systemic risk in global financial markets : a professional guide
    to accounting arbitrations / Aron Gottesman and Michael Leibrock.
Description: Hoboken, New Jersey : Wiley, [2017] | Series: Wiley finance series; 1935 |
    Includes bibliographical references and index. |
    Identifiers: LCCN 2017010796 (print) | LCCN 2017023709 (ebook) |
    ISBN 9781119348542 (pdf) | ISBN 9781119348467 (epub) |
    ISBN 9781119348504 (cloth : alk. paper) | ISBN 9781119348542 (ePDF)
Subjects: LCSH: Financial risk management. | Financial crises. | Risk. |
    Financial institutions.
Classification: LCC HD61 (ebook) | LCC HD61 .G67 2017 (print) |
    DDC 332/.0415—dc23
LC record available at https://lccn.loc.gov/2017010796

Cover Design: Wiley
Cover Images: (top) © jijomathaidesigners/Shutterstock; © arosoft/Shutterstock;
    (bottom) © NPFire/Shutterstock

Printed in the United States of America.

10 9 8 7 6 5 4 3 2 1

ML

To my wife, Roseann, and my children,
Jaclyn, Victoria, and Michael

AG

In memory of my mother, Susan Rachel Raizel
Gottesman z'l

Contents

Preface

This book provides an in-depth introduction to systemic risk. Systemic risk is the risk that developments in the financial system will disrupt financial stability and the economy. We've written this book because the topic of systemic risk is arguably the most critical issue facing the financial services industry today and one whose impact can spill over into the broader economy with devastating effect on individual consumers and investors.

The Credit Crisis of 2007–2009 was an important catalyst for this book. Yet financial crises have been occurring for centuries, often driven by very similar factors to the Credit Crisis of 2007–2009. One of our objectives is to help you develop a deep understanding of systemic risk through meaningful exploration of the lengthy history of crises and the commonalities across the crises.

We also feel there is a need for systemic risk to be viewed by practitioners as a distinct risk discipline, one that can be analyzed and monitored in an organized and repeatable fashion, much like longstanding risks such as market risk, credit risk, and operational risk have been for decades. Hence, another of our objectives is to provide you the contours of the discipline of systemic risk.

This book can be used either as an introductory text or as an accompaniment to a quantitative treatment of risk. We do not assume that the reader has sophisticated understanding of finance or math, nor have we assumed that he or she has hours to decipher our arguments. Instead, this book provides straightforward, plain-talking explanations that are directly related to those issues that matter most to practitioners. Audiences for this book include:

- Individuals and university students learning about risk management for the first time who do not have extensive math or finance backgrounds.
- Practitioners in "middle-office" and "back-office" roles in financial institutions, such as those in risk management, operations, technology, information security and compliance that require a broad understanding of the types of risks posed by systemically important financial institutions and who have a need to identify such risks to do their jobs.

■ Practitioners, regulators, and academics who want to understand how regulation and clearinghouses function as risk-mitigating utilities for the financial industry.

This book consists of 16 chapters and an appendix. Here is a brief summary of the material that is covered in each chapter.

The first three chapters of this book introduce the concept of systemic risk and explore its history. *Chapter 1* provides a high-level introduction to the topic of systemic risk, including definitions provided by industry, academic, and regulatory experts, and explains the importance of enhancing understanding of systemic risk. *Chapter 2* provides a summary of prior systemic events and identifies common drivers of these events based on several hundred years of evidence. *Chapter 3* provides an overview of the events surrounding the Credit Crisis of 2007–2009, which had a devastating impact on the both the financial industry and economies of the United States and Europe.

Chapters 4–6 delve deeper into systemic risk. *Chapter 4* explores one of several theories that help explain why financial crises have been occurring for centuries, including those that address economic cycles, behavioral biases, and the role the human brain plays in risk taking and decision making. *Chapter 5* discusses the critical role that data plays in the effective monitoring of systemic risks, including key industry advancements such as the Legal Entity Identifier and the creation of the Office of Financial Research, aimed at addressing certain information gaps that contributed to the Credit Crisis of 2007–2009. *Chapter 6* defines macroprudential and microprudential oversight and offers important distinctions between the two regulatory oversight approaches.

Chapters 7 and 8 introduce regulatory regimes in various jurisdictions. *Chapter 7* provides an introduction to U.S. financial regulation and the approaches of the various U.S. regulators and introduces the Dodd-Frank Act of 2010. *Chapter 8* turns to international regulatory regimes, providing an introduction to several key international regulators and standards that facilitate international approaches and coordination.

Chapters 9–14 explore in detail many elements of how systemic financial risk is managed. *Chapter 9* delves into the designation of entities as systemically important, including Systemically Important Financial Institutions (SIFIs), Systemically Important Financial Market Utilities (SIFMUs), and Globally Systemically Important Banks (G-SIBs). *Chapter 10* explores the Volcker Rule of the Dodd-Frank Act, which sets prohibitions, requirements, and limitations in relation to the trading and private fund activities of banking entities and systemically risky non-bank financial companies. *Chapter 11* provides an introduction to counterparty credit risk, and studies sources of counterparty credit risk and how counterparty credit risk is managed. *Chapter 12* explores Title VII of the Dodd-Frank Act, which works to reduce the counterparty exposure faced by participants in the OTC derivatives market through setting mandatory clearing and other requirements. *Chapter 13* explores the Basel Accords—multinational accords that set minimum capital requirements for banks—that were established in order to strengthen the soundness and stability of the international banking system. *Chapter 14* studies the concept of "lender of last resort," including its benefits, risks, various views of its function, and its application.

Chapters 15 and 16 tie together the concepts explored throughout this book. *Chapter 15* introduces the topic of interconnectedness, explains how this risk manifested itself during the Credit Crisis of 2007–2009, and illustrates the ways in which interconnectedness has become a key consideration in several post-crisis regulatory developments. *Chapter 16* looks ahead to the outlook and likelihood of future systemic events and includes a number of recent examples of top systemic concerns as published by several large financial institutions and regulatory bodies.

This book also includes an appendix that provides a detailed taxonomy and literature review of some of the key quantitative models that are used to measure systemic risk in different ways.

To allow you to test your understanding, each chapter concludes with a number of *Knowledge Check* questions, the solutions to which are provided in the appendix. The *Knowledge Check* questions can be used to ensure absorption of the material both when you learn the material for the first time and also when you review.

We hope this book provides you with a comprehensive understanding of systemic risk!

Acknowledgments

ML

I'm grateful to my former professors at Pace University's Lubin School of Business for providing me the foundation of scientific research I relied upon when completing this book. A special thanks to my co-author and doctoral advisor, Aron Gottesman, whose guidance and vision was critical to the success of this book. I'm also grateful to many former industry colleagues from whom I learned so much over the years, particularly while working together through some of the financial crises covered in this book. Finally, this book would not have been possible without the tremendous support of my wife, Roseann, and the patience of my children, Jaclyn, Victoria, and Michael.

AG

I am delighted to have had the opportunity to coauthor this book with Michael Leibrock. I have benefited tremendously from Mike's deep practitioner and academic knowledge. Thank you to the team at Wiley. Thank you to my colleagues at Pace University, including Niso Abuaf, Lew Altfest, Neil Braun, Arthur Centonze, Burcin Col, Ron Filante, Natalia Gershun, Elena Goldman, Iuliana Ismailescu, Padma Kadiyala, Maurice Larraine, Sophia Longman, Ed Mantell, Jouahn Nam, Joe Salerno, Carmen Urma, PV Viswanath, Tom Webster, Berry Wilson, and Kevin Wynne, and a special thank-you to Matt Morey. I also wish to thank Niall Darby, Stephen Feline, Allegra Kettelkamp, John O'Toole, Patrick Pancoast, Carlos Remigio, Lisa Ryan, and the entire team at Intuition. Thank you to Moshe Milevsky, Eli Prisman, and Gordon Roberts of York University and Gady Jacoby of the University of Manitoba, who helped spark my career. Thank you to my many students, from whom I've learned tremendously. Finally, thank you to my wife, Ronit, and our children, Moshe and Libby, Yakov, Raphi, Tzipora, and Kayla, for providing so much love and support.

About the Authors

Aron Gottesman is Professor of Finance and the Chair of the Department of Finance and Economics at the Lubin School of Business at Pace University in Manhattan. He holds a PhD in Finance, an MBA in Finance, and a BA in Psychology, all from York University. He has published articles in academic journals including the *Journal of Financial Intermediation, Journal of Banking and Finance, Journal of Empirical Finance*, and the *Journal of Financial Markets*, among others. He has also previously authored or co-authored several books including, most recently, *Derivatives Essentials: An Introduction to Forwards, Futures, Options, and Swaps* (Wiley Finance, 2016). Aron Gottesman's research has been cited in newspapers and popular magazines, including the *Wall Street Journal,* the *New York Times, Forbes* magazine, and *Business Week*. He teaches courses on derivative securities, financial markets, and asset management. Aron Gottesman also presents workshops to financial institutions. His website can be accessed at www .arongottesman.com.

Michael Leibrock is managing director, chief systemic risk officer, and head of Counterparty Credit Risk for the Depository Trust & Clearing Corporation (DTCC). Michael Leibrock currently serves as co-chair of DTCC's Systemic Risk Council and as chair of the Model Risk Governance Committee. He has conducted numerous newspaper and magazine interviews on risk topics, as well as several video interviews on *TabbForum.com*, which include "Building an Interconnectedness Risk Program" (Dec. 2016), "Unintended Risks of Regulations" (Dec. 2014), and "The Top Systemic Threats to the Capital Markets" (Aug. 2013). Michael Leibrock holds an MBA in Finance from Fordham University and a doctorate in Finance and International Economics from Pace University's Lubin School of Business. He has previously served as an adjunct professor at New Jersey City University and Monmouth University. Michael Leibrock's prior academic research has covered topics such as predictors of bank defaults, sovereign default analysis, and a doctoral dissertation titled "Systemic Risk and an Extension of the Black Scholes Merton Option Pricing Model for U.S. Banks."

Understanding Systemic Risk in Global Financial Markets

CHAPTER 1

Introduction to Systemic Risk

The topic of systemic risk should be of critical importance to the numerous actors and stakeholders that make up the global financial ecosystem. This includes, among others, financial institutions such as banks, investment banks, and asset managers, financial regulators, policymakers, and central banks, as well as individual investors. It is also important to the general consumer, given that systemic events have the potential of spilling over from the financial system and impacting the real economy. Many historical systemic events have led to national or even global recessions, significant loss of employment, and a spike in both corporate and personal bankruptcies and taxpayer losses. Clearly, the most widely known and recent example of a systemic event was the Credit Crisis of 2007–2009, which involved, among other events, the collapse of the U.S. residential real estate and asset-backed securities markets, as well as the bankruptcy or bailout of many globally recognizable financial institutions, including Lehman Brothers, Bear Stearns, and American International Group (AIG), among others.

Given the high-profile failure or effective failure of these long-established financial firms, combined with the fact that financial crises have occurred with far greater frequency over the last several decades, some people may assume that systemic risk is only a recent phenomenon. However, it is important to understand that systemic events have been occurring for many centuries. Some well-known and relatively recent examples of such events include the U.S. savings & loan crisis, the bursting of Japan's real estate bubble, the Latin American debt crisis, the collapse of the U.S. junk bond market, the failure of hedge fund Long-Term Capital Management, and the bursting of the dot-com bubble.

Before the Credit Crisis the topic of systemic risk was rarely discussed within the financial services industry. Furthermore, organized research on the topic was limited and occurred only within academia and the research divisions of certain financial regulators or central banks. However, given the devastating impact of this event globally and the massive response by global financial regulators, the focus on systemic risk has skyrocketed over the past five years and is now the subject of regular discussion, analysis, and monitoring by all stakeholders across the globe.

This chapter introduces the topic of systemic risk, explores the many definitions that have been published or discussed in recent years, summarizes the key drivers of historical systemic events, and explains why it is critical that this topic be further analyzed and understood.

After you read this chapter you will be able to:

- Describe the common definitions of systemic risk.
- Understand the key drivers of prior systemic events.
- Explain the different impacts a systemic event can have on the financial industry and real economy.

WHAT IS SYSTEMIC RISK?

The area of systemic risk analysis is still in its very nascent stages and there currently is no single, universally accepted definition employed by those involved in analyzing and monitoring systemic risk. Moreover, as research on this topic evolves over time, it is likely that existing definitions will morph or that new definitions will be put forth by the various constituents who have an interest in this topic. Furthermore, it is important to note that having a single definition of systemic risk is not a prerequisite for studying and enhancing one's knowledge of this topic or benefiting from some of the existing approaches to measuring and monitoring systemic risks covered in this book. To provide some context and a foundation for the remainder of this book, listed here are examples of some definitions publicly communicated in recent years by well-known regulators and academics:

- "Systemic risks are developments that threaten the stability of the financial system as a whole and consequently the broader economy, not just that of one or two institutions."[1]
- "In the context of our economic environment, systemic risk is the threat that developments in the financial system can cause a seizing up or breakdown of this system and trigger massive damages to the real economy. Such developments can stem from the failure of large and interconnected institutions, from endogenous imbalances that add up over time, or from a sizable unexpected event."[2]
- "Systemic Risk is the risk of a disruption in the market's ability to facilitate the flows of capital that results in the reduction in the growth of GDP globally."[3]

- "One or more global financial centers are mired in a severe crisis that spans two or more distinct regions, with at least three countries impacted in each region. There must also be a corresponding and significant impact on a composite GDP index."[4]
- "A risk of disruption to financial services that (i) is caused by an impairment of all or parts of the financial system and (ii) has the potential to have serious negative consequences for the real economy. Fundamental to the definition is the notion of negative externalities from a disruption or failure in a financial institution, market or instrument."[5]
- "Systemic risk emerges when the financial sector as a whole has too little capital to cover its liabilities. This leads to widespread failure of financial institutions and/or the freezing of capital markets, which greatly impairs financial intermediation, both in terms of the payment systems and in terms of lending to corporates and households."[6]
- "Credit risk, liquidity risk, market risk and operational risk are often difficult to quantify, and more so when the interaction of different types of risk leads to systemic risks. Systemic risks affect a financial system's stability when idiosyncratic shock to an individual financial institution generates contagious effects on others in the system."[7]

One common aspect of these definitions is that to be characterized as a systemic threat, the underlying risk(s) should have the potential to severely impact the financial system and real economy. In contrast to the characteristics of a systemic event, an event that might not rise to the level of a systemic risk is one that may have a significant impact on an industry sector or geographic region, but does not spill over into the broad economy. For purposes of this book we will treat the terms *systemic event* and *financial crisis* as synonymous.

SYSTEMIC RISK DRIVERS

Under the broad topic of systemic risk, there have been a wide range of causes for past events. While these events will be discussed in more detail in Chapters 2 and 3, we introduce this topic by providing some of the more common themes behind the many crises that have impacted countless countries and economies across the world.

One of the earliest recorded crises occurred in the middle of the 1200s and was referred to as a *currency debasement*,[8] which can be thought of as the predecessor to today's foreign exchange crisis or devaluation. Occurring during the Middle Ages, when metallic coins represented the primary medium of exchange, currency debasements involved the intentional significant reductions in the silver content of coins. This action helped provide a critical source of war financing for governments.

Currency crashes have been a significant source of past crises, which we will define as an annual depreciation versus the U.S. dollar or the relevant anchor currency for that time (most frequently the U.K. pound, French franc, or German deutsche mark) of 15% or more. While there are many currency crashes throughout history that exceeded this threshold, the largest single crash was experienced by Greece in 1944.

Another frequent driver of systemic events throughout history is the bursting of asset bubbles. A commonly employed definition of a bubble is a non-sustainable pattern of price changes or cash flows. Historically, many asset bubbles have been observed in the real estate sector, particularly over the past 30 years. Major real estate bubbles have burst in Japan, non-Japan Asia, and most recently in the United States, in connection with the Credit Crisis. The bursting of Japan's real estate bubble in the early 1990s led to the widespread failure of banks and a prolonged period of sluggish growth, which came to be known as the "lost decade."

It is noteworthy that bubbles in real estate and stock markets are often closely linked.[9] Three prominent examples of such linkages include (i) the fact that stock markets of many emerging market countries are heavily weighted toward real estate and construction companies, reflecting the growth stage of such nations, (ii) the fact that the wealth obtained by successful real estate investors is often invested into the stock market, and (iii) that the same high-net-worth individuals referenced in the second example deploy profits made from stock market increases into additional real estate holdings.

There are longstanding economic theories that posit asset bubbles are fueled by significant increases in the pro-cyclical supply of credit during economic booms. This "easy money" climate facilitated by central banks has contributed to a spike in investor speculation, leverage, and hence unsustainable increases in asset prices, which eventually "burst."

There have also been numerous historical financial crises brought on by the default by governments on both their external debt (e.g., default on payment to creditors under another country's jurisdiction) as well as domestic debt. There were at least 250 sovereign external defaults during 1800–2009 and at least 68 instances of default on domestic public debt. A couple of the most well-known examples of the former include Argentina's 2001 default on $95 billion of external debt and Mexico's 1994–1995 near default on local debt.[10] The negative impact on a country that defaults on its debt can be significant and long lasting. For example, it took Russia decades to finally resolve its 1918 external default with creditors. In addition, because of Greece's default in 1826, the country's access to global capital markets was very limited for the next half century.

As one of the goals of this book is to identify tools that will help financial industry participants identify the early signs of a financial crisis, it is worth noting that episodes of sovereign default have exhibited some noticeable macroeconomic trends prior to the actual default event. The average total decline in domestic GDP during the three years prior to domestic debt defaults is 8%, compared to an average decline of 1.2% for external defaults.[11]

Banking crises, another frequent driver of systemic events, may be defined as either the failure, takeover, or forced merger of one of the largest banks in each nation or, absent such corporate events, a large-scale government bailout of a group of large banks in that nation. Using this definition, there have been a tremendous number of banking crises that have occurred globally throughout history. Dating back to the year 1800, 136 countries have experienced some form of banking crisis.[12]

An important point to note is that banking crises have historically been intertwined with other categories of financial crises. For example, many banking crises have been fueled, at least in part, by the bursting of asset bubbles in real estate and national stock markets. However, many of these same bubbles were enabled by the banking sector itself as banks are often the main provider of credit and liquidity for real estate financing. This point is supported by the following statement:

> *Interconnections among financial firms can also lead to systemic risk under crisis conditions. Financial institutions are interconnected in a variety of networks in bilateral and multilateral relationships and contracts, as well as through markets.*[13]

Arguably the most important and practical benefit of studying the common drivers and details associated with previous systemic events is to learn from the past and the potential for using facts and statistics related to such events to help identify the buildup of emerging systemic threats.

WHY SYSTEMIC RISK MUST BE UNDERSTOOD, MONITORED, AND MANAGED

As previously mentioned, systemic events have been occurring for centuries and with devastating impact. Using events such as the Great Depression and the Credit Crisis as just two examples, both events led to the failure of hundreds of banks and other financial institutions in the United States and globally, deep and long-lasting global recessions, the seizing up of global credit markets, the need for massive government bailouts, and a tremendous loss of jobs in the private sector that in turn led to significant spikes in personal bankruptcies.

As we cover in more detail later in this book, there have been a multitude of causes for such events, many of which are extremely complex for several reasons. For example, what differentiates systemic risks from the more traditional forms of risk is that the former are typically classified by their impacts as opposed to their causes. Systemic risks can arise in many forms, can develop rapidly, and can be unpredictable. Another major difference is that systemic risk can involve interconnectedness of markets and industry participants, rather than a single, discrete source of risk. By its nature, systemic risk is also an extremely broad topic, subject to many different definitions, sources, and impacts. One of the reasons that systemic risk analysis has not yet evolved into a standard component of risk management practices in the financial industry is the lack of a roadmap that summarizes these many components and available tools to help support repeatable identification and monitoring processes.

Because of these significant challenges, and in consideration of the devastating effect systemic events have been shown to have on global economies, it is imperative that such risks become better understood and monitored so there is a greater likelihood they can be detected early to protect global financial institutions, the stability of financial markets, and individual taxpayers.

If history is any indicator, it is unlikely that all or even many future systemic events can be predicted ahead of time. That said, given the significant amount of data and other facts available concerning the root causes of the Credit Crisis and other financial events, this information has proven to be very helpful in the creation of models and other tools that may serve as early warning indictors in the future. In addition, as covered in detail in the second half of this book, new financial regulations have been enacted in the United States and internationally at a rate not seen since the Great Depression. Multiple new regulatory bodies and agencies have been created globally to oversee and enforce these new rules, most of which are aimed at the banking industry. In addition, financial institutions have vastly expanded their focus on systemic risk identification and mitigation.

While this clearly heightened global focus on systemic risk is certainly encouraging, the analysis and quantification of systemic risk remains a relatively nascent area. There is still a need for new and enhanced tools to assist the industry in its efforts to better understand, quantify, monitor, and mitigate systemic threats. While longstanding risk management disciplines such as credit risk, market risk, liquidity risk, and operational risk are all critically important pillars of the risk governance frameworks employed by nearly all large financial institutions, systemic risk warrants acceptance in the industry as a distinct risk discipline that can be monitored and managed in an organized fashion.

KEY POINTS

- No single, universally accepted definition of *systemic risk* exists globally.
- Although the Credit Crisis of 2007–2009 was one of the worst financial events in history, systemic risk events have been occurring for centuries, with currency crises representing one of the oldest categories of systemic risk.
- Some of the more common causes of past financial crises include currency crashes, currency debasements, bursting of asset bubbles, banking crises, and sovereign defaults.
- Even though systemic risk events have been taking place for centuries, the financial industry and regulatory bodies have only recently started to approach systemic risk identification, monitoring, and mitigation in a formal way.
- Since systemic risk events typically involve a significant dislocation in securities markets and adversely affect the real economy (e.g., recession, unemployment, taxpayer-funded bailouts, personal bankruptcies, etc.), it is critical that systemic risk drivers be understood to increase the likelihood that early warning indicators anticipate future events to minimize these negative impacts.

KNOWLEDGE CHECK

Q1.1: What development differentiates a systemic risk event from other types of financial crisis?

Q1.2: Are systemic events only a phenomenon of modern history?

Q1.3: What are the six most common causes of systemic events throughout history?

Q1.4: Significant failures within which segment of the global financial sector have fueled several of the worst systemic events in history?

Q1.5: Why is it important that the level of understanding, monitoring, and managing of systemic risks improves globally?

NOTES

1. Ben Bernanke in a letter to Senator Bob Corker, dated Oct. 30, 2009.
2. Text of the Clare Distinguished Lecture in Economics and Public Policy by Mr. Jean-Claude Trichet, President of the European Central Bank, organized by Clare College, University of Cambridge, Cambridge, Dec. 10, 2009.
3. Fouque, J.P., and Langsam J., 2013, *Handbook of Systemic Risk*. Cambridge University Press, 2013, p. xxi.
4. Reinhart, Carmen M., and Rogoff, Kenneth S., 2009, *This Time Is Different: Eight Centuries of Financial Folly*. Princeton, NJ: Princeton University Press.
5. www.fsb.org/what-we-do/policy-development/systematically-important -financial-institutions-sifis/.
6. Acharya, V.V., Pedersen, L.H., Philippon, T., and Richardson, M., 2010, "Measuring Systemic Risk." Working paper, New York University Stern School of Business.
7. International Monetary Fund, 2000.
8. Reinhart, Carmen M., and Rogoff, Kenneth S., 2009, *This Time Is Different: Eight Centuries of Financial Folly*. Princeton, NJ: Princeton University Press.
9. Kindlelberger, C.P., and Aliber, R., 2005, *Manias, Panics and Crashes: A History of Financial Crisis*, 5th ed. Hoboken, NJ: Wiley.
10. Reinhart, Carmen M., and Rogoff, Kenneth S., 2009, *This Time Is Different: Eight Centuries of Financial Folly*. Princeton, NJ: Princeton University Press, pp. 129–132.
11. Ibid.
12. Kindlelberger, C.P., and Aliber, R., 2005, *Manias, Panics and Crashes: A History of Financial Crisis*, 5th ed. Hoboken, NJ: Wiley, p. 3.
13. Acharya, V.V., Pedersen, L.H., Philippon, T., and Richardson, M., 2010, "Measuring Systemic Risk." Working paper, New York University Stern School of Business.

CHAPTER 2

How We Got Here: A History of Financial Crises

INTRODUCTION

Financial crises are far from a new phenomenon, having occurred as long as money and financial markets have been in existence. On the surface, it may appear that there is little to be learned from any event that occurred hundreds of years ago. Clearly the global financial services industry that exists today bears little resemblance to the one that existed even 50 years ago, due to changes in market structures, technological advances, the sophistication of risk analytical tools, and the highly developed nature of global financial regulatory frameworks.

It is outside the scope of this book to categorize every crisis throughout history, or to draw definitive conclusions about their primary causes. However, despite the vast differences in the way financial markets operate today, a brief review of key past events will reveal some common themes with respect to the nature and causes of such events. An understanding of these themes can assist the many actors involved in the study of systemic risk (e.g., risk managers, academics, policymakers, or regulators) to obtain a broader perspective on certain risks that have manifested themselves repeatedly throughout history and potentially identify the buildup of these risks before they become a full-fledged crisis. Consider the following remarks by well-known academics Carmen Reinhart and Kenneth Rogoff;

> Until very recently, studies of banking crisis have focused either on episodes drawn from the history of advanced countries (mainly the banking panics before World War II) or on the experience of modern day emerging markets. This dichotomy has perhaps been shaped by the belief that for advanced economies, destabilizing, multi-country financial crises are a relic of the past. Of course, the Second Great

Contraction, the global financial crisis that recently engulfed the United States and Europe, has dashed this misconception, albeit at a great social cost.[1]

After reading this chapter you will be able to:

- Cite examples of some of the most noteworthy financial crises in history.
- Explain some of the common themes behind prior systemic events.
- Understand what is meant by an "asset bubble" and describe the economic conditions that typically lead to a bubble.
- Describe which countries have been the source of most sovereign defaults in history.
- Understand the ways in which international contagion either fueled or contributed to the severity of prior financial crises, including the Great Depression.

COMMON DRIVERS OF HISTORICAL CRISES

Table 2.1 presents a timeline of select historical crises. In nearly all cases, a close examination of each of the crises listed in Table 2.1 will result in a myriad of causes. Furthermore, in all cases the occurrence of just one of the underlying events likely wouldn't have led to the full-fledged crisis that ensued. Rather, it was often the simultaneous occurrence of multiple underlying events or the spillover and linkages among multiple countries or markets that ultimately caused these systemic events to take place. Given the multitude of underlying causes and the inherent complexity of every crisis, we attempt to group such causes into higher-level themes as a starting point for trying to understand, analyze, and identify tools that might help avoid similar events in the future.

Bursting of Asset Bubbles

Table 2.1 provides several examples of asset bubbles throughout history. One definition of an asset bubble is an upward price movement of an asset over an extended time period of 15–40 months, which then implodes. Economists use the term to mean any deviation in the price of an asset, security, or commodity that can't be explained solely by fundamentals. Asset price bubbles are most often fueled by a combination of a rapid growth in the availability of credit and the irrational behavior of investors and markets.

TABLE 2.1 Timeline of Selected Historical Crises

Year	Event	County/Region	Broad Category
1636	Dutch Tulip Crisis	Europe	Asset Price Bubbles
1720	South Street Sea Bubble	Europe	Speculative Mania
1763	End of Seven Years War	Amsterdam	Asset Price Bubbles
1825	Crisis of 1825–1826	Europe/Latin America	Sovereign Default
1837	Crisis of 1836–1839	America/England	Price of Cotton
1857	Hamburg Crisis of 1857	Sweden/Hamburg	Expansion of Credit
1873	Panic of 1873	U.S., Austria, Germany	Global Contagion
1907	Panic of 1907	Global	Banking Crisis
1929	Great Depression	U.S./Europe	Banking Crisis
1977	"Big Five" Crisis	Spain	Real Estate Bubble/ Banking Crisis
1980s	Debt Crisis of the 1980s	U.S.	Sovereign Default, Currency Crash
1987	"Big Five" Crisis	Norway	Real Estate Bubble/ Banking Crisis
1990s	"Big Five" Crisis	Finland, Sweden, Japan	Real Estate Bubble/ Banking Crisis
1990s	Junk Bond Market Crash	U.S.	Asset Price Bubbles
1994	Mexican Debt Crisis	Mexico	Currency/Banking Crisis
1997	Asian Financial Crisis	Asia	Currency Crash
1998	Long-Term Capital Mgt.	U.S.	Credit
1990s	Latin American Debt Crisis	Latin America	Sovereign Default
2000	Dot-Com Tech Bubble	U.S.	Asset Bubble
2008	Credit Crisis	U.S./Europe	Asset Bubble

Although bubbles can theoretically take place with respect to any asset that has an observed value, most bubbles have tended to occur within a securities asset class, individual security, or real estate. In the past 30 years alone, major real estate bubbles have burst in Japan, non-Japan Asia, and most recently in the United States.

The following sequence of events are representative of a typical model of a financial crisis fueled by an asset bubble:

- Economic expansion/boom
- Euphoria and rapid increase in asset prices
- Pause in asset-price increases
- Distress/panic/crash

Asset price bubbles, at least the large ones, are almost always associated with economic euphoria. In contrast, the bursting of bubbles leads to a downturn in economic activity and is often associated with the failure of financial institutions, frequently on a large scale. The failure of these institutions disrupts the channels of credit, which in turn can lead to a slowdown in economic activity. As mentioned previously, bubbles in stock markets and real estate are often closely linked with three prominent examples of linkages and connections between these two asset markets:[2]

1. In many countries, and especially smaller nations and those in early stages of industrialization, a substantial amount of the stock market valuation consists of real estate companies and construction companies and firms in other industries that are closely associated with real estate, including banks.
2. Another connection is that individuals whose wealth has increased sharply because of the increase in real estate values want to keep their wealth diversified and so they buy stocks.
3. The third connection is the mirror-image of the second: the individual investors who have profited extensively tend to buy larger and more expensive homes.

Dutch Tulip Crisis: One of the earliest financial crises that was documented extensively is often referred to as the Dutch Tulip Crisis or Mania, when the prices of tulip bulbs increased by several hundred percent in the autumn of 1636. For more exotic and rare bulbs, price increases were even more dramatic.

In the mid-16th century tulips were introduced to Holland via the Ottoman Empire and quickly became a status symbol among its citizens, setting off a frenzy of speculative behavior across the country. The speculation became rampant in September 1636 as the bulbs were in their normal planting cycle and therefore could no longer be physically inspected by potential buyers who had to commit to purchases long before the spring bloom. This led to many investors purchasing bulbs at extraordinary prices that they had never seen.

> *Nobles, citizens, farmers, mechanics, footman, maid-servants, even chimney sweeps and old clothe woman dabbled in tulips.*[3]

This frenzy was accompanied by the introduction of call options that further fueled speculative buying, resulting in a 20-fold increase in prices between November 1636 and February 1637.

As traditional bank financing was not fully developed at that time, most investors used *in-kind* down payments, which included things such as tracts of land, houses, furniture, silver and gold vessels, paintings, and so on. When the prices of tulip bulbs crashed, it led to the complete loss of savings of many citizens and fueled an overall decline in the European economy with the Dutch economy suffering into the 1640s.

Dot-Com Bubble of 2000: Another more recent example of the bursting of an asset bubble was the dramatic rise and fall of Internet stocks in the late 1990s. Per one index that tracked the performance of Internet stocks, prices of this sector rose 1,000% from October 1998 to February 2000.[4] Prices started to drop in February 2000 and ultimately lost 80% of their peak value by the end of 2000, equating to approximately $8 trillion in lost market value. The Internet bubble exhibited similar characteristics of previous bubbles, including over-inflated prices driven by speculative buying, subsequent selling by insiders, short selling made easier by significant increases in asset float, and an eventual crash in prices.

Speculative Manias: Many crises throughout history can be traced to the rampant speculation by investors in any number of assets or investment opportunities. Herbert Simpson in a 1933 paper discusses the urban boom and collapse in the period 1921–30:

> *The economic history of this country is colorful with recurring speculative epochs and episodes, growing out of varying conditions and with varying effects upon our economic structure and welfare. We have had periods of gigantic speculation in western lands; periods of oil and mining speculation; periods of bank speculation; and of railroad speculation.*[5]

The term *mania* implies that investors are behaving irrationally. This contrasts with the *rational expectations* assumption, which holds that investors behave rationally and react to changes to economic variables as if they are fully aware of the long-term implications of such changes. This is an example of the long-used axiom that all available information about a company is fully reflected in its security price, as investors theoretically react immediately to any new news about the company. Many theories exist as to why investment manias occur. One example is *groupthink*, when all investors in a market change their views simultaneously and act together.

The South Sea Company of 1720: An example of an event that can be categorized as a speculative mania, which in turn led to an asset bubble, occurred in Britain in 1720. The South Sea Company had been given special rights by the British government to trade with Spain's American colonies, which resulted in an effective monopolistic position. The price of the company's stock rose 330% in a five-month period to £550. Following its success, several other companies attempted to enter this market and trade in the same stock market. The South Sea Company successfully convinced Parliament to approve what was called the Bubble Act of 1720, which prevented such firms from becoming publicly traded, further boosting their stock price to over £1,000. Insiders of South Sea Company realized the company's business opportunities did not support a price so high and started to sell, fueling a dramatic decline in the share price to below £100 before end of the year. Consider the following comment by Adam Smith about the South Sea Company crisis:

> The evils of reckless trading are always apt to spread beyond the persons immediately concerned. When rumors attached to a bank's credit they make a wild stampede to exchange any of its notes which they may hold; their trust has been ignorant, their distrust was ignorance and fierce. Such a rush often caused a bank to fail which might have paid them gradually. The failure of one caused distrust to rage around others and to bring down banks that were really solid.[6]

The Great Depression: The 1921–30 period of investment speculation in the United States was fueled mainly by growth of urban populations and wealth. The rural sections of the country had been in a state of depression throughout most of this period, and the very cities in which active real estate speculation had been carried on had been surrounded by rural populations in severe distress. It was the agricultural depression that led to shifting population, income, and wealth to the cities, in addition to the numerous other factors contributing to the urban growth of this period. The urban population of the United States increased 14.5 million in the decade 1920–30. It was this growth of urban population and wealth that provided the basis for real estate speculation.

As such, real estate, real estate securities, and real estate affiliations in some form were the largest single factor in the failure of the thousands of banks that closed their doors during the Great Depression. We discuss the Great Depression in detail in Chapter 14.

Banking Crises

Systemic events often occur not because of a single idiosyncratic event, but rather the linkages or spillovers that occur among several different segments of the financial system or global economy. A good example of such a common linkage is the prior discussions about asset booms in real estate, often fueled by speculative behavior on the part of investors, which is financed by the banking sector.

Banking crises may be defined as either the failure, takeover, or forced merger of one of the largest banks in a given nation or, absent such corporate events, a large-scale government bailout of a group of large banks in that nation. Using this definition, there have been a tremendous number of banking crises that have occurred globally throughout history. Dating back to the year 1800, 136 countries have experienced some form of banking crisis.[7]

A high rate of banking failures occurred during the Great Depression of the 1930s in the United States. Following this period of extreme global banking stress, there was a prolonged hiatus of failures between 1940 and the 1970s, after which several events such as the breakup of Bretton Woods fixed exchange rate system and a spike in oil prices led to an extended global recession and a renewal of bank failures.

The volume of bank failures during the past 30 or 40 years has been much larger in scope than in previous decades. For example, between 1970 and 2011 there have been 147 episodes of systemic banking crises around the globe and the costs to society have been substantial.[8] While not every recent banking crisis was of equal magnitude, with some representing isolated events, many have had systemic implications for a nation or even the global economy.[9]

During the 1980s, many Mexican banks failed as a result of the country's currency devaluation and credit losses to local banks. Also during the 1980s, U.S. taxpayers suffered losses of more than $100 billion due to the failure of approximately 3,000 U.S. savings & loan associations and thrift institutions. In Japan, the economy continues to recover from the collapse of its banking system in the 1990s, fueled by the bursting of asset bubbles in real estate and stocks. The Japanese banking crisis led to 25% reduction to the gross domestic product (GDP).[10] In March 2001, a bank run occurred in Argentina that led to partial withdrawal restrictions and the restructuring of fixed-term deposits to stem the outflow of funds. Lastly, the recent Credit Crisis resulted in hundreds of bank failures and set off a prolonged economic contraction in both the United States and Europe. During this crisis, the stock market in the United States fell by 42%, and the U.K. market fell by 46% (in dollar terms). Similarly, the global GDP fell by 0.8%, representing the first decline experienced in many years, while international trade fell 12%.

Sovereign Debt Crisis

There have been numerous prior crises brought on by the default by governments on both their external debt (e.g., default on payment to creditors under another country's jurisdiction), as well as domestic debt. There were at least 250 sovereign external defaults during 1800–2009 and at least 68 instances of default on domestic public debt. Perhaps the most well-known example of the former was Argentina's 2001 default on $95 billion of external debt, while a notable example of the latter was Mexico's 1994–1995 near default on local debt.

During the 500-year period ended 1799, both France and Spain could be considered serial defaulters, with these nations defaulting on their external debt on eight and six occasions, respectively (see Table 2.2). The dominance of France and Spain as serial defaulters pre-1800 may be explained by the basic fact that these countries were the only ones that had the resources and stability to engage in international trade and borrowing on a large scale.

The negative impact on a country that defaults on its debt can be significant and long lasting. For example, it took Russia decades to finally resolve its 1918 external default with creditors. In addition, because of Greece's default in 1826, the country's access to global capital markets was very limited for the next half century.

As one of the goals of this book is to identify tools that will help financial industry participants identify the early signs of a financial crisis, it is worth noting that episodes of sovereign default have exhibited some noticeable macroeconomic trends prior to the actual default event. The average total decline in domestic GDP during the three years prior to domestic debt defaults is 8%, compared to an average decline of 1.2% for external defaults. Meanwhile, inflation averages 170% during the year of a domestic default versus 33% for external debt crises.[11]

As shown in Table 2.3, Spain and France led Europe in defaults between 1800 and 2008, similar to what occurred prior to 1800. Furthermore, starting in 1800 there was a significant increase in the volume of external defaults globally. This trend may be attributed to many factors, including the development of international capital markets and the establishment of many new nations.

TABLE 2.2 European External Defaults: 1300–1799[12]

Country	Years of Default	Number of Defaults
France	1558, 1624, 1648, 1661, 1701, 1715, 1770, 1788	8
Spain	1557, 1575, 1596, 1607, 1627, 1647	6
England	1340, 1472, 1594*	2*
Austria	1796	1
Germany (Prussia)	1683	1
Portugal	1560	1

*Unclear if England's default was external or internal.

TABLE 2.3 Cumulative Defaults and Reschedulings: Europe and Latin America (Year of Independence to 2008)[13]

Country	Number of Defaults or Reschedulings	Share of Years in Default since Independence or 1800
Europe		
Spain	13	23.7%
France	9	4.3
Germany	8	13.0
Hungary	7	37.1
Austria	7	17.4
Portugal	6	10.6
Turkey	6	15.5
Greece	5	50.6
Latin America		
Venezuela	10	38.4
Brazil	9	25.4
Chile	9	27.5
Costa Rica	9	38.2
Ecuador	9	58.2
Peru	8	40.3
Uruguay	8	12.8
Mexico	8	44.6
Argentina	7	32.5
Columbia	7	36.2
Dominican Republic	7	29.0
Guatemala	7	34.4
Paraguay	6	23.0
Nicaragua	6	45.2
Bolivia	5	22.0
El Salvador	5	26.3
Panama	3	64.0
Honduras	3	27.9

Since 1800 there have been several distinct periods of high sovereign defaults:

- Napoleonic wars
- 1820s–1840s
- 1870s–1890s
- Great Depression era: 1930s–early 1950s
- Emerging markets: 1980s–1990s

INTERNATIONAL CONTAGION

Financial crises throughout history were often not an isolated event geographically. This is because countries around the world are often linked in a number of ways. Furthermore, very often crises are fueled by more than one of the categories we are discussing in this chapter. Often it is the combination of several of these drivers that ultimately leads to systemic events. As one example, during the period of 1900 to 2008, there was a high correlation between the percentage of all countries experiencing a default on their external debt and those countries that suffered a banking crisis in the same year. Some potential explanations for this linkage include:

- When a developed nation experiences a banking crisis it tends to have a substantially negative impact on global growth, which hurts exports of smaller emerging market countries, making it more challenging to service external debt.
- Banking crises in large countries tend to lead to reduced lending and capital flows to less-developed nations, which can strain their debt service capacity.[14]

Arbitrage connects national markets; the implication of the law of one price is that the difference in the prices of identical or similar goods in various countries cannot exceed the costs of transport and trade barriers. Similarly, the security markets in the various countries are also linked, since the prices of internationally traded securities available in different national markets must be virtually identical after a conversion of prices in one currency into the equivalent in other currencies at the prevailing exchange rates. Some examples of international transmission mechanisms include:

- Inflation and capital flows
- Exchange rates
- Securities prices and markets
- The gold exchange standard in the 1920s

Let's explore each of these examples.

Inflation and Capital Flows: The security and asset markets in various countries are linked by movements of money. An economic boom in one country almost always attracts money from abroad. To some extent, such capital flows depend on the extent of *globalization*. For example, high inflation rates in the United States during the 1960s and 1970s fueled a substantial capital outflow to countries such as Germany and Japan, both of which eventually suffered from inflation as their money supply increased.

Exchange Rates: Appreciation of a currency and deflation in that country's goods market or the increase in the foreign exchange value of the national currency leads to declines in the prices of internationally traded goods and to bankruptcies and the de-capitalization of financial firms. For example, from the 1997 Southeast Asian crisis one can make the following transmission connections: Thailand, Malaysia, Indonesia, Philippines, South Korea, Russia, Brazil, and Argentina.

Securities Prices/Markets: A common mechanism of international contagion is the extent to which a decline in one country's stock market leads to a similar decline or crash in one or more other countries' stock markets. For example, during the U.S stock market crashes of 1929 and October 1987, global stock markets crashed simultaneously. Investors who likely sought portfolio diversification by owning stocks in different securities markets around the world lost significant sums of money during these two events since correlations increased significantly across world stock markets.

Gold Exchange Standard in the 1920s:[15] Perhaps one of the most noteworthy and analyzed examples of international contagion occurred during the Great Depression due to the gold standard. The *gold standard* refers to a monetary system in which the standard unit of currency is freely convertible into gold at a fixed rate. The gold standard was adopted in Britain in 1821 and later in the 1870s by Germany, France, and the United States. Eventually, given large U.S. gold deposits and stock of bullion and uneven supplies of gold within nations, many countries moved to an international, rather than a purely domestic, gold standard. As a result, they began to hold U.S. dollars as a supplement to their own gold bullion reserves. The gold standard served to provide stability in the international markets for goods and services by establishing fixed prices of exchange for currencies linked to gold.

One of the effects of the international gold standard was that it created linkages between nations and could serve as a medium for transmission of financial contagion. The gold standard was put in place to provide the United States with a self-regulating tool to promote economic stability and control the U.S. money supply. The intended impact of the gold standard was to create confidence in our nation's currency as a stable store of value and to create a self-regulating mechanism to support international trade. The gold standard also was intended to limit the supply of money created by any nation and act as a control over inflation. Countries on the gold standard could not create money unless they held gold stock or other currencies in reserve that were convertible into gold. The gold standard prevented countries from inflating their way out of their debts to other nations by expanding the money supply.

The establishment of the Federal Reserve in 1913 was intended to supplement, not replace, the gold standard. The Federal Reserve Act in 1913 included a requirement that "nothing in this act shall be considered to repeal the parity provisions contained in the Gold Act of 1890." The Federal Reserve assumed many responsibilities previously undertaken by the Treasury. It had a mandate to back the U.S. currency by gold or eligible commercial, agricultural, or industrial loans, or loans secured by U.S. government securities rediscounted by member banks; loans to member banks secured by paper eligible for rediscount or by government securities; or bankers' acceptances. Outright government securities owned by the Federal Reserve did not count as collateral reserves to support the U.S. currency until the Glass-Steagall Act was passed in 1932. The amount of gold held by the Fed in excess of its reserve requirement was referred to as "free gold."

The United States held a significant amount of "free" or excess gold reserves during the 1920–1930s. This allowed the United States to grow its economy rapidly in the 1920s. During this period the United States experienced a significant increase in the supply of free gold, had rising asset prices, and could expand the money supply. Bubbles were created in several asset classes, including stocks and real estate. By 1931, the Fed's stock of gold was almost 40% of the world monetary gold stock.

In the panic following the stock market crash of 1929, it became difficult for the United States to act unilaterally to control the U.S. money supply as global investors sold U.S. assets and demanded gold payment. The Federal Reserve had to honor its liability to deliver gold to nations that were selling U.S. assets, receiving U.S. currency, and demanding payments in gold. Many assets were sold at panic prices and dollars were exchanged for gold, causing price deflation. Stopping the outflow of gold would have required the Federal Reserve to aggressively raise interest rates to retain gold and maintain the money supply.

The Federal Reserve's power to expand the money supply and inflate or support asset prices was further eroded by a decline in the market prices of eligible collateral. Eventually deflationary pressure and declining prices overtook the U.S. economy. The inability of the Fed to accept expanded forms of collateral or deviate from the terms of the gold standard left the Federal Reserve paralyzed. They were also unable or unwilling to create currency to offer liquidity to its member banks or the public, which was withdrawing deposits for hard currency. The public demand for hard currency further drained the Federal Reserve's resources during this period and led to significant lending contraction, bank holidays, and bank failures.

There is little debate in the literature that monetary contraction was a primary cause of the Great Depression. The money supply contracted 33%

from 1929 to 1933. The Federal Reserve's strict adherence to the gold standard and a hoarding of free gold was in part due to the Fed's fear of an attack by speculators on the U.S. dollar if excess reserves fell too quickly. There was also a great concern that the Fed would use its free gold to over-expand the money supply and create excessive inflation and a rapid rise in interest rates.

KEY POINTS

- Some of the more common causes of past financial crises include the bursting of asset bubbles, speculative manias, banking crises, sovereign defaults, and international contagion.
- There are usually four stages to an asset bubble that leads to a systemic event: economic expansion/boom; euphoria and rapid increase in asset prices; pause in asset-price increases; and distress/panic/crash.
- While asset bubbles have originated from many sources throughout time, the most common forms include real estate and stock market bubbles.
- Speculative manias contradict the *rational expectations* assumption, which posits that investors always behave rationally.
- One of the first well-documented examples of a financial crisis has been referred to as the "Dutch Tulip Crisis" that occurred in early 1600s. Like many historical crises, this event was fueled by rampant speculation by a wide array of institutional and individual investors. In this case, the asset bubble that drove the event was the price of rare tulip bulbs in Europe, in which many ordinary citizens wagered life savings on the price of a single tulip bulb in the futures market.
- There were at least 250 sovereign external defaults during 1800–2009.
- Between the years of 1300 and 1799 and from 1800 to 2008, France and Spain accounted for most recorded external sovereign defaults in Europe.
- Between 1800 and 2008, Venezuela defaulted on external debt on 10 occasions, leading all Latin American countries.
- There are many factors that fuel international contagion, including inflation and capital flows, exchange rate changes, and securities price changes.
- Dating back to the year 1800, 136 countries have experienced some form of banking crisis.
- Although bank failures have occurred for centuries, the volume of bank failures during the past 30 or 40 years has been much larger in scope than in previous decades.

■ A famous example of international contagion was the use of the gold standard leading up to the Great Depression. The inability of the Fed to accept expanded forms of collateral or deviate from the terms of the gold standard left the Federal Reserve paralyzed. It was also unable or unwilling to create currency to offer liquidity to its member banks or the public, which was withdrawing deposits for hard currency. The public demand for hard currency further drained the Federal Reserve's resources during this period and led to significant lending contraction, bank holidays, and bank failures.

KNOWLEDGE CHECK

Q2.1: What is a commonly used definition of an *asset bubble*?

Q2.2: What characteristics typically exist in the period leading up to the bursting of an asset bubble?

Q2.3: While asset bubbles have occurred in many different types of assets in history, what are the two most common forms of bubbles, particularly in the 20th century?

Q2.4: Explain a linkage between real estate speculation/bubbles and the stock market.

Q2.5: What are some of the more common transmission mechanisms that have turned localized financial events into an international contagion?

Q2.6: Which two European countries have recorded the highest number of external defaults or reschedulings since the year 1300?

Q2.7: What were the five primary periods of high external sovereign default since the start of 1800?

Q2.8: What is the definition of the *gold standard* that many feel contributed to the Great Depression?

NOTES

1. Reinhart, Carmen M., and Rogoff, Kenneth S., 2009, *This Time Is Different: Eight Centuries of Financial Folly*. Princeton, NJ: Princeton University Press, pp. 129–132.
2. Kindlelberger, C.P., and Aliber, R., 2005, *Manias, Panics and Crashes: A History of Financial Crisis*, 5th ed. Hoboken, NJ: Wiley.
3. Mackay, C., 1841, "Extraordinary Popular Delusions and the Madness of Crowds." Vol. 1. Richard Bentley, London.

4. Ofek, E., and Richardson, M., 2003, "DotCom Mania: The Rise and Fall of Internet Stock Prices," *Journal of Finance*, American Finance Association, 58(3), p. 3.

5. Simpson, H., 1933, "Real Estate Speculation and the Depression", American Economic Review.

6. Smith, Adam. An Inquiry into the Nature and Causes of the Wealth of Nations. Edwin Cannan, ed. 1904. Library of Economics and Liberty. Retrieved April 19, 2017 from the World Wide Web: http://www.econlib.org/library/Smith/smWNNotes5.html

7. Reinhart, Carmen M., and Rogoff, Kenneth S., 2009, *This Time Is Different: Eight Centuries of Financial Folly*. Princeton, NJ: Princeton University Press, pp.129–132.

8. European Systemic Risk Board, Flagship Report on Macroprudential Policy in the Banking Sector, March 2014, p. 6.

9. Kindlelberger, C.P., and Aliber, R., 2005, *Manias, Panics and Crashes: A History of Financial Crisis*, 5th ed. Hoboken, NJ: Wiley.

10. Ibid.

11. Reinhart, Carmen M., and Rogoff, Kenneth S., 2009, *This Time Is Different: Eight Centuries of Financial Folly*. Princeton, NJ: Princeton University Press, pp.129–132.

12. Reinhart, C., Rogoff, Kenneth S., and Savastano, M., 2003a, "Debt Intolerance," Brookings Papers on Economic Activity No. 1, pp. 1–74.

13. Ibid.

14. Reinhart, Carmen M., and Rogoff, Kenneth S., 2009, *This Time Is Different: Eight Centuries of Financial Folly*. Princeton, NJ: Princeton University Press, p. 74.

15. Friedman, M., and Schwartz, A.J., 1963, "A Monetary History of the United States." Princeton University Press.

CHAPTER 3

The Credit Crisis of 2007–2009

INTRODUCTION

During the Credit Crisis of 2007–2009 the failure or financial distress of many large global institutions caused reverberations across the global financial markets and economies, leading to deep recessions in the United States and continental Europe. Although the crises technically began in 2007, it wasn't until the Fall of 2008, with the failure, emergency bailout, or acquisition of some of the world's most recognizable firms such as Lehman Brothers, Bear Stearns, and American International Group Inc. (AIG), that the systemic impact of the crisis fully emerged.

This crisis has been referred to by several different labels, including the *U.S. Subprime Crisis*, the *U.S. Housing Bubble*, the *Great Contraction*, the *Great Recession*, the *Global Credit Crisis*, to name a few. Regardless of the name used, given the dramatic impact the event had on the global financial system and economies, this event is generally viewed as the worst financial crisis to occur since the Great Depression.

While in the years following the Credit Crisis many theories and opinions have emerged about its causes, it is generally acknowledged that the bursting of the U.S. residential housing bubble was the primary driver of this global financial meltdown. The U.S. residential housing market experienced a dramatic run-up in home prices between the years of 2000 and 2006, increasing by 100%, followed by a decline of over 30% during 2006–2010.[1] Dating all the way back to 1891 (e.g., inception of the S&P's Case-Shiller Housing Price Index), there was no other comparable increase in housing prices to that which occurred in the several years preceding the start of the Credit Crisis.

After reading this chapter you will be able to:

- Understand the economic, financial, and regulatory conditions that collectively led to the Credit Crisis.

- Explain the key ways in which activities of certain Wall Street investment banks contributed to a tremendous bubble in subprime mortgage bonds.
- Learn how U.S. government-sponsored enterprises and investment banks helped fuel tremendous growth in residential mortgage securitization products.
- Understand what circumstances led to the insolvency or government bailout of many large financial institutions.
- Explain the basic structure of credit default swaps and collateralized debt obligations.
- Explain the aftermath of the Credit Crisis in terms of its economic impact on the United States and Europe.

PLANTING THE SEEDS OF A BUBBLE: THE EARLY 2000s

There is ample evidence showing the linkage between the U.S housing boom, a significant inflight of cheap foreign capital due to record trade balance and current account deficits, loose monetary policies, and weak bank lending standards during the early to mid-2000s.[2]

In the years preceding the start of the Credit Crisis there were a few prominent public figures that either dismissed or countered concerns about an overheating U.S. economy. For example, in response to those who pointed to the growing U.S. current account deficit (which peaked at over 6.5% of GDP or over $800 billion in 2006), former Federal Reserve Bank Chairman Alan Greenspan characterized this as a symptom of a trend around the globe that allowed countries to maintain bigger current account deficits and surpluses than in the past.[3] Similarly, former U.S. Treasury Secretary Paul O'Neill argued that it wasn't unusual for countries to provide significant flows of capital to the United States given its high rate of productivity. Lastly, Ben Bernanke attributed the high level of U.S. borrowing to a global savings excess that occurred because of many factors outside the control of U.S. policymakers.[4]

Another of the many contributors to the Credit Crisis was the impact of "fair value" or "mark-to-market" accounting rules. FAS 157 provides a way to measure assets and liabilities on a company's balance sheet and record changes in value of those assets in the income statement. FAS 157 defines fair value as the price that would be received to sell an asset in an orderly transaction between market participants. Tremendous losses reported by banks and investment banks on subprime mortgage assets led a rigorous debate in the United States over the implementation of FAS 157 in such a unique market situation in which an orderly and liquid market simply did not exist. Critics also blamed FAS 157 for causing pro-cyclicality during the crisis in that asset prices were falling dramatically on their own and were then exacerbated by banks being forced to write down subprime mortgage securities in such a downward-spiraling market.

Proponents of the rule, including the Securities and Exchange Commission (SEC), opined that FAS 157 provided investors meaningful and transparent financial information. Opponents, such as William Isaac, former FDIC chairman, went on record publicly stating that this rule caused the Credit Crisis:

> *The devastation that followed stemmed largely from the tendency of accounting standards-setters and regulators to force banks, by means of their litigation-shy auditors, to mark their illiquid assets down to unrealistic fire-sale prices.*[5]

Mark-to-market accounting led to an estimated $500 billion loss in capital in the United States, and when the impact of leverage is considered, such rules led to a $5 trillion destruction in bank lending capacity.[6] Ultimately, the rule was relaxed to allow banks to exercise judgment in estimating a liquidation price. A report by the Financial Crisis Advisory Group in 2009 concluded that "accounting standards were not a root cause of the financial crisis," but did acknowledge that weakness in the application of the rules reduced credibility in financial reporting.

Ahead is a short list of some of the commonly discussed characterizations or assumptions that contributed to the Credit Crisis and allowed many to conclude that there was no imminent threat of a financial meltdown:[7]

- Since the United States had a very robust financial regulatory regime, the most advanced and liquid capital markets in the globe, and an extremely innovative financial system, it could withstand the huge inflows of capital that were occurring.
- Expansions in financial integration globally meant that capital markets were deep enough to permit countries like the United States to go heavily into debt.
- The United States has superior monetary policymakers and institutions.

According to some, the Federal Reserve (the Fed) could have been more aggressive in addressing what in retrospect was clearly an overheating U.S. economy in the years leading up to the Credit Crisis.[8] For example, one of many potential actions might have been to utilize the *Taylor Rule*, which is a theory that real interest rates should be raised to cool the economy when inflation increases (requiring the nominal interest rate to increase more than inflation does). Specifically, the Taylor Rule says that an increase in inflation by 1% should prompt central banks to raise the nominal interest rate by more than 1%. Since the real interest rate is (approximately) the nominal interest rate minus inflation, stipulating $a_\pi > 0$ implies that when inflation rises, the real interest rate should be increased.

The Taylor Rule involves just three variables: inflation rate, GDP growth, and the interest rate. If inflation were to rise by 1%, the proper response would be to raise the interest rate by 1.5% (Taylor explains that it doesn't always need to be exactly 1.5%, but being larger than 1% is essential). If GDP falls by 1% relative to its growth path, then the proper response is to cut the interest rate by 0.5%.

A sharp boom and bust in the housing markets would be expected to have had impacts on the financial markets as falling house prices lead to delinquencies and foreclosures. These effects were amplified by several complicating factors, including the use of subprime mortgages, especially the adjustable rate variety, which led to excessive risk taking. In the United States, this was encouraged by government programs designed to promote homeownership.

It is important to note, however, that the excessive risk taking and low interest rates or "easy credit" monetary policy decisions are connected. Empirical evidence supports the idea that government actions and interventions caused, prolonged, and worsened the financial crisis. They caused it by deviating from historical precedents and principles for setting interest rates, which had worked well for the preceding 20 years.

WALL STREET'S ROLE

The financial sector in general, and more specifically, U.S. investment banks, took a significant amount of blame for the Credit Crisis. The size of the U.S. financial sector more than doubled from an average of about 4 percent of GDP in the mid-1970s to almost 8 percent of GDP by 2007.[9] Financial innovation had also been rapidly on the rise during the 2000s, with asset securitization representing one of Wall Street's most popular and profitable products.

Securitization represents the aggregation of numerous, sometimes thousands of individual loans into a newly created *asset-backed securities* (ABS). The benefits of securitization to investors lie in the concepts of *pooling* and *tranching*. For example, since typical ABS may be comprised of thousands of individual loans, the default on a few loans would have a minimal impact on the overall performance of the security. With tranching, investors could choose which layer of risk and expected return they are comfortable with. For example, a senior tranche would have a higher priority in the receipt of principal and interest payments on the underlying loans versus a more junior tranche and would only absorb defaults after lower tranches first took losses.

While Fannie Mae and Freddie Mac historically dominated the securitization market for fixed-rate mortgage loans for decades, during the mid-1980s Wall Street firms began to securitize other types of loans, such as adjustable-rate mortgages (ARMs) and others that the GSEs were either unwilling or unable to securitize under their rules. Wall Street firms bundled loans they purchased from banks and other lenders into new securities that were sold to investors who earned returns funded by the principal and interest payments on the underlying loans.

The types of ABS created by Wall Street in the early years were more complex than the more generic *residential mortgage-backed securities* (RMBS) created by the GSEs, as the former were comprised of many different and sometimes riskier loan types. The overall ABS securitizations grew tremendously during the 1990s and included securities comprised of assets such as student loans, manufactured housing, residential loans (mortgages and home equity loans), credit cards, and automobile loans. By 1999 the securitization market grew to $900 billion from approximately $50 billion in 1990 (excluding securitizations by the GSEs).[10] Between 2003 and 2007, U.S. home prices rose 27% and $4 trillion of RMBS were created, from which Wall Street launched approximately $700 billion of mortgage-backed CDOs.[11]

One of the earliest and most popular forms of securitization is called *collateralized debt obligations* (CDOs). CDOs were often used by banks to prudently move loans into newly created structured entities that were held off-balance-sheet. Although banks typically retained some degree of risk in the CDO, they benefited greatly by reducing their direct loan exposures and freeing up capital to reinvest in new loans or other revenue-generating activities.

Beginning in the early 2000s, Wall Street financial engineers at many investment banks began to make use of CDO-type structures much more frequently. Many of these structures had corporate bonds as their underlying collateral. However, as the U.S. residential mortgage market exploded during the period of 2004–2007, investment banks began to create and aggressively sell variations on the more generic corporate CDO structure. These were called *synthetic CDOs* and they often had a much riskier profile than CDO offerings from earlier years.

The CDOs were classified as synthetic since they were not created or funded by actual bonds but rather *credit default swaps* (CDSs) that were sold or "written" on the underlying cash bond instruments. A CDS contract was less like a traditional swap contract and more akin to an insurance contract. For example, an investor may pay $100,000 a year to buy

$100 million of five-year CDS on General Motors (GM). In this example, the CDS buyer can only lose a total of $500,000 ($100,000 annual premium × 5 years) and can make a maximum of $100 million should General Motors default (assuming zero recovery value on the underlying bonds). Meanwhile, the seller of any CDS contract can only earn a maximum of the $500,000 of total premiums received, but can lose $100 million in a worst-case scenario.

In the early years of CDS activity most trading was for hedging purposes. For example, if a firm felt that GM had a high risk of credit default, they might purchase CDS "protection" that would pay them upon a GM credit event. However, in the years leading up to the Credit Crisis more and more firms began using CDS to speculate on firm defaults rather than the more conservative practice of hedging against such events.

While many variations of RMBS collateral existed in the market at that time, the percentage of subprime securities[12] began to increase dramatically and became an ever-increasing proportion of new synthetic-CDO collateral pools. To provide a sense of the growth in subprime mortgage origination and the linkage to CDOs, in 2000 there was $130 billion of subprime origination of which $55 billion was repackaged into RMBS. In 2005 there were $625 billion of subprime originations of which $507 billion became RMBS.[13]

Even though a growing percentage of the CDO reference collateral was below investment grade, by repackaging these securities into new CDO tranches, they could be sold to investors with ratings that usually ranged from BBB all the way to AAA. This was possible because the ratings were based largely on the level of *subordination* or loss absorption beneath each tranche. For example, an A-rated tranche investor might not suffer any losses unless 15% of the total collateral pool defaulted. An AA tranche might have subordination of 25%, and so on. As such, owners of these tranches felt they were taking very little risk due to the very strong public ratings assigned by rating agencies. However, the collateral that was supporting their investment often contained very low-rated individual bonds made to subprime borrowers. For example, most subprime-backed CDOs were created by the lowest rated tranches of RMBS (mainly B and BB). Such risky mortgage loans were effectively transformed into highly rated CDO tranches due to perceived benefits imbedded in the typical waterfall structure of CDOs.

The creation of synthetic CDOs became an extremely big business for Wall Street as they could earn tremendous fees for structuring and selling these investments. Between 2003 and 2007, during a period in which home prices rose 27% nationally and $4 trillion of mortgage-backed securities were created, about $700 billion in CDOs were issued by Wall Street.[14]

In 2007 the losses on subprime collateral began to spike and hence the underlying collateral to the synthetic CDOs began to deteriorate. Rating agencies continued to provide very strong ratings to CDO tranches as the agencies relied too heavily on analyses provided to them by the investment banks or relatively crude assessments of the notional size of the subordination pool rather than the credit quality of the bonds themselves.

Given the superior public ratings that were assigned to certain CDO tranches, many investors came to view these tranches as near riskless. Rating agencies were greatly criticized following the Credit Crisis for reportedly not sufficiently analyzing or modeling the expected losses on the CDOs. For example, the rating agencies assumed that securitizers could create safer financial products by diversifying among many mortgage-backed securities, when these securities weren't that different to begin with and the agencies based their CDO ratings on ratings they themselves had assigned on the underlying collateral.

There were a lot of things (the credit rating agencies) did wrong. They did not consider the appropriate correlation between (and) across the categories of mortgages.[15]

Rating CDOs was an extremely profitable business for the agencies. One rating firm reported revenues from structured products, which included mortgage-backed securities and CDOs, that grew from $199 million in 2000, or 33% of total revenues, to $887 million in 2006, or 44% of overall corporate revenue. The overall surge in structured finance activity during the first half of the 2000s helped fuel an increase in the firm's revenues and profits, as revenues spiked from $602 million in 2000 to $2 billion in 2006 while profit margins jumped from 26% to 37%.[16]

According to the conclusion found by the Financial Crisis Inquiry Council, the high ratings erroneously given CDOs by credit rating agencies encouraged investors and financial institutions to purchase them and enabled the continuing securitization of nonprime mortgages, and there was a clear failure of corporate governance at certain rating agencies, which did not ensure the quality of its rating on tens of thousands of mortgage-backed securities and CDOs.

THE U.S. GOVERNMENT TAKEOVER OF THE GSEs

A *government-sponsored enterprise* is a financial services corporation created by the U.S. Congress. Its intended function is to enhance the flow of credit to targeted sectors of the economy and to make those segments of the capital market more efficient and transparent, and to reduce the risk to investors and other suppliers of capital. The desired effect of the GSEs is to enhance the availability and reduce the cost of credit to the targeted borrowing sectors primarily by reducing the risk of capital losses to investors: agriculture, home finance, and education.

The two best-known GSEs are the Federal National Mortgage Association (Fannie Mae) and Federal Home Loan Mortgage Corporation (Freddie Mac). Fannie Mae was founded in 1938 by the Reconstruction Finance Corporation during the Great Depression to buy mortgages insured by the Federal Housing Administration (FHA). Meanwhile, in 1970 Congress chartered the creation of Freddie Mac to serve as a second GSE. Fannie and Freddie were authorized to buy "conventional"[17] fixed-rate mortgages that had to conform to the GSE's underwriting standards that had limits on debt-to-income, loan size, and minimum down payments, among other criteria.

Fannie Mae and Freddie Mac's primary mission was to purchase residential mortgages from banks operating in all 50 U.S. states. As such, the GSEs did not originate mortgages but rather purchased them in the secondary mortgage market by providing ongoing liquidity to support homeownership. The GSEs purchased mortgage loans from banks, thrifts, and mortgage companies and held them in their portfolios. As individual banks across the country booked new individual mortgage loans, they sold many of these loans to the GSEs relatively quickly, freeing up capital to write more loans.

Laws enacted between 1968 and 1970 gave the GSEs the option of securitizing mortgages rather than holding all loans on their respective balance sheets. Now the GSEs could assemble a pool of mortgages and issue securities backed by them. Ginnie Mae was the first GSE to securitize mortgages, followed by Freddie Mac in 1971 and Fannie Mae in 1981. Throughout most of their histories, the GSEs' residential mortgage business and closely related RMBS securitization activities were both focused on generally low-risk fixed-rate mortgages that were subject to national underwriting standards that stipulated, among other criteria, conservative minimum down payments. Congress granted Fannie Mae and Freddie Mac certain benefits such as exemptions from state and local taxes and substantial lines of credit to support ongoing activities.

In 1995, President Bill Clinton announced an initiative to boost homeownership from 65.1% to 67.5% of U.S. families by 2000. Also in 1995, Clinton loosened housing rules by rewriting the Community Reinvestment Act,[18] which put added pressure on banks to lend in low-income neighborhoods. The political drive to increase homeownership increased under the George W. Bush administration by the introduction of the Zero Down Payment Initiative,[19] which in certain cases removed the minimum 3% required down payment on FHA mortgages that carried U.S. government guaranty.[20]

In the early 2000s, there was a rapid increase in U.S. homeownership, combined with a significant increase in competition among banks, mortgage companies, and other entities for new business. Durinig this period of increased home ownership, subprime loan origination jumped from 7.6% of all mortgage origination to a peak of 23.5% between 2001-2006. This decline in credit standards occurred during the same period in which U.S. home prices soared. Between 1997 and their peak in 2006 the average home price jumped 152%, more than in any decade since the 1920s.[21]

Another contributing factor to the growing asset bubble in the residential mortgage sector was the easy credit conditions that existed in the early 2000s. For example, from 2000 to 2003 the Federal Reserve lowered the Fed Funds target rate from 6.5% to 1%, making mortgages much more accessible to millions of additional Americans.

Moving into early 2008, the U.S. economy continued to suffer, with GDP falling to an annual rate of just 0.7%, which was the worst result recorded in the United States since the 1990s. Meanwhile, the unemployment rate increased to 5% in the first quarter from 4.4% in the Spring of 2007.

Given that Fannie Mae and Freddie Mac were a key national source of liquidity in the mortgage market, the U.S. government feared that a potential failure of the GSEs would cause a systemic event. Trillions of dollars of GSE debt was owned across the globe and a tremendous amount of MBS carried guaranties from the GSEs.

On September 4, the FHFA agreed with Treasury that the GSEs needed to be placed into conservatorship,[22] and on September 6 the management of of Fannie Mae and Freddie Mac received notification from the FHFA recommending that the regulator be appointed conservator of the companies.

THE TIPPING POINT: LEHMAN BROTHERS' FAILURE

Lehman Brothers Holdings Inc. (Lehman) was one of the longest running financial services firms in the United States, having been founded in 1850. During 2008, Lehman ranked as the fourth largest investment bank in the United States, ranking behind Goldman Sachs, Morgan Stanley, and Merrill Lynch and focused mainly on investment banking, equity, and fixed-income sales and trading.

Lehman was one of the largest Wall Street players in the residential real estate market, including the subprime CDO sector. In addition, the firm had a very high reliance on short-term funding (e.g., nearly $8 billion of commercial paper and nearly $200 billion of repos), which exposed it to a "run" by creditors who could quickly cease such funding, putting tremendous pressure on the firm to quickly replace billions of short-term financing. Additionally, as one of the world's biggest players in over-the-counter (OTC) derivatives, Lehman's estimated 900,000 derivatives contracts with hundreds of counterparties across the world were a cause for growing concern on the part of regulators, investors, and creditors worldwide.

On June 9, 2008, Lehman reported a second-quarter loss of $2.8 billion, its first loss since it went public in 1994. A few days later Lehman announced they would be replacing both their chief operating officer, Joe Gregory, and chief financial officer, Erin Callan. The company's share price fell to $30 per share.[23]

On June 25, 2008 the results of the most recent stress tests showed that Lehman would need $15 billion more than the $54 billion in liquidity resources to survive the potential loss of all unsecured funding and certain portions of its secured borrowings.[24] In July, a couple of very large and important repo counterparties of Lehman, indicated they would no longer provide such funding to Lehman, which only served to fuel concerns of Lehman's stakeholders.[25]

During the summer months of 2008, U.S. regulators had many meetings and attempted to find solutions to save Lehman from what was becoming an ever-increasing risk of failure due to the firm's tremendous real estate exposure and its vulnerable funding structure, combined with a growing loss of confidence in the firm by its most critical counterparties and liquidity providers.

Just a few of the numerous potential options that were considered by Lehman, in coordination with its regulators, included an investment in the firm by Korea Development Bank, an acquisition by Barclays Bank, the sale of Lehman's investment management division, bulk sale of real estate assets, and splitup of the firm into a "good bank"/"bad bank" structure in which its riskiest assets would get segregated into a newly created entity.

However, the most heavily debated and most controversial of all options was an outright bailout by the U.S. government. Treasury Secretary Paulson repeatedly made the case that a private sector solution was the only feasible approach and that the government was not going to provide any extraordinary credit support for Lehman, in part due to the substantial criticisms it received following the bailout of Bear Stearns.[26] Paulson made several attempts to coordinate an effective bailout of Lehman by its largest counterparties, which included firms such as Bank of America, Barclays, and other major banks and investment banks. One of the most significant obstacles was the refusal of the Fed to consider an interim guaranty of Lehman's debts until a potential Barclays acquisition could be approved by its shareholders and completed. The overriding concern was that should a run on Lehman by its counterparties continue during this transition period, the Fed could find itself owning an insolvent entity, greatly exposing U.S. taxpayers to losses.[27]

During the first two weeks of September, some of Lehman's most important short-term funding counterparties began demanding significant increases in collateral to offset credit risk concerns that were reaching a critical stage, putting additional stress on the company.

On September 15, 2008, the firm filed for Chapter 11 bankruptcy protection following the massive exodus of most of its clients, drastic losses in its stock, and devaluation of assets by credit rating agencies, largely sparked by Lehman's involvement in the subprime mortgage crisis and subsequent allegations of negligence and malfeasance.[28] The following day, Barclays announced its agreement to purchase, subject to regulatory approval, Lehman's North American investment-banking and trading divisions along with its New York headquarters building.[29] The next week, Nomura Holdings announced that it would acquire Lehman Brothers' franchise in the Asia-Pacific region, including Japan, Hong Kong, and Australia,[30] as well as Lehman Brothers' investment banking and equities businesses in Europe and the Middle East. The deal became effective on October 13, 2008.

Lehman's bankruptcy filing is the largest in U.S. history and clearly played a major role in exacerbating the Credit Crisis. The day Lehman filed for bankruptcy, the Dow Jones Industrial Average dropped more than 500 points while approximately $700 billion in value disappeared from retirement plans, government pension funds, and other investment portfolios. For Lehman itself, the bankruptcy impacted 8,000 subsidiaries and affiliates worldwide, approximately 100,000 creditors, and its 26,000 employees worldwide.[31] Immediately following Lehman's failure and in the years since then, there has been significant debate and in some cases criticism toward the Fed for the decision to help rescue firms like Bear Stearns, AIG, and the GSEs but not to directly intervene to avoid Lehman's collapse. The Fed has defended its role by stating, among other things, that it lacked the legal authority to provide the type of extraordinary support that would have been required to save Lehman. In testimony before the FCIC, Bernanke admitted that the considerations behind the government's decision to allow Lehman to fail were both legal and practical, stating, "We are not allowed to lend without a reasonable expectation of repayment. The loan has to be secured to the satisfaction of the Reserve Bank. Remember, this was before TARP. We had no ability to inject capital or make guarantees."[32]

AFTERMATH OF THE CREDIT CRISIS

Most historical financial crises, particularly those involving the failure of many banks, are typically followed by a prolonged economic downturn. The Credit Crisis was no exception as it plunged both the United States and Europe into significant recessions and led to historically large declines in housing prices, stock market performance, and personal household net worth.

Impact on Housing Prices: As previously discussed, many historical financial and banking crises were fueled by an unsustainable runup in real estate prices followed by a bursting of the price bubble. Table 3.1 illustrates the peak-to-trough changes in real housing prices associated with some of the larger financial crises of the past hundred-plus years. According to the S&P/Case Shiller Home Price Index, peak-to-trough decline in the quarterly index of national U.S. housing prices fell from 189.9 in 2Q 2006 to 125.7 in 1Q 2011. As devastating as this real estate crash was on the U.S. economy, 7 of the 12 worst peak-to-trough housing declines globally were worse than the decline that occurred during the Credit Crisis.

In addition to the greater than 30% decline in home prices during the Credit Crisis, homeownership rate declined from a peak of 69.2% in 2004 to 66.9% in late 2010.[33] Mortgage delinquency rates rose dramatically during this period, as evidenced by third-quarter 2010 serious delinquency rates,[34] such as 19.5% in Florida, 17.8% in Nevada, 10.8% in Arizona, and 10.3% in California. Note that these states were collectively referred to as the "sand states," which were the states most negatively affected by the Credit Crisis.[35]

TABLE 3.1 Changes in Real Housing Prices[36]

Country	Year of Crisis	Duration in Years	Peak to Trough Decline
United States	2007	Three	−33.4%
Columbia	1998	Six	−51.2
Hong Kong	1997	Six	−58.9
Indonesia	1997	Five	−49.9
Philippines	1997	Seven	−53.0
Japan	1992	Ongoing	−40.2
Finland	1991	Six	−50.4
Sweden	1991	Four	−31.7
Norway	1987	Five	−41.5
Spain	1977	Four	−33.3
United States	1929	Seven	−12.6
Norway	1898	Six	−25.5

Impact on Growth: A study of the average real GDP growth for advanced nations experiencing a banking crisis shows that GDP starts at about 2.5% in *T minus 3* years (where "*T*" denotes the year of the banking crisis) and steadily falls to just under 1% in *T* and *T plus 1*. This drop is even more pronounced when analyzing five of history's most significant banking crises, in which the average GDP of the involved countries starts at approximately 4.5% in T minus 3 years and drops to a low of almost minus1% in *T plus 1*.[37] The average downturn in GDP following severe financial crises is 4.8 years.

Regarding the Credit Crisis, GDP fell at an annual rate of 4% in the third quarter of 2008 and 6.8% in the fourth quarter, representing the largest decline since 1946.[38] In June 2009 the United States officially emerged from the recession that had started in December 2007. Overall, in advanced economies, the median cumulative loss in output relative to its pre-crisis trend has been 33% of GDP. In the European Union, through 2013, GDP remained below its pre-crisis level and is about 13% below its pre-crisis trend.[39]

Impact on Equity Prices: The average downturn phase of an equity market decline following a crisis is 3.4 years. Equity prices typically reach their highest level the year before the onset of a banking crisis and experience double-digit declines for two or three years as the crisis develops and occurs, but then quickly recover in a V-shaped manner reaching or exceeding the original peak within three years following the crisis. Regarding the Credit Crisis, equity prices as measured by the Dow Jones Industrial Average fell over half (−51.1%) from a peak of 14,165 on October 9, 2007, to a low of 6,926 on March 5, 2009.[40] Meanwhile, the S&P 500 Index dropped by one-third in 2008, the largest annual decline since 1974. Similarly, worldwide stock prices plunged over 40% in 2008 per the MSCI World Index stock fund.[41]

Impact on Unemployment: Historically, unemployment rises for an average of five years because of financial crises, with an average increase of 7%. Concerning the Credit Crisis, the recession in the United States officially began in December 2007 and the fallout on the U.S economy was dramatic. In 2008, the United States lost 3.8 million jobs, the greatest annual decline since records were first kept in 1940. By December 2009, the economy lost another 4.7 million jobs. Meanwhile, the underemployment rate, the measure of those who are actively seeking jobs, those working part-time but who prefer full-time, and those who have abandoned job searches, nearly doubled to 17.4% in October 2009 from December 2017. The amount of time it took unemployed workers to find a job skyrocketed to 25.5 weeks in June 2010 from 9.4 weeks in June 2008. The overall unemployment rate increased to 10.1% by October 2009, the highest rate since 1983 and about double the rate prior to the Credit Crisis.

COST OF GOVERNMENT BAILOUTS

The amount of funds injected by the U.S. Treasury via numerous bailout programs or directly to certain financial institutions totaled $609 billion. Table 3.2 presents the allocation of bailout funds disbursed by the U.S government to a total of 935 individual firm recipients under various bailout programs because of the Credit Crisis. Note that approximately 40% of the total funds were received by banks and other financial institutions, followed by government-sponsored entities at 31%.

Despite the massive scale of the bailout funds disbursed, as of February 2014, the U.S. Treasury had earned an estimated net profit of $12.5 billion because of outright repayments of funds by bailed-out firms ($384 billion), dividends payments received from bailed-out firms ($206 billion), interest payments ($1.8 billion), warrants ($9.5 billion), and other miscellaneous proceeds ($19.5 billion). Two of the largest recipients of TARP funding, Fannie Mae and Freddie Mac, repaid $192 billion as of 2014.

Although the sheer dollar amount of the TARP program was massive, it did not result in direct losses to U.S. taxpayers. In a similar vein, the Reconstruction Finance Corporation[42] ultimately achieved a cumulative profit of $160 million on its capital of $500 million during the Great Depression. The FDIC, created in 1933 during the Great Depression, also contributed heavily to fighting contagion risk during the Credit Crisis. Consistent with its original mandate of providing sufficient insurance to depositors of banks to minimize the likelihood of a run, during the Credit Crisis the FDIC expanded the amount of insurance by granting unlimited insurance to transaction accounts and higher limits for other accounts.[43]

About the regulatory failures that occurred before and during the Credit Crisis, the Financial Crisis Inquiry Commission (FCIC) pointed to a series of errors that included the mistaking of concentrated risk for

TABLE 3.2 Allocation of U.S. Government Bailout Funds[44]

Program	Disbursements
Banks and Other Financial Institutions	$245 billion
GSEs	$187 billion
Auto Companies	$79.7 billion
AIG	$67.8 billion
Toxic Asset Program	$18.6 billion
Mortgage Modification Program	$6.4 billion
State Housing Programs	$3.1 billion
Small Business Loan Aid	$368 million
FHA Refi Program	$50 million

diversification, the lack of a comprehensive framework for assessing systemic risk, and the failure to account for the growing asset bubble in U.S. housing prices:

> We conclude collapsing mortgage-lending standards and the mortgage securitization pipeline lit and spread the flame of contagion and crisis. When housing prices fell and mortgage borrowers defaulted, the lights began to dim on Wall Street. This report catalogues the corrosion of mortgage-lending standards and the securitization pipeline that transported toxic mortgages from neighborhoods across America to investors around the globe.[45]

KEY POINTS

- During the Credit Crisis of 2007–2009 the failure or distress of many large global financial institutions caused reverberations across the global financial markets and economies, leading to deep recessions in the U.S and continental Europe.
- In the couple of years preceding the start of the Credit Crisis there were several prominent public figures who either dismissed or countered concerns about an overheating U.S. economy.
- The size of the U.S. financial sector more than doubled from an average of about 4 percent of GDP in the mid-1970s to almost 8 percent of GDP by 2007.[46] Financial innovation had been rapidly on the rise during the 2000s, with securitization representing Wall Street's most popular and profitable products.
- Between 2003 and 2007, U.S. home prices rose 27% and $4 trillion of RMBS securities were created, from which Wall Street launched approximately $700 billion of mortgage-backed CDOs.
- In the early years of CDS trading, the clear majority were used as hedging tools. However, in the years leading up to the Credit Crisis more and more firms began using CDS to speculate on firm defaults rather than hedging against such events.
- Even though a growing percentage of the CDO reference collateral was below investment grade, by repackaging these securities into new CDO tranches, they could be sold to investors with ratings that usually ranged from BBB all the way up to AAA.
- Given the superior public ratings that were assigned to certain CDO tranches (e.g., AAA or AA), many investors came to view these tranches as near riskless, leading to criticism of certain rating agencies following the Credit Crisis for not sufficiently analyzing or modeling the expected losses on CDOs.

- Certain U.S. government policy actions dating back to the 1990s were aimed at increasing U.S. homeownership. In 1995 President Bill Clinton announced an initiative to boost U.S. homeownership from 65.1% to 67.5% of families by 2000. Also in 1995, Clinton loosened housing rules by rewriting the Community Reinvestment Act, which put added pressure on banks to lend in low-income neighborhoods.
- Another contributing factor to the growing asset bubble in the residential mortgage sector was the easy credit conditions that existed in the early 2000s. For example, from 2000 to 2003 the Federal Reserve lowered the Fed Funds target rate from 6.5% to 1%, making mortgages much more accessible to millions of additional Americans.
- Subprime loan origination jumped from 7.6% of all mortgage origination to a peak of 23.5% between 2001 and 2006.
- On September 4, the FHFA agreed with Treasury that the GSEs needed to be placed into conservatorship.
- Lehman was one of the most active Wall Street firms in the residential real estate sector and particularly in the risky subprime mortgage business. The firm also had an extremely large dependence on short-term financing structures to fund its daily operations (e.g., repos and commercial paper).
- Despite reporting equity capital of about $28 billion in mid-2008, many of Lehman's key counterparties lost confidence in the firm and began to change the terms of their funding arrangements with Lehman by restricting additional funding or significantly increasing the collateral Lehman had to post to continue such arrangements.
- While months of discussions and negotiations took place during the summer of 2008 between the U.S. Federal Reserve, Treasury, Lehman, and several of its largest counterparties, a government-arranged bailout or takeover of the firm could not be agreed to by any of these stakeholders.
- Just a couple of weeks after the U.S. government takeover of the GSEs, on September 15, one of Wall Street's largest and oldest investment banks, Lehman Brothers Inc., declared bankruptcy, the largest such bankruptcy in the history of the United States.
- While over 300 U.S. banking institutions ultimately failed because of the Credit Crisis, the failure of Lehman is universally viewed as the most significant firm failure during that period and is considered the event that triggered the worst of the fallout from the crisis.
- The TARP program in the United States was utilized to provide bailouts to many institutions, with the largest percentage of funds going to the U.S. GSEs in the total amount of $187 billion.
- The aftermath of the Credit Crisis was devastating in many ways. Among other impacts, it sent both the United States and Europe into

deep recessions, led to >30% average decline in U.S. home prices, a similar decline in U.S. equity markets, a spike in U.S. unemployment to over 10%, and a tremendous loss in personal household net worth.

KNOWLEDGE CHECK

Q3.1: During what years did the Credit Crisis occur?

Q3.2: A bubble in which asset class is generally blamed for precipitating the Credit Crisis?

Q3.3: Which industry term was used to describe a sub-segment of mortgage-backed securities that consisted of loans to borrowers with below-average credit scores?

Q3.4: What were some of the factors that were believed to have contributed to the aforementioned asset bubble?

Q3.5: Which structured investment product sold by Wall Street investment banks played a significant role in Credit Crisis?

Q3.6: What potential role did U.S. policy actions play in the years leading up to the Credit Crisis?

Q3.7: What reason(s) were cited by U.S. officials for not providing any direct financial support for Lehmann Brothers Inc., despite recognizing that a bankruptcy by Lehman would likely have a catastrophic impact on global economies and financial markets?

Q3.8: Provide some of the key impacts of the Credit Crisis on the U.S. economy, unemployment, housing prices, and equity markets.

Q3.9: Did the TARP bailout program in the United States lead to direct losses to U.S. taxpayers?

NOTES

1. Xiong, W., 2013, "Bubbles, Crises, and Heterogeneous Beliefs," NBER Working Paper #18905, March 2013.

2. Rajan, R., 2010, *Fault Lines*. Princeton University Press, August.

3. Alan Greenspan, "International Imbalances" (speech, Advancing Enterprise Conference, London, England, December 2, 2005), www.federalreserve.gov/boarddocs/speeches/2005/200512022/default.htm.

4. Bernanke, Ben, 2005, "Remarks by Governor Ben S. Bernanke at the Sandridge Lecture," Virginia Association of Economists, Richmond, Virginia, www.federalreserve.gov/boarddocs/speeches/2005/200503102.

5. David M. Katz, Former FDIC Chief. Fair Value Caused the Crisis, CFO.COM, Oct. 29, 2008, http://www.cfo.com/article.cfm/12502908?f=members_110508.

6. Testimony provided by William Isaac to the Subcommittee on Capital Markets, Insurance, and Government Sponsored Enterprises on March 12, 2009.

7. Reinhart, Carmen M., and Rogoff, Kenneth S., 2010, "Growth in a Time of Debt," Working Paper #15639, National Bureau of Economic Research, January, pp. 1–26.

8. Taylor, J.B., 2008, "The Financial Crisis and the Policy Responses: An Empirical Analysis of What Went Wrong." Critical Review: A Journal of Politics and Society Volume 21, Issue 2-3, 2009 Special Issue: Causes of the Financial Crisis.

9. Almeida, H., and Philippon, T., 2007, "The Risk-Adjusted Cost of Financial Distress," *Journal of Finance* 62(6), Blackwell.

10. Financial Crisis Inquiry Report, "Final Report of the National Commission on the Causes of the Financial and Economic Crisis in the United States," Official Government Edition, 111-21 January 2011, p. 45.

11. Ibid., p. 129.

12. The average credit score of the underlying mortgage borrowers is below average.

13. Lewis, M., 2010, *The Big Short: Inside the Doomsday Machine*, W.W. Norton & Company, p. 23.

14. Financial Crisis Inquiry Report, "Final Report of the National Commission on the Causes of the Financial and Economic Crisis in the United States," Official Government Edition, 111-21 January 2011, p. 129.

15. Federal Reserve Chairman Ben Bernanke to the Financial Crisis Inquiry Commission, November 17, 2009.

16. Financial Crisis Inquiry Report, "Final Report of the National Commission on the Causes of the Financial and Economic Crisis in the United States," Official Government Edition, 111-21 January 2011, p. 149.

17. The Federal Housing Finance Agency (FHFA) publishes annual conforming loan limits that apply to all conventional mortgages delivered to Fannie Mae, including general loan limits and the high-cost area loan limits. High-cost area loan limits vary by geographic location. In 2016, $424,100 was the maximum residential loan size in most U.S. states to qualify as a conventional loan that would be accepted by Fannie Mae and Freddie Mac.

18. A U.S. federal law designed to encourage commercial banks and savings associations to help meet the needs of borrowers in all segments of their communities, including low- and moderate-income neighborhoods.

19. A 2004 legislation under George W. Bush's administration to allow the Federal Housing Administration to insure mortgages for first-time homebuyers without a down payment with the goal of increasing homeownership in the United States.

20. Financial Crisis Inquiry Report, "Final Report of the National Commission on the Causes of the Financial and Economic Crisis in the United States," Official Government Edition, 111-21 January 2011, p. 41.

21. Ibid., p. 156.

22. *Source:* www.fhfa.gov/Conservatorship/Pages/History-of-Fannie-Mae–Freddie-Conservatorships.aspx. On September 6, 2008, FHFA used its authorities to place Fannie Mae and Freddie Mac into conservatorship. A key component of

the conservatorships is the commitment of the U.S. Department of the Treasury to provide financial support to Fannie Mae and Freddie Mac to enable them to continue to provide liquidity and stability to the mortgage market. The Treasury Department has provided $189.5 billion in support, which includes an initial placement of $1 billion in both Fannie Mae and Freddie Mac at the time of the conservatorships and an additional cumulative $187.5 billion investment from the Treasury Department. In accordance with the Federal Housing Enterprises Financial Safety and Soundness Act of 1992 as amended by HERA, FHFA is authorized to "take such action as may be: (i) necessary to put the regulated entity in a sound and solvent condition; and (ii) appropriate to carry on the business of the regulated entity and preserve and conserve the assets and property of the regulated entity." In addition, as conservator, FHFA assumed the authority of the management and boards of Fannie Mae and Freddie Mac during the period of the conservatorship. However, Fannie Mae and Freddie Mac continue to operate legally as business corporations and FHFA has delegated to the chief executive officers and boards of directors responsibility for much of the day-to-day operations of the companies. Fannie Mae and Freddie Mac must follow the laws and regulations governing financial disclosure, including the requirements of the Securities and Exchange Commission.

23. Financial Crisis Inquiry Report, "Final Report of the National Commission on the Causes of the Financial and Economic Crisis in the United States," Official Government Edition, 111-21 January 2011, p. 327.
24. Federal Reserve Bank of New York, "Primary Dealer Monitoring: Liquidity Stress Analysis," June 2008.
25. Financial Crisis Inquiry Report, "Final Report of the National Commission on the Causes of the Financial and Economic Crisis in the United States," Official Government Edition, 111-21 January 2011, p. 328.
26. Baxter, Tom, "Speaker Notes: Financial Community Meeting." Attached to email from Helen Pala, NYFRB, to Steven Sharon, Treasurer, September 12, 2008.
27. Paulson, H. M., "On the Brink: Inside the Race to Stop the Collapse of the Global Financial System." New York: Business Plus, 2010, ISBN 978-0-7553-6054-3, pp. 209–210.
28. Malloy, M.P., 2010, "Anatomy of a Meltdown: A Dual Financial Biography of the Subprime Mortgage Crisis," *Wolters Kluwer Law & Business*, ISBN 978-0-7355-9458-6.
29. "Barclays Buys Core Lehman Assets," BBC News, September 17, 2008.
30. "Nomura to Acquire Lehman Brothers' Asia Pacific Franchise" (press release). Nomura Holdings, September 22, 2008. Retrieved 2012-02-15.
31. Financial Crisis Inquiry Report, "Final Report of the National Commission on the Causes of the Financial and Economic Crisis in the United States," Official Government Edition, 111-21 January 2011, p. 339.
32. Ibid., p. 340.
33. Financial Crisis Inquiry Report, "Final Report of the National Commission on the Causes of the Financial and Economic Crisis in the United States," Official Government Edition, 111-21 January 2011, p. 392.

34. Single-family mortgages that are 90 days or more past due.

35. Financial Crisis Inquiry Report, "Final Report of the National Commission on the Causes of the Financial and Economic Crisis in the United States," Official Government Edition, 111-21 January 2011, p. 393.

36. *Source:* www.bis.org.

37. Reinhart, Carmen, and Rogoff, Kenneth S., 2009, *This Time Is Different: Eight Centuries of Financial Folly,*" Princeton, NJ: Princeton University Press, pp. 129–132.

38. Financial Crisis Inquiry Report, "Final Report of the National Commission on the Causes of the Financial and Economic Crisis in the United States," Official Government Edition, 111-21 January 2011, p. 391.

39. European Systemic Risk Board, "Flagship Report on Macro-Prudential Policy on the Banking Sector," p. 6.

40. Bloomberg.

41. The MSCI World is a stock market index of 1,643 world stocks. It is maintained by MSCI Inc., formerly Morgan Stanley Capital International, and is used as a common benchmark for "world" or "global" stock funds. The index includes a collection of stocks of all the developed markets in the world as defined by MSCI. The index includes securities from 23 countries.

42. The Reconstruction Finance Corporation was a government corporation in the United States between 1932 and 1957 that provided financial support to state and local governments and made loans to banks, railroads, mortgage associations, and other businesses. Its purpose was to boost the country's confidence and help banks resume daily functions after the start of the Great Depression

43. Scott, Hal S., *Connectedness and Contagion: Protecting the Financial System from Panics*, MIT Press, May 2016.

44. *Source:* projects.propublica.org/bailout/list.

45. Financial Crisis Inquiry Commission, 2011.

46. Almeida, H., and Philippon, T., 2007, "The Risk-Adjusted Cost of Financial Distress," *Journal of Finance* 62(6), Blackwell.

CHAPTER 4

Systemic Risk, Economic and Behavioral Theories: What Can We Learn?

INTRODUCTION

This chapter explores the issue of systemic events in the context of some longstanding academic theories related to economic cycles and human behavior. By studying the characteristics of the numerous crises that have occurred throughout history, certain common themes emerge related to the economic climate that existed leading up to these events. For example, several theories exist around the impact of monetary policy on the development of asset bubbles. Some argue that so-called "easy credit" conditions have fueled investors' speculative buying of risky assets, which may have artificially inflated prices to unsustainable levels. That said, economic factors alone cannot be blamed for events such as the Great Depression or the Credit Crisis. The occurrence of these catastrophic financial events required the interplay between economic factors and the actions of individual consumers, investors, or corporations. Regarding the latter, this chapter discusses some theories related to human behavior and investment risk taking, speculative borrowing, and even the role that fear and the human brain may have played in contributing to financial crises.

After reading this chapter you will be able to:

- Describe the key components of Hyman Minsky's model of financial crises.
- Define and distinguish between homogeneous and heterogeneous beliefs.
- Describe the Rational Expectations Theory and how its key tenets were challenged following the Credit Crisis.

- Understand how theories such as Familiarity Bias and Risk Aversion may have played a role with respect to investor risk taking and decision making during periods of market stress.
- Explain the role that the human brain plays in risk taking and decision making.

MINSKY THREE-PART MODEL

Hyman Minsky was an economist and academic whose research tried to explain the economic drivers and characteristics of crises. Minsky's economic theories became a subject of focus following the Credit Crisis as many acknowledged that such theories could help at least partially explain its causes.

Minsky focused on credit market conditions and how access to credit can change over a business cycle. Minsky's belief was that surges in availability of credit in favorable time periods and reductions of such supply in weak economic periods cause volatility in financial activities and raise the possibility of a systemic crisis. Minsky's model was like that of other economists such as Fischer, Mill, Marshall, and Wicksell, who also focused on the instability in the supply of credit.

Minsky argued that a key mechanism that pushes an economy toward a crisis is the accumulation of debt by the non-government sector. He identified three types of borrowers who contribute to the accumulation of insolvent debt: hedge borrowers, speculative borrowers, and Ponzi borrowers.

- The *hedge borrower* can make debt payments (covering interest and principal) from current cash flows from investments.
- For the *speculative borrower*, cash flow from investments can service the interest due on debt, but the borrower must regularly roll over, or re-borrow, the principal, which subjects them to partial refinancing risk.
- The *Ponzi borrower* (named for Charles Ponzi) borrows based on the belief that the appreciation of the value of the asset will be sufficient to refinance the debt, but could not make sufficient payments on interest or principal with the cash flow from investments; only the appreciating asset value can keep the Ponzi borrower afloat.

The environment that existed during the Credit Crisis, in which millions of Americans borrowed frequently and excessively against the value of homes, best illustrates the *Ponzi borrower theory*. If the use of Ponzi finance is widespread enough in the financial system, then when the asset prices stop increasing, the speculative borrower can no longer refinance the principal even if able to cover interest payments. This scenario can cause the system to seize up: when the asset bubble eventually bursts, collapse of the speculative borrowers can then bring down even hedge borrowers, who are unable to find loans despite the apparent soundness of the underlying investments.

According to Minsky, outside shocks to the macroeconomic system are often the starting point for financial crises. These shocks will vary crisis to crisis, but all have similar characteristics that lead to a sort of *euphoria* on the part of investors. For example, leading up to the Great Depression in the United States there was quick growth of auto manufacturing and related expansion of the highways system, all at the same time the country began its rapid expansion of electricity use. Minsky argued if the shocks were large enough and wide in scope, the general populace expects increased profits from certain segments of the economy and may become overly aggressive in their risk taking. The corollary regarding the Credit Crisis was the tremendous runup in prices in the housing sector.

This euphoria leads to heightened and typically impractical views of the future economic climate and corporate profits. For example, in the late 1990s when the U.S. equity markets were booming because of the dot-com phenomenon, certain U.S. securities analysts called for a massive 15% annual growth in corporate profits over the next five-year period. This was clearly unrealistic, because if these analysts were correct, the GDP in the United States after that five-year period would be nearly 50% higher than at any point in history.[1] In response to these economic booms, banks begin to lend aggressively and new banks are created to fill the growing need for financing.

When inevitably the buyers become more conservative and sellers become more aggressive, this forms the beginning stages of the impending crisis. Banks and other forms of financing begin to quickly dry up as lenders fear credit losses on their loan portfolios. This *instability* of credit and early declines in asset prices led to recognition on the part of a large sector of the economy that it is time to increase their liquidity, and this fuels further selling by investors until eventually the asset bubble bursts.

DEBT DEFLATION CYCLE

A theory of economic cycles developed by Irving Fisher following the Great Depression holds that recessions and depressions are due to the overall level of debt shrinking (deflating). It holds that a decline in prices of assets and commodities leads to a reduction in the value of collateral and induces banks to call loans or refuse new ones; firms sell commodities and inventories because their prices are in decline, and the decline in prices causes more and more firms to fail. The debt–deflation cycle describes the fall in prices as firms/investors deleverage as they realize that they are overleveraged relative to a declining economy. Prices will continue to fall until leverage reaches normal levels.

BENIGN NEGLECT

The premise behind the *Theory of Benign Neglect* is that a financial crisis or panic will work itself out if allowed to follow its own course. One of the primary arguments that economists use to support this theory is the *moral hazard* scenario, whereby the very speculative behavior that might have fueled the crisis will only be further encouraged as investors observe a possibility that they will be bailed out by the government. There is also a longstanding argument that the more government authorities intervene regarding the current crisis, the more likely it is that individuals, having come to rely on public bailouts to limit or insulate their downside risk, will fuel an even greater asset bubble in the future. Note the following quote by Andrew Mellon in his advice to President Herbert Hoover:

> *When people get an inflationary brainstorm, the only way to get out of their blood is to let it collapse. It will purge the rottenness out of the system. High cost of living and high living will come down. People will work harder, live a moral life. Values will be adjusted, and enterprising people will pick up the wrecks from less competent people.*[2]

The opposing view often cited is that the risk of a panic that might ensue from the lack of government intervention would spread to the broader economy and wipe out investments of non-speculators as well. History tells us that panics are almost never left to their own devices. For example, during the crisis of the South Sea Company, the Bank of England promised to absorb payment of £400 of bonds issued by the company.[3] Before the existence of the U.S. Federal Reserve System, a key tool used by the United States to address the risk of bank runs was the use of clearinghouse certificates, a currency replacement that represented the joint obligation of debt of a group of banks. In the early period of World War I in 1914, to stem panic selling, trading on the New York Stock Exchange (NYSE) was temporarily ceased in many global exchanges, including London. Similarly, following the bombing of the World Trade Center in 2001, the NYSE and other U.S stock exchanges were closed for a week.

A recent example of government intervention was the Credit Crisis in which the U.S. government intervened on a massive scale, providing over

$600 billion of bailout funds to approximately 950 entities under its Treasury Asset Relief Program (TARP) and other similar programs.

A famous example of a contrarian view to the doctrine of benign neglect is that of Walter Bagehot, who felt that "loans should be granted to all comers" based upon sound collateral "as largely as the public asks for them," and "however sudden the demand may be, it does not appear to us that there is any objection on principle to sudden issues of paper money to meet sudden and large extensions of demand."[4]

BEHAVIORAL THEORIES

The impact of human behavior on the performance of financial markets and economic issues has been studied for a long time. Consider the following quote from a British economist:

> Far be it for me to say that we ever shall have the means of measuring directly the feelings of the human heart. A unit of pleasure or of pain is difficult even to conceive; but it is the amount of these feelings which is continually prompting us to buying and selling, borrowing and lending, laboring and resting, producing and consuming; and it is from the quantitative effects of the feelings that we must estimate their comparative amounts.[5]

Among the many likely contributors to many crises throughout history, behavioral factors have been the subject of frequent industry and academic discussion. Some researchers argued that most of the causes of the crises are closely linked to behavioral factors[6] while others found that subprime mortgage models suffered severe flaws in predicting consumer behavior given the significant underestimation of predicted default rates on more complex mortgages.[7]

Before discussing the role that human behavior may have played in the recent Credit Crisis, we must first discuss the *Efficient Market Hypothesis* (EMH) and the related *Rational Expectations Theory*, as behavioral finance challenges most of the assumptions associated with these theories.

EMH assumes, among other things, that market prices should fully reflect all available information about a particular asset or company up to that point in time. Another EMH assumption is that given the prior assumption, informed investors and traders identify any deviations between current prices and fundamental value and achieve quick arbitrage profits. Behavioral theory challenges these EMH assumptions, including the idea that EMH cannot adequately explain the frequent market anomalies that occur and that the influence of arbitrage on keeping markets efficient is limited.

The Rational Expectations Theory assumes that investors and markets are rational and that their beliefs change immediately in response to each market change. Investors who make optimal decisions under the assumption that they form their expectation about the future rationally has been an existing theory of macroeconomics for decades.[8] Rational expectations do not require that an agent's predictions about the future always be correct. In fact, such predictions may turn out to be incorrect in every period, but still be rational. Instead, the primary test is whether, on average, over a long period time, expectations are correct. Agents are assumed to consider all relevant information and to make unbiased predictions based on this information. Some criticize the Rational Expectations Theory because it requires agents to possess too much knowledge. For example, to form rational expectations, agents must know the true structure and probability distribution of the economy.[9] Given the inability of econometricians to estimate the economic model perfectly, it is unrealistic to expect agents to have such ability.[10]

History is full of all types of crises, panics, and manias, which on the surface would seem to contradict the assumption of rational behavior by market participants. Consider the following quote concerning the South Street Sea Bubble of 1720:

> *They had an immense capital dividend among an immense number of proprietors. It was naturally to be expected, therefore, that folly, negligence, and profusion should prevail in the whole management of their affairs. The knavery and extravagance of their stock-jobbing operations are sufficiently known (as are) the negligence, profusion and malversation of the servant of the company.*[11]

RISK AVERSION BIAS

In the seminal Sharpe-Lintner Capital Asset Pricing Model (CAPM),[12] which derives equilibrium prices for all risky assets, all agents are assumed to be risk-averse. All agents are expected to agree on the expected returns and on the variance/covariance matrix. Risk aversion is the tendency to feel the negative impact of a loss more acutely than the pleasure of an equal-sized gain.[13] This phenomenon is captured by the *Prospect Theory*.[14] Under this theory, decision makers' reaction to changes in wealth are modeled and are approximately twice as sensitive to perceived losses than gains. Under the tenets of the Prospect Theory, investors underweight outcomes that are deemed likely versus those that are viewed with near certainty. For example, during the Great Depression era Moody's ratings on stocks were considered the gold standard in terms of assessing the quality of securities. As such, many investors relied entirely on such ratings for decisions without doing the necessary due diligence.[15] The massive drying up of liquidity in the credit markets during the Credit Crisis, particularly in structured products, led to fire-sale prices, availability of high interest rates, and unique profit opportunities for sophisticated investors. The fact that few such investors took advantage of these once-in-a-generation price anomalies and arbitrage opportunities is evidence of *loss aversion bias*, as EMH and related theories of rational investing would suggest that investors would have recognized that some of these price dislocations were temporary or even unjustified in some cases and would have jumped in to buy, thereby adjusting prices to more realistic levels.

ASSET PRICES

A fundamental idea behind the Rational Expectations Theory is that each trader is able to make inferences from market price about the profitability of his or her trade. Assuming a stock market with homogeneous information, all traders have at each period the same information, and the asset price conveys no extra information.[16] This scenario is often referred to as the *Martingale Property*.

If this property held true, one would not expect to see significant volatility in observed historical asset returns, in particular, equity returns. However, agents may be boundedly rational about their beliefs about future payoff on risky assets and may have homogeneous views about future cash flows. But agents often disagree about the speed the asset price will mean-revert back to its fundamental value and expect that a mispricing will adjust at different time horizons.[17]

Many models have been proposed that incorporate the assumption that heterogeneity of expectations may play a significant role in asset pricing.[18] Some studies have also suggested the combination of differences in beliefs and short sale constraints can explain persistent deviations of stock prices from intrinsic values.

Asset prices are known to experience significant increases in correlation during periods of market stress. A potential explanation for this phenomenon is the fact that traders come to the realization that the market price that they felt contained all pertinent information about a company, actually may not. As a result, they quickly adjust their behavior, exhibiting traits such as herding and homogeneous beliefs, which help to fuel increased asset correlations.

HOMOGENEOUS EXPECTATIONS VERSUS HETEROGENEITY

Heterogeneous beliefs represent a scenario whereby investors do not agree on the basic value of an asset. For example, an investor may be agreeable to overpay for a security today with respect to their analysis of its true worth, on the belief the security can be resold for a profit to another optimistic investor in the future. This behavior is blamed for helping to fuel prior asset bubbles.

> *In a dynamic environment with time-varying heterogeneous beliefs and short sale constraints, an asset buyer may be willing to pay more than his own expectation of the asset's fundamentals because he believes he can resell to an even more optimistic buyer for a speculative profit. This motive leads the asset owner to value the asset at a price higher than his already optimistic belief and therefore helps to fuel bubble.*[19]

A key assumption in the seminal *Modern Portfolio Theory* is that all investors will have the same expectations and make the same choices given a set of circumstances.[20] The assumption of *homogeneous expectations* states that all investors will have the same expectations regarding inputs used to develop efficient portfolios, including asset returns, variances, and covariances. For example, if shown several investment plans with different returns at a particular risk level, all investors will choose the plan that boasts the highest return. Similarly, if investors are shown plans that have different risks but the same returns, all investors will choose the plan that has the lowest risk.

Agents are *boundedly rational* in that they choose from a variety of methods with which to form expectations, with homogeneous expectations representing just one choice.[21] One of many reasons why an agent might shift from homogeneous to heterogeneous expectations is that agents analyze the past performance of their chosen predictor(s) and, if such choices performed poorly, in the future they might exhibit behavior that is less homogeneous with other agents. Agents can be heterogeneous in several ways:[22]

- *Preference* (risk aversion)
- *Agent-specific noise:* Agent is an expected utility maximizer but may deviate from the optimal investment strategy due to random noise.
- *Expectation:* Even if all investors have the same preferences, they may have heterogeneous expectations regarding the future distribution of the random variable (returns in the stock market). For example, all agents estimate future distribution of returns looking at historical rates

of return, but they are heterogeneous regarding their memory spans; some use the last 5 years' returns while others may analyze the past 10 years' returns.

■ *Strategy:* Agents may have different investment strategies. Some may adjust their expectations and their investment policies frequently while others may take a longer-term approach.

Ahead are some examples of behavioral theories that have each played a role in explaining bubbles and crashes.

Anchoring Heuristic

Behavioral studies, including those by cognitive psychologists, have found that investors tend to *anchor* their views to their initial values or judgments and, therefore, even when presented with overwhelming evidence supporting an adjustment to such judgments, refuse to take rational actions.[23] As it relates to the Credit Crisis, most investors held a view that U.S. housing prices would only continue to rise, based on recent history. This anchored belief likely caused many to continue speculating on further increases to home prices and related MBS even as data in early 2007 showed significant signs of weakening in the U.S. housing market. Consider the following quote on the theory of anchoring:

> *Anchoring may be a particular influential cognitive process in making judgments about the value of a financial security and the direction of its future market price. Likely anchors in this regard may include a security's current price, its most recent prices and the prices of related securities, whether or not the relationship is relevant and whether the relationship points to a relationship in fundamental valuation or changes in values.*[24]

Excessive Optimism

Substantial psychological literature exists that supports the theory that human beings can be excessively optimistic and refuse to properly account for downside risk. For example, some research suggests that financial regulators failed to require firms to use conservative enough stress testing scenarios. Consider the following:

"The regulators required the institutions to run tests under a 'baseline' and 'more adverse' scenario. However, the latter scenario only assumed for the worst scenario over the next two years: −3.3% real GDP growth, 10.3%

unemployment, and an approximately 22% decline in home prices. In short, even in the middle of one of the worst financial catastrophes in decades, financial regulators could not even assume an extremely adverse scenario for planning purposes."

Indeed, history has shown that that over time investors' memories of prior crises seem to fade as good economic times return.[25]

Familiarity Bias

Familiarity bias represents a subconscious process in which the brain essentially substitutes newer information for previously understood patterns and successful outcomes.[26] Research finds that *familiarity bias* played a significant negative role in the recent Credit Crisis, as homeowners became accustomed to rising home values and failed to prudently account for the possibility that home prices might actually fall. Among other problems, such bias led to homeowners taking excessive amounts of cash out of their homes when refinancing and drawing down too much on home equity lines of credit and loans.[27]

Fallacy of Composition

The theory of *fallacy of composition* states that the actions of each investor are rational, or would be if many other investors did not act in the exact same way. An example related to the recent Credit Crisis might apply to the practice of leveraged investing in real estate. While on an individual basis this practice may lead to profits, it is bad for the economy as a whole. Residential property is not productive from an economic standpoint; therefore speculative investment in such properties crowds out investment in productive activities that would benefit the entire economy. In addition, when all investors behave the same, the result is an overleveraged market that is highly susceptible to a price bubble. Subprime investors may have acted individually rational in certain cases, but didn't anticipate that the production of a large volume of subprime loans would be destabilizing to the overall economy as higher default rates brought down house prices.

Fight or Flight

It has long been an accepted fact that fear has helped protect the human species throughout history from physical harm. Perhaps the most common example of the latter is the scientifically proven *fight-or-flight* response that is imbedded in the human brain. This innate response often consists of significant changes in blood pressure and a rush of adrenaline to protect against physical threats. For example, it can lead to very poor decisions such as the common behavior of *doubling down* rather than limiting further investment losses.[28]

A detailed chemical study of the brain found that only one of its four regions, the amygdala, was the final place where the path of fear ended and determined that fear had several important implications for financial crisis. Perhaps the most significant of these is that the neuropathway for fear response circumvents the brain's higher capabilities, including those associated with rationality. The pathway leads to an area of the brain that processes the emotional significance of stimuli. Thus, people often behave and make decisions subconsciously driven by this emotional state, which has had clear implications with respect to prior financial crises.[29]

On the one hand, the fear of losing money can cause an investor to rationally manage his risks in relation to potential rewards. Meanwhile, extreme fear may cause investors to liquidate more risky securities faster than they ordinarily would, even at losses, in exchange for safer investments. This decision may not be in the best interest of the investor in the long term. When you consider that this behavior is sometimes widespread, such as during a banking panic, it can lead to a systemic event.

Akin to the study of the brain to better understand fear impulses, scientists have long studied the so-called *reward center* of the brain. The neurological pathways of this area of the brain all transmit the same chemical signal, dopamine. When injected with the drug L-DOPA, a chemical converted to dopamine in the brain, patients often became addicted to gambling.[30]

In another study, a technique known as *functional magnetic resonance imaging* (fMRI) identified portions of the brain that were impacted when a person achieved financial rewards or losses. In one experiment, it was found that the nucleus accumbens, which is part of the brain's reward system, the amygdala, evidenced enhanced activity associated with financial gains.[31]

Some additional researchers who attempted to leverage fMRI technology to project economic behavior include those who theorized that since certain sections of the brain become stimulated prior to certain behaviors taking place, these changes might be studied to develop a sort of psychological roadmap of decision making. While fMRI has dramatically improved the ability of researchers to explore the brain in detail never before possible, helping to link neuroscience to economics and finance, there is still a considerable way to go before the role the brain plays in financial decision making is fully understood.[32]

KEY POINTS

- Minsky identified three types of borrowers who contribute to the accumulation of insolvent debt: hedge borrowers, speculative borrowers, and Ponzi borrowers. The *hedge borrower* can make debt payments (covering interest and principal) from current cash flows from investments. For the *speculative borrower*, the cash flow from investments can service the debt, that is, cover the interest due, but the borrower must regularly roll over, or re-borrow, the principal. The *Ponzi borrower* (named for Charles Ponzi) borrows based on the belief that the appreciation of the value of the asset will be sufficient to refinance the debt but could not make sufficient payments on interest or principal with the cash flow from investments; only the appreciating asset value can keep the Ponzi borrower afloat.

- The premise behind the *Theory of Benign Neglect* is that a financial crisis or panic will work itself out if allowed to follow its own course. *Efficient Market Hypothesis* assumes that market prices should fully reflect all available information about a particular asset or company up to that point in time. The *Rational Expectations Theory* assumes that investors and markets are rational and that their beliefs change immediately in response to each market change.

- Theories such as Efficient Market Hypothesis and Rational Expectations have been the subject of substantial challenge since history is full of all types of market anomalies that occur, including numerous crises, panics, and manias, which on the surface would seem to contradict the assumption of efficient markets and rational behavior by market participants.

- Under the *Prospect Theory,* decision makers' reaction to changes in wealth are modeled and are approximately twice as sensitive to perceived losses than gains and investors' underweight outcomes that are deemed likely versus those that are viewed with near certainty.

- *Heterogeneous beliefs* represent a scenario whereby investors do not agree on the basic value or expected return of an asset. For example, an investor may be agreeable to overpay for a security today relative to their view of its fundamental value, on the belief the security can be resold for a profit to another optimistic investor in the future, earning a speculative profit.

- *Fight or flight* represents innate response that involves significant changes in blood pressure and a rush of adrenaline to protect humans against physical threats. A detailed chemical study of the brain found that only one of its four regions, the amygdala, was the final place where the path of fear ended and determined that fear had several important implications for financial crisis. For example, extreme fear or panic may cause investors to liquidate more risky securities faster than they ordinarily would, even at losses, in exchange for safer investments.

- *Familiarity bias* played a significant negative role in the Credit Crisis as homeowners became accustomed to rising home values and failed to prudently account for the possibility that home prices might fall.
- A detailed chemical study of the brain found that fear had several important implications for financial crises. Perhaps the most significant of these is that the neuropathway for fear response circumvents the brain's higher capabilities, including those associated with rationality.

KNOWLEDGE CHECK

Q4.1: What are the three parts to Hyman Minsky's theory regarding the role excessive supply of credit and borrowing plays in most historical crises?

Q4.2: Which economic theory posits that there shouldn't be any extraordinary government intervention or bailout during a crisis?

Q4.3: Please explain the concept of Moral Hazard.

Q4.4: What is the main tenet of the Efficient Market Hypothesis?

Q4.5: What evidence has often been cited to refute the validity of the Efficient Market Hypothesis?

Q4.6: Please explain the Theory of Anchoring Heuristics and what role it may have played during the Credit Crisis.

Q4.7: How does the Prospect Theory attempt to explain investor risk aversion?

Q4.8: Describe the main difference between the theories of *heterogeneous* and *homogeneous* beliefs.

Q4.9: Which of the four regions of the brain may help explain why individual investors make irrational investment and borrowing decisions?

NOTES

1. Kindleberger, C.P., and Aliber, R., 2005, *Manias, Panics and Crashes: A History of Financial Crisis*, 5th ed. Hoboken, NJ: Wiley, p. 28.
2. Hoover, Herbert. 1952. The memoirs of Herbert Hoover: the Great Depression 1929–1941. New York: Macmillan Co.
3. Andreades, Bank of England, p. 137, citing Henrey D. McLeod, *Theory and Practice of Banking*, 3rd ed. London: Longman Green, Reader & Dyer, 1879, p. 428.

4. Bagehot, W., 1873, *Lombard Street: A Description of the Money Market*, reprint ed., London: John Murray, 1917, p. 160.
5. Jevons, W.J., 1871, *The Theory of Political Economy*. London: Macmillan and Co.
6. Avgouleas, E., 2009, "The Global Financial Crisis, Behavioral Finance and Financial Regulation: In Search of Orthodoxy," *Journal of Corporate Law Studies*, 9(1): 23–59.
7. Gerding, E.F., 2009, "Code, Crash, and Open Source: The Outsourcing of Financial Regulations to Risk Models and the Global Financial Crisis," *Washington Law Review*, 84: 127–188.
8. Ormerod, P., 2009, "The Current Crisis and the Capability of Macroeconomic Theory," working paper.
9. Sargent, T., 1993, "Bounded Rationality in Macroeconomics," Clarendon Press.
10. Branch, W.A., 2004, "The Theory of Rationally Heterogeneous Expectations: Evidence From Survey Data on Inflation Expectations," *Economic Journal*, 114: 592–621.
11. Smith, A., 1776, *An Inquiry into the Nature and Causes of Wealth of Nations* (reprinted). New York: Modern Library, 1937, p. 703.
12. The capital asset pricing model developed by William Sharpe and John Lintner represents the origin of asset pricing theory and is widely used in applications such as estimating the cost of capital for firms and evaluating the performance of managed portfolios.
13. Rabin, M., and Thaler, R.H., 2001, "Anomalies: Risk Aversion," *Journal of Economic Perspectives*, 15(1): 219–232.
14. Kahneman, D., and Tversky, A., 1979 (Mar.), "Prospect Theory: An Analysis of Decision under Risk," *Econometrica*, 47(2): 263–292.
15. Donnellan, J.T., 2013, "An Analysis of the Stability and Accuracy of Moody's Bond Ratings and Stock Picking During the U.S. Great Depression," dissertation. Pace University Lubin School of Business, p. 77.
16. Tirole, J., 1982, "On the Possibility of Speculation under Rational Expectations," *Econometrica*, 50(5): 1163–1181.
17. Boswijk, P., Hommes, C., and Manzan, S., 2005, "Behavioral Homogeneity in Stock Prices," Tinbergen Institute Discussion Paper No. 05-052/1.
18. Hong, H., and Stein, J.C., 2003, "Differences of Opinion, Short-Sales Constraints, and Market Crashes," *Rev. Finance. Stud.*, 16(2): 487–525.
19. Harrison, M., and Kreps, D.M., 1978, "Speculative Investor Behavior in a Stock-Market with Heterogeneous Expectations," *Quarterly Journal of Economics*, 92: 323–336.
20. Markowitz, H., 1952, "Portfolio Selection," *Journal of Finance*, 7(1): 77–91.
21. Branch, W.A., 2004, "The Theory of Rationally Heterogeneous Expectations: Evidence from Survey Data on Inflation Expectations," *Economic Journal*, 114: 592–621.
22. Levy and Soloman, 1995, "A Microscopic Model of the Stock Market: Cycles, Booms, and Crashes," *Economics Letters*, 45(1): 103–111.
23. Lynch, T.E., 2009, "Deeply and Persistently Conflicted: Credit Rating Agencies in the Current Regulatory Environment," *Case Western Reserve Law Review*, 59(2).

24. Barberis, N., and Thaler, R., 2003, "A Survey of Behavior Finance," in *Handbook of the Economics of Finance*, Constantinides, G., Harris, M., Stulz, R. (eds.). North Holland, Amsterdam.
25. Fanto, J., 2009, "Anticipating the Unthinkable: The Adequacy of Risk Management in Finance and Environmental Studies," *Wake Forest Law Review*, 44(3): 731–755.
26. Kahneman, D., and Tversky, A., 1979 (Mar.), "Prospect Theory: An Analysis of Decision under Risk," *Econometrica*, 47(2): 263–292.
27. Seiler, M.J., Seiler, V., Harrison, D.M., and Lane, M.A., 2013, "Familiarity Bias and Perceived Future Home Price Movements," *Journal of Behavioral Finance*, 14: 9–24.
28. Lo, A.W., 2011, "Fear, Greed, and Financial Crises: A Cognitive Neurosciences Perspective," October.
29. LeDoux, J.E., 1996, *The Emotional Brain*. New York: Simon & Schuster.
30. Carlsson, A., Lindqvist, M., and Magnusson, T., 1957, "3,4-Dihyroxyphenyl-alanine and 5- Hydroxtryptophan as Reserpine Antagonists," *Nature*, 180: 1200.
31. Breiter, H.C., Aharon, I., Kahneman, D., Dale, A., and Shizgal, P., 2001, "Functional Imaging or Neural Responses to Expectancy and Experience of Monetary Gains and Losses," *Neuron*, 30: 619–639.
32. Knutson, B., and Bossaerts, P., 2007, "Neural Antecedents of Financial Decisions," *Journal of Neuroscience*, 27: 8174–8177.

CHAPTER 5

Systemic Risk Data

INTRODUCTION

The Credit Crisis revealed significant gaps in the data available for regulators and risk managers to identify vulnerabilities and emerging threats that ultimately led to the crisis. These gaps were widespread and related to insufficient information about individual financial institutions and a lack of data about interconnections across the financial system. Concerning the latter, the Credit Crisis illustrated how a shock or dislocation in one company, asset class, or region can quickly spread to other markets and firms across borders. Because of the catastrophic impact that historical crises have had on financial institutions and consumers, the need to close data gaps to enhance systemic risk measurement and monitoring has been a top priority for global regulators in recent years. This chapter will discuss some of the responses by regulators and policymakers in terms of new entities created to address data gaps, some of the new metrics developed to track the buildup of systemic risks in the financial system, and some of the challenges that still exist with respect to maximizing the use of data to identify and monitor systemic threats.

After reading this chapter you will be able to:

- List the key characteristics that data should possess to aid in the monitoring of systemic risks.
- Identify examples of economic data sources that can prove useful in the identification of systemic risk buildup.
- Explain the various systemic risk indices and metrics that are publicly available.
- Explain the mandate of the Office of Financial Research.
- Understand data standardization initiatives such as the Legal Entity Identifier (LEI).

KEY DATA ATTRIBUTES

Given the heightened focus on systemic risk research and supervision, particularly a shift from the more traditional institution-based or microprudential analysis to macroprudential supervision, there has been a greater need for the analysis of the broader financial system and contagion risk.

> *Thus, regulators performing systemic risk oversight will be tasked with receiving and monitoring types of information which they have typically not received before. Measures and information which enable assessment of network effects and concentrations will be needed. Information long used in risk management may be viewed and used in new ways. A focus on counterparty risk exposures, with more information about interactions between counterparties, will likely be needed.*[1]

Driven largely by the fallout from the Credit Crisis, there has been an increasing need for more data and more flexible risk analysis capabilities that would allow the many different constituents involved in systemic risk monitoring to have better transparency into counterparty exposures and potential asset bubbles. While clearly each actor will have different data and information requirements, in the spirit of outlining a reasonable foundation for all participants in the systemic risk arena, the following represents a taxonomy of attributes that would make measures of systemic risk valuable to all researchers:[2]

- Simplicity
- Specificity
- Comparability
- Aggregate and firm specific
- Forward looking
- International
- Encompasses financial institutions broadly (not limited to banks)
- Linked to theory

In the appendix of this book, we provide a taxonomy and literature review of some of the key quantitative models that are used to measure systemic risk in different ways.

KEY POLICY CHANGES TO ADDRESS DATA GAPS

Because of the widespread impact of the Credit Crisis, there were calls for significant changes in the way that financial supervisors monitor systemic risk indicators that might help provide an early warning of future crises. One of the main responses to this problem in the United States was the creation of the Office of Financial Research (OFR) in 2010 under the powers of the Dodd-Frank Wall Street Reform and Consumer Protection Act. The OFR was given the authority to collect data to support the work of the Financial Stability Oversight Council (FSOC) and to set standards for reporting such data. To support the FSOC in identifying interconnections among market participants and monitoring systemic risk, the OFR strives to standardize how parties to financial contracts are identified in the data it collects on behalf of the FSOC. The FSOC is chaired by the U.S. Treasury Secretary and is comprised of eight federal financial regulators and an insurance expert as well as state regulators and other non-voting members. The mission of the FSOC is to identify risks to financial stability, respond to emerging threats, and promote market discipline. See Chapter 9 for more details on the FSOC.

In 2015, the OFR identified eight programs covering the following broad mandates:

- Improving the quality, scope, and accessibility of financial data
- Assessing, measuring, and monitoring threats across the financial system
- Performing essential research
- Supporting the FSOC and its member organizations

Through the collection and analysis of data the OFR strives to anticipate emerging threats to financial stability or assess how shocks to one financial firm could impact the system. The OFR collects information and analyzes data on the financial system to assess the current and potential future states of the system and explore potential government interventions.

OFR Programs Focused on Data: The OFR's three programs focused directly on data include data accessibility, data quality, and data scope.

1. *Data Accessibility:* The Dodd-Frank Act requires the OFR to collect data on behalf of the FSOC, provide data to the FSOC and its member agencies, and maintain data security and confidentiality. After consulting with member agencies, the OFR provides data to financial industry participants and the public to increase transparency and facilitate research on the financial system. For the OFR to achieve these objectives, secure and appropriate data sharing must be a key priority.
2. *Data Quality:* Data quality is particularly important to the OFR and to the FSOC because complete, accurate, and timely data are essential to identify and analyze vulnerabilities in the U.S. financial system. Data standards do not assure quality, but without standards, comparing, aggregating, and analyzing the data essential for financial stability

analysis are nearly impossible. That's why the OFR has a mandate to standardize the types and formats of data it reports and collects, and to assist FSOC member agencies with the development and use of data standards. The financial crisis demonstrated to regulators and industry that standardizing data collected from financial services companies is necessary for effective oversight of the financial system and its parts.

3. *Data Scope:* The OFR has a mandate to collect from any financial company the data necessary to assess to what extent a financial activity or financial market poses a threat to U.S. financial stability. To assess data gaps and to prioritize filling them, it collaborates with other regulatory bodies to identify key questions and the data needed to answer them. The OFR uses data inventories or catalogs to compare the needs to the available data and to prevent the duplication of existing data collection efforts. Before building permanent data collections, the OFR will engage with industry and the sources for financial data, and conduct pilot projects to ensure that the data collected are defined precisely and meet specific data-quality criteria.

To measure financial activity for financial stability monitoring, data scope must be both comprehensive and detailed. It must be comprehensive to analyze sources and uses of funds, the behavior of borrowers and lenders, and risks wherever they arise. It must be detailed, at times even to the transaction level, because assessing vulnerabilities involves measuring risk throughout the distribution of outcomes, not just at the mean or median. For example, an analysis of average lending terms and conditions might hide important concentrations of risk. Taking these factors into consideration, the OFR collects highly detailed data when they are essential for such analysis.[3]

Stress-Testing Programs: In addition to the work of the OFR, stress-testing programs such as the U.S. Comprehensive Capital Analysis and Review (CCAR) and the European Union–wide bank stress tests coordinated by the European Banking Authority (EBA) illustrate the need for improved risk analytics and strong risk and transaction data. Under the post-crisis European systemic risk management framework, the European Central Bank (ECB) has been tasked with collecting, processing, and providing statistical information and analytical support to the European Systemic Risk Board (ESRB),[4] whose mandate is to recommend macroprudential policies aimed at preventing and mitigating systemic risks to financial stability. See Chapter 8 for more details on the European systemic risk regulatory regime.

A core component of macroprudential policy strategy involves the risk identification stage, in which relevant indicators help detect and assess vulnerabilities and the buildup of systemic threats and where indicative thresholds can be used to help guide policy.[5]

DATA SOURCES

It is outside the scope of this book to list all potential sources of data and metrics that can be used to assist financial regulators and other market participants in monitoring the buildup of systemic risks. However, the important point is that the future technology infrastructure of the industry will need to support an extremely wide array of data requirements and will need to have the ability to store large volumes of data that will be updated with frequencies that can range from once per quarter to possibly many times each second.[6] The specific data sources needed will, of course, be driven by the input requirements of specific models. Sources will include data on specific industries and markets as well as national-level data such as:

- Key interest rates
- Equity and commodity indices
- Labor productivity
- Employment rates
- Inflation rates
- Capital productivity

Table 5.1 provides a partial example of some metrics and indices that measure changes to markets and economic data relative to historical norms and flag changes that represent outliers and may provide an early warning of a market dislocation or systemic event.

DATA COLLECTION CHALLENGES AND REMAINING GAPS

In recent years, many financial firms have undertaken major initiatives aimed at improving the quality and accuracy of their internal data and reporting capabilities. The plethora of new regulatory demands, among other reasons, has drawn attention to the fact that there are significant gaps in data quality both at the individual firm level as well as industry-wide. The FSB noted the following:

> *Supervisors observe that aggregation of risk data remains a challenge for firms despite being essential to strategic planning, risk monitoring and decision-making.... While firms are working toward improving their data aggregation capabilities, supervisors would like to see more progress and some are raising expectations for what is considered acceptable in firms' risk reporting capabilities, particularly at SIFIs.*[16]

TABLE 5.1 Financial Turbulence and Systemic Risk Metrics

Index Title	Description
Chicago Fed National Financial Conditions Index[7]	Provides a comprehensive weekly update on U.S. financial conditions in money markets, debt and equity markets, and the traditional and shadow banking systems.
St. Louis Fed Financial Stress Index[8]	Measures the degree of financial stress in the markets and is constructed from 18 weekly data series: seven interest rate series, six yield spreads, and five other indicators. Each of these variables captures some aspect of financial stress. Accordingly, as the level of financial stress in the economy changes, the data series are likely to move together.
Kansas City Financial Stress Index[9]	A monthly measure of stress in the U.S. financial system based on 11 financial market variables.
CBOE Volatility Index[10]	The VIX Index is a key measure of market expectations of near-term volatility conveyed by S&P 500 stock index option prices. Since its introduction in 1993, the VIX Index has been considered by many to be the world's premier barometer of investor sentiment and market volatility. Several investors expressed interest in trading instruments related to the market's expectation of future volatility, and so VIX futures were introduced in 2004, and VIX options were introduced in 2006.
Global Financial Stress Index[11]	The Global Financial Stress Index is a Bank of America Merrill Lynch–calculated, cross-market measure of risk, hedging demand, and investor flows in the global financial system. Levels greater/less than 0 indicate more/less financial market stress than normal. Apart from the headline GFSI, there are three sub-indices: Risk, Flow, and Skew.
CBOE/S&P 500 Implied Correlation Index[12]	Using SPX options prices, together with the prices of options on the 50 largest stocks in the S&P 500 Index, the CBOE S&P 500 Implied Correlation Indexes offer insight into the relative cost of SPX options compared to the price of options on individual stocks that comprise the S&P 500.

Citi Economic Surprise Index[13]

The Citigroup Economic Surprise Indices are objective and quantitative measures of economic news. They are defined as weighted historical standard deviations of data surprises (actual releases vs. Bloomberg survey median). A positive reading of the Economic Surprise Index suggests that economic releases have on balance [been] beating consensus. The indices are calculated daily in a rolling three-month window. The weights of economic indicators are derived from relative high-frequency spot FX impacts of 1 standard deviation data surprises. The indices also employ a time decay function to replicate the limited memory of markets.

Put/Call Ratio[14]

The put/call ratio is an indicator ratio that provides information about the trading volume of put options to call options. The put/call ratio has long been viewed as an indicator of investor sentiment in the markets. Technical traders use the put/call ratio as an indicator of performance and as a barometer of the overall market sentiment.

CBOE Skew Index[15]

An index derived from the price of S&P 500 tail risk. Similar to the VIX, the price of S&P 500 tail risk is calculated from the prices of S&P 500 out-of-the-money options. SKEW typically ranges from 100 to 150. A SKEW value of 100 means that the perceived distribution of S&P 500 log-returns is normal, and the probability of outlier returns is therefore negligible. As SKEW rises above 100, the left tail of the S&P 500 distribution acquires more weight, and the probabilities of outlier returns become more significant. One can estimate these probabilities from the value of SKEW. Since an increase in perceived tail risk increases the relative demand for low strike puts, increases in SKEW also correspond to an overall steepening of the curve of implied volatilities, familiar to option traders as the "skew."

Furthermore, any framework for data collection needs to consider the massive global scale of the world's largest financial institutions and their extremely complex organization structures. Based on public annual reports of the 10 largest global banks, these institutions have on average 3,500 subsidiaries located in 80 countries. Additionally, in some cases the greatest systemic risk within a global institution may be located within its non-home-country subsidiary. An example of the latter would be the significant deterioration in the financial condition of the U.S. branches of European banks during the Credit Crisis because of their substantial involvement in subprime real estate activities.[17]

These data challenges are further supported by the results of an industry survey that asked risk managers what they viewed as their most significant concern regarding risk information systems, and *risk data quality and management* was cited as the largest concern.[18] Additionally, no more than 8% of risk executives rated any area of data management as *extremely effective* and no more than 31% rated any area as *very effective.*

One challenge relates to the global nature of most large financial institutions that operate in many different jurisdictions. Financial supervisors will have access to very detailed data for banks operating in their jurisdiction. However, with laws that limit the availability of data sharing across geographic borders, it is a challenge for a bank's home supervisor to obtain a complete view of all risk exposures and interconnections such a bank might have across multiple countries and regions.

Per the Bank for International Settlements (BIS) there are four main challenges that arise internationally concerning the use of data for systemic risk mitigation:[19]

1. *Measurement of Bank's Foreign Credit Exposures:* Although aggregated bank data, such as BIS international banking statistics, track banks' exposures to countries and sectors, they lack granularity necessary to identify which specific subsidiaries are the main source of risk.
2. *Measurement of Borrowers' Reliance on Foreign Bank Credit:* Many banks experienced disruptions in international capital flows during the Credit Crisis. This was largely due to creditor banking systems' unwillingness to roll over all cross-border credit as they were having their own balance sheet problems.
3. *Measurement of Cross-Currency Funding and Maturity Transformation:* During the lead-up to the Credit Crisis, many international banks invested heavily in U.S. dollar-denominated assets that were funded through short-term interbank borrowings. When concerns over asset quality increased, especially in asset-backed securities, these banks found it very difficult to roll over their dollar-funding positions. BIS did

provide data that helped demonstrate the aggregate size of the risk. For example, just before the Credit Crisis it was estimated that European Banks were reliant on about $1 trillion of short-term funding. However, such data only showed broad trends as there were no data available on residual maturities or the use of the FX swaps market.

4. *Modeling Systemic Risk for International Banks:* BIS consolidated banking data are used to model losses due to direct exposures of banking systems to the public sector, banking sector, non-bank private sector, and indirect exposures via off-balance-sheet contingent positions. However, due to a lack of bank-level data, this limits the effectiveness of the analysis for policy discussions.

Another challenge related to the effective measurement of systemic risk is the growing interconnectedness among financial institutions and markets, countries, and real sectors (e.g., linkages between public and financial, household or corporate and financial, public and external). Consequently, macro-financial linkages and systemic risks are more difficult to measure than ever before.[20] This risk will be discussed in more detail in Chapter 15.

The International Monetary Fund and Financial Stability Board have issued jointly a report to the G20 finance ministers and central bank governors with 20 recommendations on reducing financial data gaps. Some of the key recommendations include:[21]

- Development of measures of system-wide macroprudential risk, such as aggregate leverage and maturity mismatches. (R4)
- Development of a common data template for systemically important global financial institutions to better understand the exposures of these institutions to different financial sectors and national markets. (R8 and 9)
- Enhancement of BIS consolidated banking statistics, including the separate identification of non-bank financial institutions in the sectoral breakdown, and the tracking of funding patterns of international financial systems. (R11)
- Development of a standardized template covering the international exposure of large non-bank financial institutions. (R14)

The OFR has identified several projects as top priorities for addressing remaining data gaps. These include projects related to repos, securities lending, and swaps. Let's explore each.

Bilateral Repo Data Collection Pilot Project: The OFR has a partnership with the Fed and the Securities and Exchange Commission (SEC) to fill gaps in data about repurchase agreements, or *repo*. A repo is essentially a collateralized loan where one party sells a security to another party with an agreement to repurchase it later at an agreed price. The project promises to improve understanding of a short-term funding market that is instrumental in providing liquidity that helps to keep the global financial system operating smoothly.

Securities Lending Data Collection Pilot Project: In partnership with the Fed and SEC, the OFR conducted a pilot project to fill gaps in data about securities lending. This pilot project followed the OFR's collaboration with the same two agencies to collect data about repurchase agreements, or repos. In securities lending, securities owners lend stocks or bonds to other parties. These loans are secured by collateral, which can be cash, other securities, or other financial assets. Securities lending makes financial markets more liquid by increasing the supply of securities, and facilitates price discovery. Securities lending allows investors who believe that a security is overvalued to borrow the security and sell it short, hoping to buy it back later at a lower price.

Data Quality in Swap Data Repositories: Financial reform sought to improve transparency in derivatives markets by requiring that data related to transactions in swaps be reported to swap data repositories. Swap data are critical to understand exposures and connections across the financial system, and the repositories are designed to be high-quality, low-cost data collection points.

The credit default swap data reported to these repositories exemplify new sources of data that supervisors are getting to know for the first time. Because centralizing and reporting these data are so new, some issues are arising in establishing consistent, well-understood data definitions and data structures so supervisors can reliably combine and analyze the information.

In 2016, the OFR and the Commodity Futures Trading Commission (CFTC), to promote the use of data standards in swap data reporting to assure data quality and utility, announced a memorandum of understanding for a joint project to enhance the quality, types, and formats of data collected from registered swap data repositories.

MOVE TOWARD STANDARDIZATION: LEGAL ENTITY IDENTIFIER INITIATIVE

When Lehman Brothers failed in 2008, its thousands of counterparties globally struggled to assess their total exposure to Lehman. Financial regulators were also unclear about the consequences of a Lehman failure in part because no industry-wide standards existed for identifying and linking financial data representing entities or instruments. Standards are needed to produce high-quality data. And high-quality data are essential for effective risk management for financial companies, especially to assess their connections and exposures to other firms and regulatory oversight.

The Legal Entity Identifier (LEI) is a data standard, like a bar code for precisely identifying parties to financial transactions. The OFR has led the global LEI initiative as it has progressed from conception to full-fledged operational system in just a few years.

The LEI can help the financial industry, regulators, and policymakers trace exposures and connections across the financial system. It also generates efficiencies for financial companies in internal reporting, risk management, and in collecting, cleaning, and aggregating data. In addition, the LEI is expected to ease companies' regulatory reporting burdens by reducing overlap and duplication with respect to the multiple identifiers reporting firms must manage.

Although the worldwide LEI system reached significant milestones in 2014 as the final components of the governance framework of the LEI system were introduced, only some aspects of financial reporting in the United States and abroad require use of the LEI and these in substantial part rely on voluntary implementation. Although these steps have driven LEI adoption across the globe, with more than 300,000 LEIs issued to entities in 180 countries as of January 2015, regulators should mandate the use of the LEI in regulatory reporting. Universal adoption is necessary to bring efficiencies to reporting entities and useful information to the FSOC, its member agencies, and other policymakers.[22]

It is important to stress that the LEI initiative is not a cure-all for the data challenges since it still needs to be accompanied by accurate and timely underlying data. However, without first establishing the accurate identity of a counterparty and the organizational *family tree* to which it belongs, the industry can never achieve the goal of producing aggregated exposure reports that are accurate. Such aggregated information is now a requirement under the Dodd-Frank Act, with respect to the mandated development of *global data repositories* around the world, which will provide supervisors ongoing exposure reports concerning derivatives trading activities conducted by Systemically Important Financial Institutions.

KEY POINTS

- The Credit Crisis revealed significant gaps in the data available for regulators and risk managers to identify vulnerabilities and emerging threats that ultimately led to the crisis. These gaps were widespread and related to insufficient information about individual financial institutions, as well a lack of data about interconnections across the financial system.

- Although firm-level or microprudential supervision remains critically important, systemic risk buildup across the financial system (e.g., macroprudential supervision) has taken on increased focus.
- A taxonomy of attributes would likely make measures of systemic risk valuable to all researchers: (i) simplicity, (ii) specificity, (iii) comparability, (iv) aggregate and firm specific, (v) forward looking, (vi) international, (vii) financial institutions broadly (not limited to banks), and (viii) linked to theory.
- Post Credit Crisis, both the United States and Europe have taken substantial steps to ensure that supervisors have improved access to data to monitor systemic risk via the creation of the Financial Stability Oversight Council and the Office of Financial Research in the United States and the European Systemic Risk Board in Europe.
- Two of the most important regulatory attempts to improve existing data gaps have been (i) the requirement that all systemically important financial institutions complete comprehensive recovery and resolution plans that outline, among many things, how these institutions could be unwound in the event of a crisis and (ii) the creation of global swap repositories, intended to hold the vast majority of global swaps data between counterparties and provide global regulators a view into potential concentration and other risks in the financial system.
- One of the numerous challenges preventing the collection and aggregation of data on financial institutions is the massive global scale of the world's largest financial institution and their extremely complex organization structures. The 10 largest global banks have on average 3,500 subsidiaries located in 80 countries.
- According to the Bank for International Settlements there are four main challenges that arise internationally concerning the use of data for systemic risk mitigation: measurement of bank's foreign credit exposures; measurement of borrowers' reliance on foreign bank credit; measurement of cross-currency funding and maturity transformation; and modeling systemic risk for international banks.
- The OFR has also identified the following projects as top priorities for addressing remaining data gaps: the bilateral repo data collection pilot project; the securities lending data collection pilot project; and the data quality in swap data repositories.
- Recognizing the industry-wide need for more data, more granular data, greater frequency of exposure reporting, and greater accuracy of such data, a global data standardization project called Legal Entity Identifier was created by the OFR in 2011. The LEI will assign a unique identifier

to individual legal entities. LEIs are intended to assist global financial regulators in their efforts to better identify and mitigate systemic risk in the financial system by helping to accurately identify a counterparty and the organizational *family tree* to which it belongs.

KNOWLEDGE CHECK

Q5.1: What did the Credit Crisis reveal as it relates to data gaps?

Q5.2: Is microprudential or macroprudential supervision more associated with monitoring of data on broad economic and financial data to identify the buildup of potential systemic threats?

Q5.3: Which governmental agency was created under the powers of the Dodd-Frank Act and specifically mandated with identifying and using data to help mitigate systemic risk?

Q5.4: What characteristic of large, global banks makes the aggregation and monitoring of systemic risk they may pose very challenging?

Q5.5: Which public index has been considered by many to be the world's premier barometer of investor sentiment and market volatility over many years?

Q5.6: Cite 4 of the 20 recommendations made in a joint report by the IMF and FSB on reducing financial data gaps.

Q5.7: Name three of the top remaining data-related priorities cited by the Office of Financial Research.

Q5.8: Which historic U.S. bankruptcy in 2008 highlighted significant data gaps that limited transparency into the full extent of that entity's global credit exposure by financial supervisors and market participants?

NOTES

1. Hida, E.T., 2013, "Systemic Risk Information Requirements," *Current Environment, Needs and Approaches for Development*, p. 35.
2. Stern, G., and Feldman, R.J., 2013, "Handbook on Systemic Risk," Cambridge University Press. p. 745.
3. www.financialresearch.gov/programs-overview/.
4. European Central Bank, "Analytical Models and Tools for the Identification and Assessment of Systemic Risk," *Financial Stability Review*, June 2010.
5. European Systemic Risk Board, "Flagship Report on Macro-Prudential Policy in the Banking Sector," p. 8, https://www.esrb.europa.eu/pub/reports/html/index.en.html

6. Worrell, C., Guharay, S., McMahon, M., Seligman, L., and Shenoy, R., 2013, "Operational Considerations in an Analytical Environment for Systemic Risk," Elsevier B.V. July 2013.
7. www.chicagofed.org/publications/nfci/index.
8. fred.stlouisfed.org/series/STLFSI.
9. www.kansascityfed.org/research/indicatorsdata/kcfsi.
10. www.cboe.com/micro/vix/vixintro.aspx.
11. www.coastlightcapital.com/global-financial-stress/.
12. www.cboe.com/micro/impliedcorrelation/.
13. www.businessinsider.com/citi-economic-surprise-index-2013–12.
14. www.investopedia.com/terms/p/putcallratio.asp.
15. www.cboe.com/micro/skew/introduction.aspx.
16. Financial Stability Board, 2014.
17. Bank for International Settlements, 81st Annual Report, p. 90.
18. Deloitte , 2011 (Feb.), "Global Risk Management Survey," Deloitte Global Services Limited, 7th ed.
19. BIS Working Paper No. 376, "Systemic Risks in Global Banking: What Can Available Data Tell Us and What Data Are Needed?" April 2012.
20. International Monetary Fund, "Systemic Risk Monitoring Toolkit: A User Guide," p. 7. **www.imf.org**/external/pubs/ft/wp/2013/wp13168.pdf
21. BIS Working Paper No. 376, "Systemic Risks in Global Banking: What Can Available Data Tell Us and What Data Are Needed?," April 2012, p. 15.
22. www.financialresearch.gov/.

CHAPTER 6

Macroprudential versus Microprudential Oversight

INTRODUCTION

This chapter will focus on two categories of regulatory supervision that are important to understand in the context of systemic risk identification and mitigation. Over the past century, financial regulators have implemented many types of requirements that financial institutions, primarily banks, must adhere to, such as minimum capital ratios, loan underwriting standards, and stock margin rules, to name a few. Historically, such tools were concerned primarily with managing risk at the individual institution level, known as microprudential supervision. However, a key lesson from the Credit Crisis was the need to put in place more robust macroprudential policies, tools, and frameworks to ensure financial stability in a marketplace that has grown significantly more complex and interconnected than in the past. These frameworks should include new and better tools to allow for early warning and intervention to help reduce the probability of systemic events and contain their impact on the economy.

After reading this chapter you will be able to:

- Define the term *microprudential supervision.*
- Define the term *macroprudential supervision.*
- Understand the key differences between both categories of supervision.
- Provide examples of the various regulatory tools that have existed for decades.
- Explain the four stages that a sound macroprudential policy strategy should follow.
- Provide examples of the capital, liquidity, and asset-side policy instruments that macroprudential supervisors utilize to help ensure financial stability.

A COMPARISON OF MACROPRUDENTIAL VERSUS MICROPRUDENTIAL

Microprudential and macroprudential authorities often make use of similar prudential policy tools that are applied at the individual firm level (e.g., capital or liquidity buffers) but these can be applied with different goals. So-called microprudential regulations tend to target individual institutions or components of the system on a stand-alone basis, regardless of the institution's impact on the financial system. Additionally, they typically apply the standards uniformly across all institutions in the financial system irrespective of the conditions prevailing at any given point in time. In effect, the microprudential approach assumes that the sources of risk are exogenous and independent of the collective impact of the interactions between individual institutions. Furthermore, prudential guidelines often apply to regulated entities and do not cover many financial entities in the systems.

By contrast, macroprudential policy aims to address the drawbacks of the microprudential approach by focusing on risks to the financial system. For example, a macroprudential policy framework would simultaneously look at the "cross-sectional" aspects of systemic risks in the financial system. Macroprudential policies are also concerned with aggregate levels of capital and economic cycles, with the main goal of avoiding systemic risks from building up. While macroprudential policies are distinct from day-to-day risk management, many macroprudential tools are in effect microprudential instruments deployed with a systemic perspective in mind.[1] Depending on the type of vulnerabilities that need addressing, policy tools can be targeted at banks' capital requirements, their liquidity, or the asset side of their balance sheet. Some liquidity-based instruments, such as haircuts and margins, can also be applied to specific markets.[2] What should become evident in reading this chapter is that there can be a tension between macro- and microprudential concerns. For example, what might appear appropriate from a micro-perspective (e.g., the shutting down of a large bank due to failure to meet minimum capital ratios) may be damaging from a macro-perspective (e.g., may lead to a systemic event and ultimately a negative impact on the real economy).[3]

Table 6.1 highlights some of the key differences between the two approaches.

MICROPRUDENTIAL POLICIES

Microprudential policies are concerned with capital adequacy and safety of individual firms. Such policies take a bottom-up approach and do not consider issues such as joint exposures, correlations, or the overall

TABLE 6.1   The Micro- and Macroprudential Perspectives Compared[4]

	Macroprudential	Microprudential
Proximate objective	Limit financial system-wide distress	Limit distress of individual institutions
Ultimate objective	Avoid output (GDP) costs	Consumer (investor/depositor) protection
Characterization of risk	Seen as dependent on collective behavior (endogenous)	Seen as independent of individual agent's behavior (exogenous)
Correlations and common exposures across institutions	Important	Irrelevant
Calibration of prudential controls	In terms of system-wide risk: top-down	In terms of risks of individual institutions: bottom-up

interconnectedness of institutions. Ensuring strength of the financial system is one of the main goals of microprudential policy and via its close attention on the stability of individual firms it therefore contributes to the safety of the overall markets. However, such actions are not always enough to avoid systemic risks due in part to the complexity of the financial system. Actions that on the surface appear appropriate regarding specific firms and circumstances can at times lead to volatility in the overall system.[5] The latter can occur because of how these actions impact the broader markets and the role the specific firm plays in the overall industry. One example could be actions taken by regulators against a large bank that provides critical services, such as securities settlement for hundreds of other banks. The actions may be perfectly prudent when viewed in isolation, but if they compromise the banks' ability to continue providing this critical service, it could lead to contagion risk in the broader industry.

To avoid systemic risk events within the financial system, the focus on individual firms needs to be complemented and supplemented by the system-wide analysis and viewpoints conducted by macroprudential supervisors, which are primarily concerned with controlling asset booms and busts.

Along the same lines expressed earlier, microprudential tools should be implemented prudently with an eye on the potential unintended impacts of such decisions:

> *Although it is clearly appropriate to strengthen the liquidity and capital standards for banks, regulatory reform needs to be comprehensive. My second concern on the regulatory reform front is that reform may be too focused on the traditional banking sector and*

not enough on other financial intermediation activities . . . . First, too much focus on raising the requirements on banks runs the risk of just forcing activity into the non-banking sector. Second, many of the problems of the financial crisis originated outside the banking sector.[6]

It is the firm view of the Institute that strong and appropriately intrusive supervision will be a central component of an effective multifaceted approach to systemic risk. We believe that an attenuation of the supervisory relationship was, in a number of cases, a contributing material factor in the development of the crisis.[7]

MACROPRUDENTIAL POLICIES

It is commonly accepted that gaps in regulations and the oversight of the financial sector in both the United States and Europe at least partially contributed to the Credit Crisis. If future crises are to be averted or more effectively contained, macroprudential policies and enforcement need to be better aligned to the underlying risks in the system.[8] This framework should include new and better tools to allow for early warning and intervention to help reduce the probability of systemic events and contain their impact on the economy.[9] In principle, macroprudential policies should be motivated by externalities and market failures arising from various financial frictions and market imperfections that exist even when microprudential supervision and monetary policy are conducted effectively.[10]

Macroprudential refers to a type of financial regulation that bridges the gap between traditional macroeconomic policy and traditional microprudential (or safety and soundness) oversight of individual financial firms.[11]

The implementation of the macroprudential policy strategy follows four stages:

1. Risk identification and assessment:
   - Selection of key risk indicators and thresholds.
   - Indicators should be interpreted with care due to the risk of misleading signals.
2. Instrument selection and calibration:
   - Must reflect underlying sources of risk.
   - Must account for possible cross-border spillovers.
   - Can dampen the upswing and downswing of financial cycles.
   - Must reflect financial cycles and structures.

3. Policy implementation:
- Decisions on instrument implementation are based on a wide range of quantitative and qualitative information, including information about the overall risk identification and assessment, key indicators and their indicative thresholds, instrument selection, and the evaluation of instruments used.
- Communication is critical to ensure rationale for macroprudential instruments is clear to banks and other stakeholders.
4. Policy evaluation:
- Evaluation is a key element of the policy cycle, especially during the first years of implementation.
- Provides feedback on the effectiveness and efficiency of macroprudential instruments.
- International organizations such as the IMF can play a key role from outside the decision-making process, including the establishment of international best practices.

A HISTORICAL PERSPECTIVE ON MACROPRUDENTIAL TOOLS

There are many macroprudential tools that have been used to varying degrees by financial regulators over the course of many decades.

Underwriting Standards: Examples include lending rules such as maturity limits, minimum down payments, or loan-to-value limits on loans offered by banks or other financial institutions to protect borrowers and as a prudential safeguard for lenders.

Stock Margin Requirements: This represents rules related to limitations on how much an investor can borrow on a specific stock(s) expressed as a percentage of the price. This rule has its roots in the Great Depression when Congress provided the Fed the authority to set margin requirements.

Reserve Requirements: Banks must keep a specific minimum amount of reserves, made up of liquid assets such as cash and near-cash assets, expressed as a percentage of deposits or liabilities. Reserve requirements are typically classified as a tool of monetary policy, as are the open market operations and the use of discount rates.

Interest Rate Ceilings: In the early part of the 20th century the United States enacted caps on the interest rates banks can pay retail depositors. This was done in connection with the state deposit insurance program. The Banking Act of 1933[12] gave the Fed the authority to set maximum rates on time and savings deposits for member banks, which it did shortly after the introduction of Regulation Q.[13] There were several reasons for the establishment of such ceilings, including (i) to change competitive behavior exhibited by many banks in the 1930s, which fueled aggressive lending and contributed to the high bank failure rate in that time period,[14] and (ii) to stimulate lending to customers at more manageable interest rate levels.[15]

Capital Requirements: Intended to protect a company against unexpected losses, capital represents a critical proxy of a firm's solvency. Before 1980, the capital requirements of commercially chartered U.S. banks were set in dollar terms, but since 1980 minimum capital ratios were introduced. Rather than make use of countercyclical capital requirements (e.g., requirements that are highly correlated with a decline in the bank's financial condition and/or economic conditions), U.S. bank supervisors have sometimes exercised forbearance (e.g., the temporary suspension of safety and soundness standards). One notable example of the latter is the actions taken by regulators to manage the U.S Savings & Loan Crisis in the 1980s, during which industry capital fell to 0.5% of assets in 1982 from 5.3% in 1980. In the face of mass bank failures, the Federal Home Loan Bank Board (supervisor of S&Ls until 1989) deregulated S&Ls and lowered the minimum capital ratio to 3%, among other actions.[16]

Throughout history these and other tools have been used to varying degrees and purposes. For example, to address excesses in specific asset sectors, the Fed made many changes to equity margin requirements between 1934 and 1974. This was done primarily in response to shifting dynamics associated with the stock market and a tremendous boom in housing in the 1950s and including actions by both the Fed and the Federal Housing Finance Administration. During World War II and the Korean War, curbs were instituted with respect to allowable expansion in bank loan portfolios, loan-to-value limits, and caps on maturities in industries unrelated to defense.

On a few occasions the president or Congress has granted the Fed broad authority to implement necessary constraints on the extension of credit by banks. A couple of examples are the wartime Trading with the Enemy Act of 1917[17] and the 1950 Defense Production Act.[18]

One critical aspect related to macroprudential policy tools is the extent to which they are considered cyclical or countercyclical. One can easily see how some of the tools, if used improperly from a magnitude or timing standpoint, can actually serve to precipitate or deepen a crisis. For example, raising margin requirements during an industry-wide liquidity crunch and a significant stock market selloff can potentially lead to a dramatic increase in margin calls to investors, many of which won't be met given the conditions in the market at that time.

TABLE 6.2 Capturing the Financial Cycle: Some Useful Indicators[19]

Macroeconomic indicators	▪ Broad credit aggregates ▪ Measures of debt sustainability (debt-to-income, debt-to-service ratio)
Banking sector indicators	▪ Stress tests, bank risk metrics ▪ Leverage ratios ▪ Maturity and currency mismatch ▪ Indicators of funding vulnerabilities ▪ Profits and losses
Market-based indicators	▪ Asset valuations in equity and property markets ▪ Corporate bond and CDS spreads and risk premiums ▪ Margins and haircuts ▪ Lending spreads
Qualitative information	▪ Underwriting standards ▪ Asset quality ▪ Credit conditions

Since the Credit Crisis, many indicators have been developed, ranging from traditional balance sheet variables, market-based indicators, and broad macro-aggregates to qualitative information available to supervisory and regulatory authorities. Some of these indicators gauge the resilience of individual players of the financial system while others are focused on system vulnerabilities. A classification and examples are provided in Table 6.2.

CHOICE OF MACROPRUDENTIAL POLICY TOOLS

The choice of macroprudential tools depends on several factors that put a premium on an appropriate set of indicators to guide the deployment and release of macroprudential measures as discussed earlier. Some tools can be used to remedy financial imbalances that are domestic in nature. Countercyclical provisions, capital and liquidity buffers, and balance sheet instruments (e.g., leverage ratios, limits on debt service, and loan-to-value ratios) applied to banks would fall into this category. They are intended to address threats to financial stability arising from excessive credit expansion and asset price booms, and limit amplification mechanisms of risks through leverage. Margining and haircut requirements are meant to achieve similar outcomes on financial markets. Table 6.3 provides an overview of such domestic instruments and the associated indicators.

TABLE 6.3   Policy Instruments and Potential Indicators[20]

Policy Instrument	Policy Indicators
Capital-based instruments:	
Countercyclical capital buffers	▪ Measures of the aggregate credit cycle
Dynamic provisions	▪ Bank-specific credit growth and specific provisions (current and historical average)
Sectoral capital requirements	▪ Measures of the price and quantity of different credit aggregates (stock and new loans) on a sectoral basis: interbank credit, OFIs, nonfinancial corporate sector, and households new loans) ▪ Measures of sectoral concentrations ▪ Distribution of borrowing within and across sectors ▪ Real estate prices (commercial and residential, old and newly developed properties) ▪ Measures of the price and quantity of different credit aggregates (stock and price-to-rent ratios)
Liquidity-based instruments:	
Countercyclical liquidity requirements	▪ Liquidity Coverage Ratio and Net Stable Funding Ratio ▪ Liquid assets to total assets or short-term liabilities ▪ Loans and other long-term assets to long-term funding ▪ Loan-to-deposit ratios ▪ Libor–OIS spreads ▪ Lending spreads
Margins and haircuts in markets	▪ Margins and haircuts ▪ Bid–ask spreads ▪ Liquidity premiums ▪ Shadow banking leverage and valuation ▪ Market-depth measures
Asset-side instruments:	
Loan to values and debt to incomes	▪ Real estate prices (commercial and residential, old and newly developed properties) ▪ Price-to-rent ratios ▪ Mortgage credit growth ▪ Underwriting standards ▪ Indicators related to household vulnerabilities ▪ Indicators of cash-out refinancing

KEY POINTS

■ Historically, financial regulators and the tools they relied upon were concerned primarily with managing risk at the individual institution level, otherwise known as "microprudential" supervision.

■ However, a key lesson from the Credit Crisis was the need to put in place more robust "macroprudential" policies, tools, and frameworks to ensure financial stability in a marketplace that has grown significantly more complex and interconnected than in the past.

■ Microprudential regulations tend to target individual institutions or components of the system on a stand-alone basis, regardless of the institution's impact on the financial system as a whole. Microprudential regulations typically apply the standards uniformly across all institutions in the financial system irrespective of the conditions prevailing at any given point in time.

■ Macroprudential refers to a type of financial regulation that bridges the gap between traditional macroeconomic policy and traditional microprudential (or safety and soundness) oversight of individual financial firms. Macroprudential policies are also concerned with aggregate levels of capital and economic cycles, with the main goal of avoiding systemic risks from building up.

■ Four stages of macroprudential policy implementation include risk identification and assessment; instrument selection and calibration; policy implementation; and policy evaluation.

■ Pre–Credit Crisis, some of the more typical tools employed by regulators throughout the 1900s to limit risk in the financial sector included underwriting standards, stock margin requirements, reserve requirements, interest rate ceilings, and capital requirements.

■ Since the Credit Crisis, many indicators have been developed, ranging from traditional balance sheet variables, market-based indicators, and broad macro aggregates to qualitative information available to supervisory and regulatory authorities. Some of these indicators gauge the resilience of individual players of the financial system while others are focused on system vulnerabilities. These new and expanded indicators and tools fall in the following broad categories: capital-based instruments, liquidity-based instruments, and asset-side instruments.

KNOWLEDGE CHECK

Q6.1: Prior to the Credit Crisis, many supervisory tools fell into which category?

Q6.2: What was a key lesson learned from the Credit Crisis as it relates to the need for new and different regulatory tools?

Q6.3: Provide a definition of microprudential regulation.

Q6.4: Provide a definition of macroprudential regulation.

Q6.5: Explain how both microprudential and macroprudential tools may be very similar but applied differently.

Q6.6: Provide three examples of commonly used categories of regulatory tools throughout most of modern financial history.

Q6.7: Identify the four stages of macroprudential policy implementation.

NOTES

1. Bank for International Settlements, "80th Annual Report," 2010.
2. Gadanecz, B., and Jayaram, K., 2015, "Macroprudential Policy Frameworks, Instruments and Indicators: A Review," Bank for International Settlements.
3. Institute of International Finance, "Systemic Risk and Systemically Important Firms: An Integrated Approach," May 2010, p. 22.
4. Borio, C., 2013, "The Macroprudential Approach to Regulation and Supervision: Where Do We Stand?" Bank for International Settlements, p. 110.
5. Hanson, S.G., Kashyap, A.K., and Stein, J.C., 2011, "A Macroprudential Approach to Financial Regulation," *Journal of Economic Perspectives*, 25(1): 3–28.
6. Remarks by Bill Dudley, president and CEO of the New York Federal Reserve, at the Council of Society Business Economists Annual Dinner, London, Mar. 11, 2010.
7. Institute of International Finance, "Systemic Risk and Systemically Important Firms: An Integrated Approach," May 2010.
8. Ibid.
9. Bernanke, B.S., 2011 (Oct.), "The Effects of the Great Recession on Central Bank Doctrine and Practice," Federal Reserve Bank of Boston 56th Economic Conference.
10. IMF working paper, "An Overview of Macroprudential Policy Tools," 2014.
11. Elliott, D. J., 2011 (June), "Choosing Among Macroprudential Tools," The Brookings Institution, pp. 1–40.
12. The Banking Act of 1933 (Pub.L. 73–66, 48 Stat. 162, enacted June 16, 1933) was a statute enacted by the U.S. Congress that established the Federal Deposit Insurance Corporation (FDIC) and imposed various other banking reforms
13. Regulation Q was Title 12, part 217 of the U.S. Code of Federal Regulations. From 1933 until 2011 it prohibited banks from paying interest on demand deposits in accordance with Section 11 of the Glass–Steagall Act (formally the Banking Act of 1933).
14. Bentson, G., 1964 (Oct.), "Interest Payments on Demand Deposits and Bank Investment Behavior," *Journal of Political Economy*, 431–449.

15. Federal Reserve Board Chairman Marriner Eccles' statement at a hearing before the Committee on Banking and Currency, House of Representatives, 74th Congress, First Session on H.R. 5357, Feb. 21–Apr. 8, 1935.
16. Elliott, D., Feldberg, G., and Lehnhart, A., 2013 (May), "The History of Cyclical Macroprudential Policy in the United States," Office of Financial Research Working Paper #008.
17. The Trading with the Enemy Act of 1917 (also known as the Trading with the Enemy Act) (40 Stat. 411, enacted October 6, 1917, codified at 12 U.S.C. §§ 95a–95b and 50 U.S.C. App. §§ 1–44), sometimes abbreviated as TWEA, is a U.S. federal law to restrict trade with countries hostile to the United States.
18. The Defense Production Act (Pub.L. 81–774) is a U.S. federal law enacted on September 8, 1950, in response to the start of the Korean War. It was part of a broad civil defense and war mobilization effort in the context of the Cold War. Its implementing regulations, the Defense Priorities and Allocation System (DPAS), are located at 15 CFR §§ 700–700.93. The Act has been periodically reauthorized and amended and remains in force as of 2014.
19. Gadanecz, B., and Jayaram, K., 2015, Bank for International Settlements, "Macroprudential Policy Frameworks, Instruments and Indicators: a Review," p. 6.
20. Ibid., p. 9.

CHAPTER 7

Introduction to the U.S. Regulatory Regime

INTRODUCTION

There are multiple U.S. financial regulators with a wide range of regulatory objectives and approaches. Further, both the architecture and approach of the U.S. regulatory regime differ from those of other international regulatory regimes. This chapter provides an introduction to U.S. financial regulation and the approaches of the various U.S. regulators, and compares the U.S. approach to that of international financial regulatory regimes. This chapter also introduces the Dodd-Frank Act.

After you read this chapter you will be able to:

- Identify the U.S. financial regulators.
- Understand the approach of U.S. financial regulators.
- Compare the U.S. financial regulatory regime to international financial regulatory regimes.
- Identify international financial institutions.
- Understand the objectives of the Dodd-Frank Act.
- Describe each of the titles of the Dodd-Frank Act.

WHO ARE THE REGULATORS?

Table 7.1 details the various U.S. federal financial regulators and organizations. In a Congressional Research Service article authored by Edward Murphy, regulators are described as focused on either certain types of financial institution, a particular financial market or activity, or systemic risk.[1] The focus of each of the regulatory entities is as follows:

- *Focus on certain types of financial institutions:* The Office of the Comptroller of the Currency (OCC), the Federal Deposit Insurance

TABLE 7.1 U.S. Federal Financial Regulators and Organizations[2]

Category	Regulator/Organization
Prudential bank, thrift, and credit union regulators	Office of the Comptroller of the Currency (OCC) Federal Deposit Insurance Corporation (FDIC) National Credit Union Administration (NCUA) Federal Reserve Board (FRB)
Securities regulator	Securities and Exchange Commission (SEC)
Derivatives regulator	Commodities Futures Trading Commission (CFTC)
GSE regulator	Federal Housing Finance Agency (FHFA)
Consumer protection regulator	Consumer Financial Protection Bureau (CFPB)
Coordinating forums	Financial Stability Oversight Council (FSOC) Federal Financial Institutions Examinations Council (FFIEC) President's Working Group on Financial Markets (PWG)

Corporation (FDIC), the National Credit Union Administration (NCUA), and the Federal Reserve Board (FRB) regulate lending institutions. The regulation of lending institutions is coordinated by the Federal Financial Institutions Examinations Council (FFIEC). The OCC is the primary prudential regulator of national banks and thrifts. The FDIC provides deposit insurance and is the primary prudential regulator of certain state-chartered banks. The NCUA is the prudential regulator of credit unions. The FRB (also known, colloquially, as "the Fed") is the primary prudential regulator of bank holding companies, certain U.S. branches of foreign banks, and certain state-chartered banks. The Federal Housing Finance Agency (FHFA) regulates government-sponsored enterprises (GSEs).

- *Focus on a particular financial market or activity:* The Securities and Exchange Commission (SEC) regulates corporations that sell securities to the public and securities markets while the Commodities Futures Trading Commission (CFTC) regulates derivatives markets. The President's Working Group on Financial Markets (PWG) (colloquially known as the "plunge protection team") studies and provides recommendations related to financial markets. The Consumer Financial Protection Bureau (CFPB) regulates financial activity related to consumers.
- *Focus on systemic risk:* The Financial Stability Oversight Council (FSOC) monitors systemic risk and coordinates the systemic risk–related activities of financial regulatory authorities.

Due to the way that regulation is organized, a given organization will often find itself regulated by multiple regulatory agencies. For example, a bank is regulated as a financial institution, its activities in securities markets and derivatives markets are regulated, its activities related to consumers are regulated, and there is careful monitoring of the financial institution as a source of systemic risk. Further, in addition to the federal financial regulators there are state financial regulators, including state banking supervisors, state insurance supervisors, and state securities regulators.

U.S. REGULATORY APPROACHES

All regulatory agencies do not share the same approach toward regulation. The differences in the approaches across regulatory agencies are driven by their distinct goals. The Group of Thirty, a consultative group on international economic and monetary affairs, describes four policy goals of regulation:[3]

1. The safety and soundness of financial institutions
2. Mitigation of systemic risk
3. Fairness and efficiency of markets
4. The protection of customers and investors

Financial regulation can be broadly categorized as either prudential regulation that is focused on the health of financial institutions or conduct of business regulation that is focused on protecting users of financial services and increasing confidence in markets. The Group of Thirty describes four regulatory approaches through which regulation can be organized:[4]

1. *Institutional approach:* Financial institutions are regulated based on the type of institution that represents its legal status.
2. *Functional approach:* Financial institutions are regulated based on the type of activity they undertake.
3. *Integrated approach:* A single regulator oversees all financial institutions, markets, and activities.
4. *Twin peaks approach:* One regulator oversees prudential regulation while another regulator oversees business conduct.

The U.S. financial regulatory approach combines the institutional and functional approaches. The OCC, FDIC, NCUA, FRB, and the FHFA focus on certain types of financial institutions while the SEC, CFTC, and the

CFPB focus on certain types activities. Clearly, the financial regulatory architecture in the United States is decentralized, with multiple regulators providing a variety of regulatory functions rather than a single regulatory agency. In an article authored for the Pew Economic Policy Department's Financial Reform Project, authors Adriane Fresh and Martin Neil Baily note some of the pros and cons of the decentralized U.S. approach.[5] On the one hand, competition among multiple regulators encourages innovation and specialization. On the other hand, competition can lead a given regulator to be lenient so as to attract more customers (i.e., regulated financial institutions). This can lead to *regulatory arbitrage* whereby financial institutions shop for the most lenient regulator. As an example of regulatory arbitrage, Fresh and Baily provide the example of AIG's choice of a thrift institution through which to expand its credit default swap unit. This allowed AIG's credit default swap activity to fall under the regulation of the Office of Thrift Supervision (OTS), which was ill-suited to appropriately regulate the credit default swap activity.[6]

The approach of regulators and politicians toward regulation evolves over time, reflective of changing attitudes towards the role of regulation in financial markets. In our discussion in subsequent chapters, we will see how the evolution of changing attitudes greatly influenced—and continues to influence—financial regulation.

COMPARISON OF U.S. VERSUS INTERNATIONAL FINANCIAL REGULATORY REGIMES

We've seen that the U.S. financial regulatory approach combines the institutional and functional approaches and does not use the integrated or twin peaks approaches. The approaches used in other jurisdictions vary widely. Table 7.2 presents the approaches of a number of international jurisdictions.

The European Union has extensive supervisory authority as well. Three European Union Supervisory Authorities (ESAs) are as follows:

1. *The European Banking Authority (EBA):* A prudential regulator of the EU's banking sector.
2. *The European Securities and Market Authority (ESMA):* A conduct-of-business regulator of the EU's securities sector that works to protect investors and promote stable and orderly financial markets.
3. *The European Insurance and Occupational Pensions Authority (EIOPA):* A regulator of the EU's insurance and occupational pensions sector.

TABLE 7.2 International Examples of Financial Regulatory Approaches[7]

Jurisdiction	Approach
Australia	Twin peaks approach
Brazil	Primarily a functional approach with some institutional approach aspects
Canada	A hybrid of the integrated and functional approaches
China	Primarily an institutional approach with some functional approach aspects
France	Primarily a functional approach with some twin peaks approach aspects
Germany	Integrated approach
Hong Kong	Primarily an institutional approach with some functional approach aspects
Italy	Combination of institutional and functional approaches
Japan	Integrated approach
Mexico	Institutional approach
Qatar	Evolving toward an integrated approach
Spain	Evolving from a functional approach toward a twin peaks approach
Netherlands	Twin peaks approach
Singapore	Integrated approach
Switzerland	Evolving from a functional approach toward an integrated approach
United Kingdom	Integrated approach
United States	Combination of institutional and functional approaches

In addition, the European Systemic Risk Board (ESRB) provides macroprudential oversight of the EU's financial system and works to mitigate systemic risk.[8] Further, the European System of Financial Supervision (ESFS) is a decentralized system consisting of European and national supervisors, including the three ESAs (the EBA, ESMA, and EIOPA), the ESRB, and national supervisors. The objectives of the ESFS are to develop a common supervisor culture and to facilitate a single European market.

There are also a wide range of international financial institutions, consisting of membership across jurisdictions. Table 7.3 presents a list of such organizations.[9]

TABLE 7.3 Key International Financial Institutions

Institution	Objectives/Mandates
Basel Committee on Banking Supervision	"Enhance understanding of key supervisory issues and improve the quality of banking supervision worldwide."[10]
Committee on the Global Financial System	"Identify and assess potential sources of stress in global financial markets, to further the understanding of the structural underpinnings of financial markets, and to promote improvements to the functioning and stability of these markets."[11]
Committee on Payments and Market Infrastructures	"Promotes the safety and efficiency of payment, clearing, settlement and related arrangements, thereby supporting financial stability and the wider economy."[12]
Financial Action Task Force	"Set standards and promote effective implementation of legal, regulatory and operational measures for combating money laundering, terrorist financing and other related threats to the integrity of the international financial system."[13]
Financial Stability Board	"Promotes international financial stability ... seeks to strengthen financial systems and increase the stability of international financial markets."[14]
International Association of Deposit Insurers	"To contribute to the stability of financial systems by promoting international cooperation in the field of deposit insurance and providing guidance for establishing new, and enhancing existing, deposit insurance systems, and to encourage wide international contact among deposit insurers and other interested parties."[15]
International Association of Insurance Supervisors	"To promote effective and globally consistent supervision of the insurance industry in order to develop and maintain fair, safe and stable insurance markets for the benefit and protection of policyholders and to contribute to global financial stability."[16]
International Organization of Securities Commissions	"Develops, implements and promotes adherence to internationally recognized standards for securities regulation."[17]

INTRODUCTION TO THE DODD-FRANK ACT

On July 21, 2010, the Dodd-Frank Wall Street Reform and Consumer Protection Act, typically referred to as the "Dodd-Frank Act," was signed into law. The Dodd-Frank Act is quite extensive and its impact on financial institutions and the financial system in the United States is enormous. The preamble of the Dodd-Frank Act encapsulates the objectives of the Dodd-Frank Act as follows:[18]

> *To promote the financial stability of the United States by improving accountability and transparency in the financial system, to end "too big to fail," to protect the American taxpayer by ending bailouts, to protect consumers from abusive financial services practices, and for other purposes.*

We see that the core objectives of the Dodd-Frank Act are fourfold:

1. To promote financial stability
2. To end "too big to fail"
3. To end bailouts
4. To protect consumers from abusive financial services practices

The first three of these objectives shows that the primary purpose of the Dodd-Frank Act is to reduce the exposure of both the U.S. financial system and the U.S. government to systemic risk. The fourth objective shows that another purpose of the Dodd-Frank Act is consumer protection.

The Dodd-Frank Act is organized into 16 titles, listed in Table 7.4.

The following is a brief summary of each title of the Dodd-Frank Act.

- *Title I: Financial Stability:* Establishes the Financial Stability Oversight Council (FSOC) and the Office of Financial Research (OFR). Establishes regulation and supervision of systemically important non-bank financial institutions. We discuss the FSOC in Chapter 9 and the OFR in Chapter 15.
- *Title II: Orderly Liquidation Authority:* Establishes processes through which systemically important financial institutions in distress can be liquidated by the FDIC in an orderly fashion.
- *Title III: Transfer of Powers to the Comptroller of the Currency, the Corporation, and the Board of Governors:* Eliminates the Office of Thrift Supervision (OTS) and transfers its authorities to the Office of the Comptroller of the Currency (OCC), the Federal Deposit Insurance Corporation (FDIC), and the Federal Reserve Board (FRB). Establishes other changes to the FDIC.

TABLE 7.4   The 16 Titles of the Dodd-Frank Act

The Dodd-Frank Act			
Title I: Financial Stability	Title V: Insurance	Title IX: Investor Protections and Improvements to the Regulation of Securities	Title XIII: Pay It Back Act
Title II: Orderly Liquidation Authority	Title VI: Improvements to Regulation of Bank and Savings Association Holding	Title X: Bureau of Consumer Financial Protection	Title XIV: Mortgage Reform and Anti–Predatory Lending Act
Title III: Transfer of Powers to the Comptroller of the Currency, the Corporation, and the Board of Governors	Title VII: Wall Street Transparency and Accountability	Title XI: Federal Reserve System Provisions	Title XV: Miscellaneous Provisions
Title IV: Regulation of Advisers to Hedge Funds and Others	Title VIII: Payment, Clearing and Settlement Supervision	Title XII: Improving Access to Mainstream Financial Institutions	Title XVI: Section 1256 Contracts

- *Title IV: Regulation of Advisers to Hedge Funds and Others:* Establishes a registration requirement for private funds.
- *Title V: Insurance:* Creates the Federal Insurance Office, which monitors certain elements of the insurance industry and makes recommendations to the FSOC. Establishes other insurance industry reforms.
- *Title VI: Improvements to Regulation of Bank and Savings Association Holding Companies and Depository Institutions:* Reforms the regulation of Bank and Saving Association Holdings. Notably, includes the "Volcker Rule," which prohibits banks from engaging in proprietary trading or owning or sponsoring a private fund. We discuss the Volcker Rule extensively in Chapter 10.
- *Title VII: Wall Street Transparency and Accountability:* Heavily regulates over-the-counter (OTC) derivatives markets. We discuss Title VII extensive in Chapter 12.

- *Title VIII: Payment, Clearing and Settlement Supervision:* Establishes regulation and supervision of systemically important financial market utilities that provide payment, clearing, and settlement services.
- *Title IX: Investor Protections and Improvements to the Regulation of Securities:* Establishes a wide range of investor protections and reform of securities regulation. Impacts broker-dealers, credit rating agencies, and those engaged in securitization and collateralization. Also reforms executive compensation and corporate governance.
- *Title X: Bureau of Consumer Financial Protection:* Establishes the Consumer Financial Protection Bureau (CFPB).
- *Title XI: Federal Reserve System Provisions:* Establishes limits and audits related to the FRB's ability to engage in emergency lending. We discuss the role of the FRB as a lender of last resort in Chapter 14.
- *Title XII: Improving Access to Mainstream Financial Institutions:* Encourages initiatives to provide access to financial products and services to underserved Americans who are "not fully incorporated into the financial mainstream."
- *Title XIII: Pay It Back Act:* Sets limits to the Troubled Asset Relief Program (TARP) established under the Emergency Economic Stabilization Act of 2008 and other acts in response to the financial crisis.
- *Title XIV: Mortgage Reform and Anti–Predatory Lending Act:* Establishes reforms of the mortgage market.
- *Title XV: Miscellaneous Provisions:* Contains a variety of additional provisions. These include restrictions on the use of U.S. funds for foreign governments; provisions related to conflict minerals; reporting requirements for coals or other mine safety; payment disclosure requirements for resource extraction issuers; and certain studies.
- *Title XVI: Section 1256 Contracts:* Section 1256 contracts are marked to market for tax purposes. Title XVI establishes that certain swaps, such as an interest rate swap, currency swap, basis swap, interest rate cap, interest rate floor, commodity swap, equity swap, equity index swap, credit default swap, or similar agreements, are not deemed Section 1256 contracts.

In the subsequent chapters of this book we will delve deeply into various ways through which the Dodd-Frank Act works to reduce exposure to systemic risk. In Chapter 9 we will learn that the Dodd-Frank Act enables the designation of certain financial institutions as "systemically important." In Chapter 10 we will learn about the Volcker Rule, which has greatly curtailed certain trading and investing activities of certain financial institutions. In Chapter 11 we will learn about counterparty credit risk and in Chapter 12 we will learn how the Dodd-Frank Act addresses the counterparty credit risk

TABLE 7.5   Key Examples of Pre-Dodd-Frank Act U.S. Financial Legislation

Key Examples of U.S. Banking Legislation	Key Examples of U.S. Securities and Derivatives Legislation
National Bank Act of 1864	Securities Act of 1933
Federal Reserve Act of 1913	Securities Exchange Act of 1934
The McFadden Act of 1927	Commodity Exchange Act of 1936
Glass-Steagall Act of 1933	Trust Indenture Act of 1939
Banking Act of 1935	Investment Company Act of 1940
Federal Deposit Insurance Act of 1950	Investment Advisers Act of 1940
Bank Holding Company Act of 1956	Commodities Futures Modernization Act of 2000
International Banking Act of 1978	Securities Act of 1933
Depository Institutions Act of 1982	Securities Exchange Act of 1934
Gramm-Leach-Bliley Act of 1999	Commodity Exchange Act of 1936
Sarbanes-Oxley Act of 2002	Trust Indenture Act of 1939

that financial institutions face due to their participation in over-the-counter derivatives markets.

The Dodd-Frank Act is obviously not the first U.S. financial legislation—indeed, there is an extensive history of U.S. financial legislation before the Dodd-Frank Act, key examples of which are provided in Table 7.5. In subsequent chapters, we will learn that many aspects of the Dodd-Frank Act alter or overturn previous legislation. Our emphasis on the Dodd-Frank Act is due to its recency; its focus on systemic risk; and its tremendous impact on financial institutions and the financial system. However, in the context of exploring the Dodd-Frank Act, we will also learn about earlier legislation and the evolution of financial regulation over time.

KEY POINTS

- There are multiple U.S. financial regulators and organizations. The Office of the Comptroller of the Currency (OCC) is the primary prudential regulator of national banks and thrifts. The Federal Deposit Insurance Corporation (FDIC) provides deposit insurance and is the primary prudential regulator of certain state-chartered banks. The National Credit Union Administration (NCUA) is the prudential regulator of credit unions. The Federal Reserve Board (FRB) is the primary prudential regulator of bank holding companies, certain U.S. branches of foreign banks, and certain state chartered banks. The regulation of lending institutions is coordinated by the Federal Financial Institutions Examinations Council (FFIEC).

- The Federal Housing Finance Agency (FHFA) regulates GSEs. The Securities and Exchange Commission (SEC) regulates corporations that sell securities to the public and securities markets while the Commodities Futures Trading Commission (CFTC) regulates derivatives markets. The President's Working Group on Financial Markets (PWG) studies and provides recommendations related to financial markets. The Consumer Financial Protection Bureau (CFPB) regulates financial activity related to consumers. The Financial Stability Oversight Council (FSOC) monitors systemic risk and coordinates the systemic risk–related activities of financial regulatory authorities.
- Four policy goals of regulation are the safety and soundness of financial institutions; mitigation of systemic risk; fairness and efficiency of markets; and the protection of customers and investors. Financial regulation can be broadly categorized as either prudential regulation that is focused on the health of financial institutions or conduct-of-business regulation that is focused on protecting users of financial services and increasing confidence in markets.
- Four regulatory approaches through which regulation can be organized include an institutional approach where financial institutions are regulated based on the type of institution that represents its legal status; a functional approach where financial institutions are regulated based on the type of activity they undertake; an integrated approach where a single regulator oversees all financial institutions, markets, and activities; and a twin peaks approach where one regulator oversees prudential regulation while another regulator oversees business conduct. The U.S. financial regulatory approach combines the institutional and functional approaches. Other jurisdictions use alternative approaches.
- Three European Union supervisory authorities are the European Banking Authority (EBA), the European Securities and Market Authority (ESMA), and the European Insurance and Occupational Pensions Authority (EIOPA). The European Systemic Risk Board (ESRB) oversees the EU's financial system and works to mitigate systemic risk. The European System of Financial Supervision (ESFS) is a decentralized system consisting of European and national supervisors.
- Notable international financial institutions include the Basel Committee on Banking Supervision; the Committee on the Global Financial System; the Committee on Payment and Settlement Systems; the Financial Action Task Force; the Financial Stability Board; the International Association of Deposit Insurers; the International Association of Insurance Supervisors; the International Organization of Securities Commissions; and the Joint Forum.

■ The Dodd-Frank Act is recent U.S. legislation with extensive impact. Its objectives are to promote financial stability; to end "too big to fail"; to end bailouts; and to protect consumers from abusive financial services practices. The Dodd-Frank Act is organized into 16 titles, a number of which will be explored in detailed in subsequent chapters. While the Dodd-Frank Act is not the first U.S. financial legislation, it is of central importance due to its recency; its focus on systemic risk; and its tremendous impact on financial institutions and the financial system.

KNOWLEDGE CHECK

Q7.1: Who are the various U.S. federal financial regulators and what do they do?

Q7.2: What are the four policy goals of regulation?

Q7.3: What are the four regulatory approaches and what is the U.S. financial regulatory approach?

Q7.4: How is the European Union's financial regulation organized?

Q7.5: Who are the key international financial institutions?

Q7.6: What are the objectives of the Dodd-Frank Act?

Q7.7: What are the 16 titles of the Dodd-Frank Act?

Q7.8: What are key examples of pre–Dodd-Frank Act U.S. financial legislation?

NOTES

1. Murphy, Edward V., 2015, "Who Regulates Whom and How? An Overview of U.S. Financial Regulatory Policy for Banking and Securities Markets," Congressional Research Service.
2. *Source:* Table 1 of Murphy, ibid., 2015.
3. Group of Thirty, 2008, "The Structure of Financial Supervision: Approaches and Challenges in a Global Marketplace."
4. Group of Thirty, 2008.
5. Fresh, Adriane, and Baily, Martin Neil, 2009, "What Does International Experience Tell Us about Regulatory Consolidation?" The Pew Economic Policy Department Financial Reform Project.
6. The OTS no longer exists. Under the Dodd-Frank Act it merged with other financial regulatory agencies.
7. *Source:* Group of Thirty, 2008.
8. We will discuss the ESRB in detail in the next chapter.
9. We will discuss the international regulatory regime in greater detail in the next chapter.
10. www.bis.org/bcbs/, extracted Sept. 2016.

11. www.bis.org/cgfs/, extracted Sept. 2016.
12. www.bis.org/cpmi/, extracted Sept. 2016.
13. www.fatf-gafi.org/about/, extracted Sept. 2016.
14. www.fsb.org/about/, extracted Sept. 2016.
15. www.iadi.org/en/about-iadi/, extracted Sept. 2016.
16. www.iaisweb.org/page/about-the-iais, extracted Sept. 2016.
17. www.iosco.org/about/?subsection=about_iosco, extracted Sept. 2016.
18. *Source:* The Dodd-Frank Wall Street Reform and Consumer Protection Act.

CHAPTER 8

Introduction to International Regulatory Regimes

INTRODUCTION

The U.S. financial regulatory architecture works to meet the country's unique objectives. However, there are certain universal themes that characterize the approach toward financial regulation across all jurisdictions. Further, there are regulatory challenges that can only be addressed through international planning and coordination. This chapter provides an introduction to several key international regulators and standards that facilitate international approaches and coordination.

After you read this chapter you will be able to:

- Understand the importance of the Financial Stability Board.
- Describe the Basel Accords.
- Understand the role of the European Systemic Risk Board.
- Describe the Principles for Financial Market Infrastructures.

THE FINANCIAL STABILITY BOARD

The Financial Stability Board (FSB) is an organization, made of the member institutions presented in Table 8.1, that works to promote international financial stability. The FSB was formed by the G20—an international forum consisting of 20 major economies—following the Credit Crisis. Before the crisis, international coordination in relation to issues of financial stability was limited. There was an organization—the Financial Stability Forum—that worked to promote international financial stability, but it was ineffective. This is illustrated in the following quote from an article by Stuart P.M. Mackintosh, the executive director of the Group of Thirty:[1]

> *Before 2008, there was no effective mechanism to overcome (or at least mitigate) the tendency to diverge from, instead of converge on, common goals. An entity did exist, called the Financial Stability Forum, but it had no power or authority. In addition, its mission was unclear, it was unrepresentative, it lacked balanced advanced and emerging market membership, its resources were minimal, it did not oversee other actors' output, and it did not report upwards to political leaders.*

The FSB identifies financial systemic risks, generates policy responses, and monitors the execution of responses through the following three standing committees:

1. It identifies financial systemic risks through its Standing Committee on Assessment of Vulnerabilities.
2. It generates policy responses through its Standing Committee on Supervisory and Regulatory Cooperation.
3. It monitors the execution of responses through its Standing Committee on Standards Implementation.

The FSB's policy responses, while influential, are "soft laws" that are not legally binding on its member jurisdictions. Member jurisdictions

TABLE 8.1 Member Institutions of the FSB[2]

Type of Member Institution	Specific Jurisdictions and Organizations
Central banks and financial regulators of member jurisdictions	Argentina, Australia, Brazil, Canada, China, France, Germany, Hong Kong, India, Indonesia, Italy, Japan, South Korea, Mexico, Netherlands, Russia, Saudi Arabia, Singapore, South Africa, Spain, Switzerland, Turkey, UK, USA, EU
International financial institutions	The Bank for International Settlements (BIS) The International Monetary Fund (IMF) The Organisation for Economic Co-operation and Development (OECD)
Other international organizations	Basel Committee on Banking Supervision Committee on the Global Financial System Committee on Payments and Market Infrastructures International Association of Insurance Supervisors International Accounting Standards Board International Organization of Securities Commissions

have a number of obligations, which include periodic peer reviews and the implementation of key standards for sound financial systems as presented in Table 8.2.

A characteristic of the FSB that is distinct from other international finance regulators is the heavy participation of elected politicians or political appointees, as noted by law professor Stavros Gadinis in an article published in the Texas International Law Journal.[3] Gadinis observes that approximately a quarter of the participants in the FSB's plenary, the main decision-making authority of the FSB, is made up of finance ministers and treasury secretaries. The ability of politicians to intervene in international financial regulation represents a shift away from the pre–financial crisis approach, which focused on regulatory independence.

THE BASEL ACCORDS

The Basel Accords are multinational accords that set minimum capital requirements for banks. They are referred to as the "Basel Accords" as they were established by BIS's Basel Committee on Banking Supervision, otherwise known as the "Basel Committee." The Basel Accords have evolved over time in response to new risks and challenges. Basel I set the original minimum capital adequacy ratio requirements. Basel II revised Basel I's capital framework and is organized with the three pillars of minimum capital requirements; supervisory review of the bank's internal assessment of its capital adequacy; and market discipline through minimum disclosures requirements. Basel III implemented additional revisions to the capital framework, examples of which are constraints on the bank's ability to payout earning; a countercyclical capital buffer; standards, and monitoring in relation to liquidity; and new requirements for global systemically important banks.

This book explores the Basel Accords in detail in Chapter 13.

THE EUROPEAN SYSTEMIC RISK BOARD

The European Systemic Risk Board (ESRB) provides macroprudential oversight of the EU's financial system and works to mitigate systemic risk. The creation of the ESRB, which occurred in 2010, was driven by the 2009 de Larosière report, which is a report by a group formed by the EU that was chaired by Jacques de Larosière. The de Larosière report argued that the financial crisis was driven by several failures, including a lack of adequate macroprudential supervision; ineffective early warning mechanisms; failures to challenge supervisory practices on a cross-border basis; and no means for supervisors to take common decisions, among others.[5] To address these failures, the de Larosière report recommended the creation of a new entity at

TABLE 8.2   Key Standards for Sound Financial Systems[4]

Policy Area	Standard	Description
Macroeconomic Policy and Data Transparency	Enhanced General Data Dissemination System	Standards related to sound statistical practices
	Code of Good Practices on Fiscal Transparency	Standards related to transparency related to government structure and finances
	Code of Good Practices on Transparency in Monetary and Financial Policies	Standards related to transparency in the conduct of monetary policy
	Special Data Dissemination Standard	Standards related to the dissemination of economic and financial data
Financial Regulation and Supervision	Insurance Core Principles, Standards, Guidance and Assessment Methodology	Standards related to the supervision of the insurance sector
	Core Principles for Effective Banking Supervision	Standards related to the supervision of the banking sector
	Objectives and Principles of Securities Regulation	Standards related to securities regulation
Institutional and Market Infrastructure	International Standards on Auditing	Standards related to financial statement auditors' responsibilities
	G20/OECD Principles of Corporate Governance	Corporate governance standards
	IADI (International Association of Deposit Insurers) Core Principles for Effective Deposit Insurance Systems	Standards related to deposit insurance systems and practices
	Principles for Financial Market Infrastructures	Standards for entities that make up financial market infrastructures and their supervisors
	FATF (Financial Action Task Force) Recommendations on Combating Money Laundering and the Financing of Terrorism and Proliferation	Anti–money laundering (AML) and countering the financing of terrorism (CFT) standards
	Insolvency and Creditor Rights Standard	Standards by which to evaluate and improve insolvency and creditor/debtor regimes
	International Financial Reporting Standards (IFRS)	Accounting standards

TABLE 8.3 Voting and Non-voting Members of the ESRB[6]

Type of Member	Members
Voting	The president and the vice president of the European Central Bank (ECB)
	The governors of the national central banks of the Member States
	One member of the European Commission
	The chair of the European Banking Authority (EBA)
	the chair of the European Insurance and Occupational Pensions Authority
	The chair of the European Securities and Markets Authority
	The chair and the two vice chairs of the Advisory Scientific Committee
	The chair of the Advisory Technical Committee
Non-voting	One high-level representative per Member State of the competent national supervisory authorities
	The president of the Economic and Financial Committee

the EU level. The creation of the ESRB occurred as a result. The ESRB plays a role in EU similar to the role of the Financial Stability Oversight Council (FSOC) in the United States, and both were established in response to the Credit Crisis of 2007–2009.

The voting and non-voting members of the ESRB are presented in Table 8.3. The ESRB provides guidance and recommendations in relation to the EU's Capital Requirements Directive (CRD) and Capital Requirements Regulation (CRR). EU directives, such as the CRD, allow the Member States of the EU individually to decide how to transpose the directive into national laws. EU regulations, such as the CRR, have binding legal force throughout the EU.

To work toward its objective of mitigating systemic risk, the ESRB has identified four sources of risk to financial stability as follows, as well as indicators of each source of risk and instruments through which it can be addressed:[7]

1. *Excessive credit growth and leverage:* This source of risk is addressed through capital buffers and minimum loan-to-value and loan-to-income requirements.
2. *Excessive maturity mismatch and market illiquidity:* This refers to the risks associated with funding of long-term investments in illiquid assets using short-term funding. This source of risk is addressed through stable funding restrictions and liquidity charges.

3. *Direct and indirect exposure concentrations:* This source of risk is addressed through large exposure restrictions.
4. *Misaligned incentives and moral hazard:* This source of risk is addressed through capital surcharges for systemically risky institutions as well as a systemic risk buffer.

PRINCIPLES FOR FINANCIAL MARKET INFRASTRUCTURES

The Principles for Financial Market Infrastructures (PFMI) are international standards for the management of *financial market infrastructures* (FMIs), which are entities that facilitate the clearing, settlement, and recording of financial transactions. Specifically, the PFMI target the following entities:[8]

- Systemically important payment systems
- Central securities depositories
- Securities settlement systems
- Central counterparties
- Trade repositories

The PFMI were established by the Committee on Payments and Market Infrastructures (CPMI) and the Technical Committee of the International Organization of Securities Commissions (IOSCO). The CPMI is the BIS committee that promotes the safety and efficiency of payment, clearing, settlement, and related arrangements.[9] The IOSCO is an international organization of securities regulators that sets standards for securities markets. The main objective of the PFMI is to enhance the safety and efficiency that the CPMI promotes, with the broader objectives of limiting systemic risk, facilitating transparency, and financial stability.[10]

The PFMI are structured as 24 principles and 5 responsibilities, organized as follows:

- General organization principles
- Credit and liquidity risk management principles
- Settlement principles
- Central securities depositories and exchange-of-value settlement systems principles
- Default management principles
- General business and operational risk management principles
- Access principles
- Efficiency principles
- Transparency principles

■ Responsibilities of central banks, market regulators, and other relevant authorities for financial market infrastructures

Table 8.4 presents all of the PFMI's principles and responsibilities.

TABLE 8.4   PFMI Principles and Responsibilities[11]

Category	Principle/Responsibility
General organization principles	Principle 1: Legal basis
	Principle 2: Governance
	Principle 3: Framework for the comprehensive management of risks
Credit and liquidity risk management principles	Principle 4: Credit risk
	Principle 5: Collateral
	Principle 6: Margin
	Principle 7: Liquidity risk
Settlement principles	Principle 8: Settlement finality
	Principle 9: Money settlements
	Principle 10: Physical deliveries
Central securities depositories and exchange-of-value settlement systems principles	Principle 11: Central securities depositories
	Principle 12: Exchange-of-value settlement systems
Default management principles	Principle 13: Participant-default rules and procedures
	Principle 14: Segregation and portability
General business and operational risk management principles	Principle 15: General business risk
	Principle 16: Custody and investment risks
	Principle 17: Operational risk
Access principles	Principle 18: Access and participation requirements
	Principle 19: Tiered participation arrangements
	Principle 20: FMI links
Efficiency principles	Principle 21: Efficiency and effectiveness
	Principle 22: Communication procedures and standards
Transparency principles	Principle 23: Disclosure of rules, key procedures, and market data
	Principle 24: Disclosure of market data by trade repositories

(continued)

TABLE 8.4 (*Continued*)

Category	Principle/Responsibility
Responsibilities of central banks, market regulators, and other relevant authorities for financial market infrastructures	Responsibility A: Regulation, supervision, and oversight of FMIs
	Responsibility B: Regulatory, supervisory, and oversight powers and resources
	Responsibility C: Disclosure of policies with respect to FMIs
	Responsibility D: Application of the principles for FMIs
	Responsibility E: Cooperation with other authorities

KEY POINTS

- The Financial Stability Board is an organization that works to promote international financial stability. It identifies financial systemic risks through its Standing Committee on Assessment of Vulnerabilities; generates policy responses through its Standing Committee on Supervisory and Regulatory Cooperation; and monitors the execution of responses through its Standing Committee on Standards Implementation.
- The Financial Stability Board's policy responses are "soft laws" that are not legally binding on its member jurisdictions. Member jurisdictions have a number of obligations, which include periodic peer reviews and the implementation of key standards for sound financial systems. The Financial Stability Board is characterized by heavy participation of elected politicians or political appointees.
- The Basel Accords are multinational accords that set minimum capital requirements for banks. Basel I set the original minimum capital adequacy ratio requirements. Basel II revised Basel I's capital framework and is organized with the three pillars. Basel III implemented additional revisions to the capital framework.
- The European Systemic Risk Board (ESRB) provides macroprudential oversight of the EU's financial system and works to mitigate systemic risk through addressing excessive credit growth and leverage; excessive maturity mismatch and market illiquidity; direct and indirect exposure concentrations; and misaligned incentives and moral hazard. The ESRB provides guidance and recommendations in relation to the EU's Capital Requirements Directive (CRD) and Capital Requirements Regulation (CRR).

▪ The Principles for Financial Market Infrastructures (PFMI) are international standards for the management of financial market infrastructures (FMIs) that facilitate the clearing, settlement, and recording of financial transactions. The PFMI are structured as 24 principles and 5 responsibilities, organized as general organization principles; credit and liquidity risk management principles; settlement principles; central securities depositories and exchange-of-value settlement systems principles; default management principles; general business and operational risk management principles; access principles; efficiency principles; and transparency principles; and responsibilities of central banks, market regulators, and other relevant authorities for financial market infrastructures.

KNOWLEDGE CHECK

Q8.1: What is the Financial Stability Board?

Q8.2: What are the Financial Stability Board's standing committees and what do they do?

Q8.3: What are the member institutions of the Financial Stability Board?

Q8.4: What are the obligations of the Financial Stability Board's member jurisdictions?

Q8.5: What are the Basel Accords?

Q8.6: What is the European Systemic Risk Board?

Q8.7: Who are the members of the European Systemic Risk Board?

Q8.8: What sources of risk has the European Systemic Risk Board identified and through what instruments is each addressed?

Q8.9: What is a financial market infrastructure?

Q8.10: What are the Principles for Financial Market Infrastructures?

Q8.11: How are the Principles for Financial Market Infrastructures organized?

NOTES

1. Mackintosh, Stuart P.M., 2014, "The Global Financial and Economic Crisis, and the Creation of the Financial Stability Board," *World Economics*, 15(3): July–Sept.
2. www.fsb.org/about/fsb-members/, extracted Sept. 2016.
3. Gadinis, Stavros, 2013, "The Financial Stability Board: The New Politics of International Financial Regulation," *Texas International Law Journal*, 48(2).
4. www.fsb.org/what-we-do/about-the-compendium-of-standards/key_standards/, extracted Sept. 2016.

5. *Source:* "The High Level Group on Financial Supervision in the EU," Chaired by Jacques de Larosière, 2009.
6. www.esrb.europa.eu/about/orga/board/html/index.en.html. Extracted Sept. 2016.
7. *Source:* "Flagship Report on Macro-prudential Policy in the Banking Sector," ESRB, 2014.
8. *Source:* "Principles for Financial Market Infrastructures," Committee on Payment and Settlement Systems and Technical Committee of the International Organization of Securities Commissions (CPSS-IOSCO), 2012.
9. The CPMI was formally known as the Committee on Payment and Settlement Systems (CPSS).
10. *Source:* CPSS-IOSCO, 2012.
11. *Source:* CPSS-IOSCO, 2012.

CHAPTER 9

Systemically Important Entities

INTRODUCTION

A systemically important entity is an entity whose failure would cause financial instability that would threaten the economy. In this chapter we explore systemically important entities in depth, including Systemically Important Financial Institutions (SIFIs), Systemically Important Financial Market Utilities (SIFMUs), and Globally Systemically Important Banks (G-SIBs).

After you read this chapter you will be able to:

- Explain what makes an entity systemically important.
- Understand the role of the U.S. Financial Stability Oversight Council.
- Describe bank SIFIs, nonbank SIFIs, and SIFMUs and the requirements they face.
- Describe G-SIBs and the requirements they face.
- Understand how financial stability rules impact different types of banks.

INTRODUCTION TO SYSTEMICALLY IMPORTANT ENTITIES

A systemically important entity can be broadly defined as an entity whose failure would cause financial instability that would threaten the economy. There is widespread sentiment that one of the drivers of the credit crisis of 2007–2009 was the failure of financial regulators to adequately identify systemically important entities. Consequently there is now intense focus on both identifying systemically important entities and placing burdensome regulatory oversight and requirements on such entities.

The characterization of an entity as systemically important can be a function of a number of factors. James Thomson of the Federal Reserve Bank of Cleveland identifies the following factors:[1]

- *Size:* An entity may be characterized as systemically important—or "too big to fail"—based on the size of its assets and/or activity surpassing a given threshold.

- *Contagion:* An entity may be characterized as systemically important if its failure would cause the failure of other entities, thereby representing a source of systemic risk.
- *Correlation:* An entity may be characterized as systemically important if its performance is highly correlated with that of other entities. The combined failure of highly correlated entities can represent a source of systemic risk, known as the "too-many-to-fail problem."
- *Concentration:* An entity may be characterized as systemically important based on its concentration in a key financial market or activity. Concentration is a function of both the given entity's presence as well as the ability of other entities to expand into the given market or activity should a given entity fail.
- *Conditions:* Whether a given entity is characterized as systemically important can depend on the condition of the economy and financial markets, as the failure of a given entity may cause ruinous financial instability under certain conditions, such as a period of economic fragility or financial market distress, and have little impact under other conditions.

Thomson argues that while size can identify systemically important entities, size alone is an inadequate basis for classifying an entity as systemically important as it fails to take into account the nature of the entity's activities. Instead, classification as systemically important based on a combination of the "four Cs" (i.e., contagion, correlation, concentration, and conditions) allows for more judicious classification. In practice, however, size often plays a central role is whether a given entity is designated as systemically important.

There are a variety of systemically important entities and entities that provide such classifications. Systemically important entities can include banks, non-banks, and financial market utilities such as central counterparty clearinghouses. Further, classification of entities as systemically important can take place at the domestic level and internationally. In the remaining sections of this chapter we will look at how entities are classified as systemically important by the U.S. government, by the EU, and by the Financial Stability Board (FSB).

CLASSIFICATION OF ENTITIES AS SYSTEMICALLY IMPORTANT BY THE FSOC

As we discussed in Chapter 7, one of the core objectives of the Dodd-Frank Act is to promote financial stability. Toward this objective, the Dodd-Frank Act created a new oversight entity known as the Financial

TABLE 9.1   Members of the Financial Stability Oversight Council (FSOC)[2]

Voting Members	Nonvoting Members
Treasury Secretary (Chair of the FSOC)	Director of the OFR
Chairman of the Fed	Director of the Federal Insurance Office
Comptroller of the Currency	A state insurance commissioner selected by the state insurance commissioners
Director of the CFPB	
Chair of the SEC	A state banking supervisor selected by the state banking supervisors
Chair of the FDIC	
Chair of the CFTC	A state securities commissioner selected by the state securities commissioners
Director of the FHFA	
Chair of the NCUA	A presidential appointee with insurance expertise

Stability Oversight Council (FSOC), which is made up of the voting and nonvoting members presented in Table 9.1. Among the many duties of the FSOC is to identify systemically important banks and nonbank financial companies and make recommendations regarding heightened prudential standards for such entities, including heightened standards related to:

- Risk-based capital
- Leverage
- Liquidity
- Contingent capital[3]
- Resolution plans
- Credit exposure reports
- Concentration limits
- Enhanced public disclosures
- Overall risk management

The FSOC also has the duty to identify systemically important financial market utilities and payment, clearing, and settlement activities.

Entities designated as systemically important by the FSOC are referred to as one of the following:

- Systemically Important Financial Institutions (SIFIs), which include both systemically important banks and systemically important nonbank financial companies.
- Systemically Important Financial Market Utilities (SIFMUs). Financial market utilities are systemically important multilateral systems that comprise the infrastructure of financial markets.

Let's explore the FSOC's designation of entities as SIFIs and SIFMUs.

Bank SIFIs

Under the Dodd-Frank Act, a bank is designated as an SIFI if it has at least $50 billion in assets. Table 9.2 lists those banks with more than $50 billion in assets as of June 30, 2016.

Nonbank SIFIs

Under the Dodd-Frank Act, the FSOC determines whether to designate a nonbank financial company as systemically important based on the following considerations:[4]

- Extent of leverage
- Extent and nature of off-balance-sheet exposure
- Extent and nature of transactions and relationships with other significant entities
- The entity's importance as a source of credit and liquidity for the U.S. financial system
- The entity's importance as a source of credit for low-income, minority, or underserved communities
- The extent to which assets are managed rather than owned and the diffusion of ownership of assets under management
- The nature, scope, size, scale, concentration, interconnectedness, and mix of activities
- The degree to which the company is already regulated
- The amount and nature of the entity's assets
- The amount and type of the entity's liabilities
- Other risk-related factors

Nonbank SIFIs are subject to supervision by the U.S. Federal Reserve and are subject to heightened prudential standards. The following entities have been designated as nonbank SIFIs by the FSOC as of October 2016:[5]

- American International Group (designated July 8, 2013)
- Prudential Financial Inc. (designated September 19, 2013)
- MetLife Inc. (designated December 18, 2014)

General Electric Capital Corporation was also designated an SIFI on July 8, 2013; however, this designation was rescinded on June 28, 2016. The basis for rescinding General Electric's designation as an SIFI was due to a change

TABLE 9.2   Banks with Assets Greater than $50 Billion as of June 30, 2016[6]

Rank	Name	Assets (1000s)
1	JPMORGAN CHASE & CO.	$2,466,096,000
2	BANK OF AMERICA CORPORATION	$2,189,811,000
3	WELLS FARGO & COMPANY	$1,889,235,000
4	CITIGROUP INC.	$1,818,771,000
5	GOLDMAN SACHS GROUP INC.	$896,870,000
6	MORGAN STANLEY	$828,873,000
7	U.S. BANCORP	$438,463,000
8	BANK OF NEW YORK MELLON CORPORATION	$372,351,000
9	PNC FINANCIAL SERVICES GROUP INC	$361,528,406
10	CAPITAL ONE FINANCIAL CORPORATION	$339,247,718
11	HSBC NORTH AMERICA HOLDINGS INC.	$295,534,689
12	TD GROUP US HOLDINGS LLC	$276,317,370
13	TEACHERS INSURANCE & ANNUITY ASSOCIATION OF AMERICA	$276,045,408
14	STATE STREET CORPORATION	$255,396,733
15	BB&T CORPORATION	$221,858,615
16	SUNTRUST BANKS INC.	$199,276,480
17	CHARLES SCHWAB CORPORATION	$198,052,000
18	AMERICAN EXPRESS COMPANY	$159,632,000
19	ALLY FINANCIAL INC.	$157,931,000
20	RBC USA HOLDCO CORPORATION	$151,710,605
21	CITIZENS FINANCIAL GROUP INC.	$145,568,297
22	UNITED SERVICES AUTOMOBILE ASSOCIATION	$144,819,412
23	STATE FARM MUTUAL AUTOMOBILE INSURANCE COMPANY	$143,801,553
24	FIFTH THIRD BANCORP	$143,625,325
25	BMO FINANCIAL CORP.	$132,007,952
26	SANTANDER HOLDINGS USA INC.	$126,502,203
27	REGIONS FINANCIAL CORPORATION	$126,378,482
28	M&T BANK CORPORATION	$123,820,584
29	NORTHERN TRUST CORPORATION	$121,509,559
30	MUFG AMERICAS HOLDINGS CORPORATION	$117,205,079
31	KEYCORP	$101,406,977
32	BBVA COMPASS BANCSHARES INC.	$91,753,156
33	DISCOVER FINANCIAL SERVICES	$87,511,328
34	SYNCHRONY FINANCIAL	$82,384,173
35	BANCWEST HOLDING INC.	$80,624,408
36	HUNTINGTON BANCSHARES INCORPORATED	$73,954,016
37	COMERICA INCORPORATED	$71,440,155
38	CIT GROUP INC.	$66,783,624
39	ZIONS BANCORPORATION	$59,642,992
40	DEUTSCHE BANK TRUST CORPORATION	$54,629,000

in its business, which resulted in General Electric becoming a less significant participant in financial markets. Following the change, General Electric is no longer an owner of depository institutions nor does it provide financing. Further, General Electric is less interconnected with other significant entities. Due to this, General Electric was deemed to no longer pose a risk to financial stability and is therefore no longer designated as an SIFI.

SIFMUs

Financial market utilities are multilateral systems that comprise the infrastructure of financial markets. Under the Dodd-Frank Act, the FSOC has the duty to identify Systemically Important Financial Market Utilities (SIFMUs). The formal definition of a financial market utility, subject to certain exclusions, is an entity that[7]

> ... *manages or operates a multilateral system for the purpose of transferring, clearing, or settling payments, securities, or other financial transactions among financial institutions or between financial institutions and the person.*

An entity designated as an SIFMU is subject to standards of risk management and conduct, enhanced supervision, and liquidity requirements. The FSOC takes the following into account when determining whether to designate a given entity as an SIFMU:

- Monetary value of transactions
- Exposure to counterparties
- Relationships, interdependencies, or other interactions with other financial market utilities
- The effect of the financial market utility's failure or disruption
- Other factors that the FSOC deems appropriate

Based on these criteria, on July 18, 2012, the FSOC designated eight financial market utilities as SIFMUs. These eight SIFMUs, and a brief description of each, are presented in Table 9.3.

GLOBALLY SYSTEMICALLY IMPORTANT BANKS

A Globally Systemically Important Bank (G-SIB) is a bank whose distress or failure would threaten the global financial system and harm the economies

TABLE 9.3 FSOC-Designated SIFMUs[8]

SIFMU	Brief Description
The Clearing House Payments Company LLC as operator of the Clearing House Interbank Payments System (CHIPS)	A multilateral payment transfer system across participants, including some of the largest banks in the world
CLS Bank International (CLS Bank)	A multilateral system that settles foreign exchange transactions
Chicago Mercantile Exchange Inc. (CME)	A multilateral system that clears the vast majority of the U.S. market for futures, options on futures, and commodity options, and acts as a CCP (central counterparty clearinghouse) for futures, options, and swaps
The Depository Trust Company (DTC)*	A multilateral system for clearing and settling securities transactions related to corporate debt, municipal debt, and for equity securities; acts as a central securities depository and provides asset servicing and custodial services
Fixed Income Clearing Corporation (FICC)*	A multilateral system for clearing and settling and a CCP for U.S. Treasuries, agency debt, and non-private-label mortgage-backed securities
ICE Clear Credit LLC	A multilateral system that provides central counterparty clearing services; acts as CCP for credit default swaps
National Securities Clearing Corporation (NSCC)*	A multilateral system that provides clearing, settlement, and CCP services for broker-to-broker trades executed on U.S. exchanges
The Options Clearing Corporation (OCC)	A multilateral system that provides clearing and settlement services for the U.S. options market

*Subsidiary of The Depository Trust & Clearing Corporation.

of multiple countries. In a 2010 report, the Financial Stability Board (FSB) recommended a policy framework that sets loss-absorbency capacity requirements more stringent than those required by Basel III for entities that threaten global financial stability and also subjects such entities to more intensive supervision and resolution planning.[9] The FSB report, which was endorsed by the G20 Leaders, asked the Basel Committee on Banking Supervision (the Basel Committee) to study the measures through which global systemic importance is assessed, and the identification and implementation of the more-stringent requirements.

Based on this request, the Basel Committee developed an indicator-based measurement approach by which to identify G-SIBs, based on the following five measures, each of which receives equal weight:[10]

1. *Cross-jurisdictional activity:* Captures the bank's global footprint. Measured through evaluating the bank's cross-jurisdictional claims and cross-jurisdictional liabilities.
2. *Size*
3. *Interconnectedness*
4. *Substitutability/financial institution infrastructure:* Captures the degree to which the bank's role is that of infrastructure that cannot easily be replaced should it face distress or failure. Measured through evaluating the bank's assets under custody; payments activity; and underwritten transactions.
5. *Complexity:* Captures the fact that a more complex bank requires more time and money to resolve should it be in distress or should it fail. Measured through the bank's notional amount of OTC derivatives; its level-3 assets whose values cannot be measured using markets or models; and its trading and available-for-sale securities.

Based on the previous indicators banks receive scores, based on which they are categorized as G-SIBs or not. Those banks categorized as G-SIBs are then placed in five buckets based on their scores, with a higher score requiring higher loss absorbency. Table 9.4 lists the G-SIBs that were identified by the FSB and Basel Committee in their 2015 and 2016 updates. As discussed in Chapter 15, the OFR uses these same criteria for monitoring and measuring the systemic risk associated with GSIBs.

Total Loss-Absorbing Capacity (TLAC) Requirements

Among the FSB's recommendations for G-SIBs is the setting of loss-absorbency capacity requirements more stringent than those required by Basel III. The FSB implemented this recommendation through setting new requirements for G-SIBs, known as *total loss-absorbing capacity* (TLAC) requirements. The stated objective of the TLAC requirement is as follows:[11]

> ... *to ensure that G-SIBs have the loss-absorbing and recapitalisation capacity necessary to help ensure that, in and immediately following a resolution, critical functions can be continued without taxpayers' funds (public funds) or financial stability being put at risk.*

TABLE 9.4   Globally Systemically Important Banks[12]

Bucket	2015 G-SIBs	2016 G-SIBs
5	None	None
4	HSBC	Citigroup
	JP Morgan Chase	JP Morgan Chase
3	Barclays	Bank of America
	BNP Paribas	BNP Paribas
	Citigroup	Deutsche Bank
	Deutsche Bank	HSBC
2	Bank of America	Barclays
	Credit Suisse	Credit Suisse
	Goldman Sachs	Goldman Sachs
	Mitsubishi UFJ FG	Industrial and Commercial Bank
	Morgan Stanley	of China Limited
		Mitsubishi UFJ FG
		Wells Fargo
1	Agricultural Bank of China	Agricultural Bank of China
	Bank of China	Bank of China
	Bank of New York Mellon	Bank of New York Mellon
	China Construction Bank	China Construction Bank
	Groupe BPCE	Groupe BPCE
	Groupe Crédit Agricole	Groupe Crédit Agricole
	Industrial and Commercial Bank	ING Bank
	of China Limited	Mizuho FG
	ING Bank	Morgan Stanley
	Mizuho FG	Nordea
	Nordea	Royal Bank of Scotland
	Royal Bank of Scotland	Santander
	Santander	Société Générale
	Société Générale	Standard Chartered
	Standard Chartered	State Street
	State Street	Sumitomo Mitsui FG
	Sumitomo Mitsui FG	UBS
	UBS	Unicredit Group
	Unicredit Group	
	Wells Fargo	

The calibration of the TLAC requirement is determined by the given G-SIB's regulators. For example, in an October 2015 press release, the U.S. Federal Reserve set TLAC requirements for U.S. domestic G-SIBs and U.S. operations of foreign G-SIBs. The given G-SIB's TLAC requirement must satisfy a common minimum TLAC requirement set by the FSB among other requirements.

TABLE 9.5   Third Way Identification of Financial Stability Rules as a Function of Bank Size[13]

Bank Holding Company Size	Bank Classification	Applicable Rules
$1 Billion–$10 Billion	Large Community Bank	Volcker Rule Enhanced Capital Standards Leverage Ratio
$10 Billion–$50 Billion	Regional Banks	Volcker Rule Enhanced Capital Standards Leverage Ratio Stress Testing: One Annual Internal Test Risk Management Committee (If Publicly Traded)

$50 Billion–$250 Billion	Systemically Important Financial Institutions (SIFIs)	Volcker Rule
		Enhanced Capital Standards
		Leverage Ratio
		Liquidity Coverage Ratio of 70% +
		   Monthly Reports
		30-Day Liquidity Buffer
		Stress Testing: Two Annual Internal
		   Tests + Fed-Run Tests
		Risk Management Committee + Risk
		   Officer & Resolution Plan
		Office of Financial Research Fees

$250 Billion–$2.5 Trillion	Globally Systemically Important Banks (G-SIBs) and Advanced Approaches	Volcker Rule
		Enhanced Capital Standards
		Leverage Ratio + Supplementary
		   Leverage Ratio
		Liquidity Coverage Ratio of 100% +
		   Daily Reports
		30-Day Liquidity Buffer
		Stress Testing: Two Annual Internal
		   Tests + Fed-Run Tests
		Risk Management Committee + Risk
		   Officer & Resolution Plan
		Office of Financial Research Fees
		Basel III Proposals: G-SIB Capital
		   Surcharge, Total Loss-Absorbing
		   Capital, Net Stable Funding Ratio

BROAD IMPACT OF FINANCIAL STABILITY REQUIREMENTS

As noted at the beginning of this chapter, size alone is an inadequate basis for classifying an entity as systemically important as it fails to take into account the nature of the entity's activities. Regardless, the degree to which a bank is exposed to financial stability rules is broadly correlated with its size. The think-tank Third Way demonstrates this through illustrating the financial stability rules to which banks in the United States are subject as a function of their size, as presented in Table 9.5.

KEY POINTS

- A systemically important entity is an entity whose failure would cause financial instability that would threaten the economy. The characterization of an entity as systemically important can be a function of a number of factors, including size, contagion, correlation, concentration, and conditions.
- The U.S. Financial Stability Oversight Council (FSOC) identifies systemically important banks and nonbank financial companies and makes recommendations regarding heightened prudential standards for such entities. The FSOC also identifies systemically important financial market utilities and payment, clearing, and settlement activities. Systemically Important Financial Institutions (SIFIs) include both systemically important banks and systemically important nonbank financial companies and Systemically Important Financial Market Utilities (SIFMUs).
- A Globally Systemically Important Bank (G-SIB) is a bank whose distress or failure would threaten the global financial system and harm the economies of multiple countries. The Financial Stability Board (FSB) recommended a policy framework that sets loss-absorbency capacity requirements more stringent than those required by Basel III for entities that threaten global financial stability and also subjects such entities to more intensive supervision and resolution planning. The Basel Committee developed an indicator-based measurement approach by which to identify G-SIBs that equally weights cross-jurisdictional activity, size, interconnectedness, substitutability/financial institution infrastructure, and complexity.
- Financial stability rules have impacted banks of all sizes. The degree to which a bank is exposed to financial stability rules is broadly correlated with its size.

KNOWLEDGE CHECK

Q9.1: What is a systemically important entity?

Q9.2: What factors can be used to characterize an entity as systemically important?

Q9.3: What is the role of the FSOC in relation to identifying systemically important entities?

Q9.4: On what basis does the FSOC determine whether a bank is a SIFI?

Q9.5: On what basis does the FSOC determine whether a nonbank is an SIFI?

Q9.6: On what basis does the FSOC determine whether an entity is a SIFMU?

Q9.7: What is a G-SIB?

Q9.8: What measures does the FSB use when identifying G-SIBs?

Q9.9: What is the objective of the TLAC requirement?

NOTES

1. Thomson, James B., 2010, "On Systemically Important Financial Institutions and Progressive Systemic Mitigation." *DePaul Business & Commercial Law Journal*, 8(2).
2. *Source:* The Dodd-Frank Wall Street Reform and Consumer Protection Act, Title I Subtitle A, Section 111.
3. *Contingent capital* refers to debt that under certain circumstances converts into equity.
4. *Source:* The Dodd-Frank Wall Street Reform and Consumer Protection Act, Title I Subtitle A, Section 113.
5. www.treasury.gov/initiatives/fsoc/designations/Pages/default.aspx.   Extracted Oct. 2016.
6. www.ffiec.gov/nicpubweb/nicweb/HCSGreaterThan10B.aspx. Extracted Oct. 2016.
7. *Source:* The Dodd-Frank Wall Street Reform and Consumer Protection Act, Title VIII, Section 803.
8. *Source of SIFMUs and descriptions:* 2012 FSOC Annual Report, Appendix A.
9. *Source:* Financial Stability Board, "Reducing the Moral Hazard Posed by Systemically Important Financial Institutions: FSB Recommendations and Time Lines," Oct. 20, 2010.
10. *Source:* Basel Committee on Banking Supervision, "Global Systemically Important Banks: Updated Assessment Methodology and the Higher Loss Absorbency Requirement," July 2013.

11. *Source:* Financial Stability Board, "Principles on Loss-absorbing and Recapitalisation Capacity of G-SIBs in Resolution: Total Loss-absorbing Capacity (TLAC) Term Sheet," Nov. 9, 2015.

12. *Sources:* Financial Stability Board, "2015 Update of List of Global Systemically Important Banks (G-SIBs)," Nov. 3, 2015, and Financial Stability Board, "2016 List of Global Systemically Important Banks (G-SIBs)," Nov. 21, 2016.

13. *Source:* This table is formed using elements of Liner, Emily, and Jackson, Clare, "Making Sense of SIFIs," Infographic, Third Way, May 20, 2015, available at www.thirdway.org/infographic/making-sense-of-sifis.

CHAPTER 10

The Volcker Rule

INTRODUCTION

Section 619 of the Dodd-Frank Act, known as the Volcker Rule, sets prohibitions, requirements, and limitations in relation to the trading and private fund activities of banking entities and systemically risky nonbank financial companies. The Volcker Rule is wide-ranging and complex, with activities that are permitted despite the prohibitions and many elements that are subject to rulemaking and interpretation. In this chapter we explore the Volcker Rule in-depth.

After you read this chapter you will be able to:

- Explain the Volcker Rule.
- Understand the Volcker Rule's motivation and objectives.
- Describe the Volcker Rule's prohibition of proprietary trading by banking entities.
- Describe the Volcker Rule's prohibition of ownership or sponsorship of hedge funds and private equity funds by banking entities.
- Explain the impact of the Volcker Rule on systemically risky nonbank financial companies.
- Describe activities that are permitted despite the Volcker Rule.
- Understand how the Volcker Rule was implemented.
- Explain criticism of the Volcker Rule.

INTRODUCTION TO THE VOLCKER RULE

The "Volcker Rule" is the commonly used title of Section 619 of the Dodd-Frank Act. Section 619 is referred to as the "Volcker Rule" in recognition of Paul Volcker, a former chair of the U.S. Federal Reserve and the driving force behind Section 619. Specifically, Paul Volcker had chaired a Group of Thirty Steering Committee that formed recommendations in response to the credit crisis of 2007–2009. The resulting report, which was largely authored by Volcker, includes recommendations that formed the basis of the Volcker Rule.[1]

The Volcker Rule prohibits banking entities from engaging in two broad types of activities. First, the Volcker Rule prohibits banking entities from engaging in proprietary trading, in which the banking entity trades for its own account to generate short-term profits. Second, the Volcker Rule prohibits banking entities from owning or sponsoring hedge funds and private equity funds. The Volcker Rule also sets limits and requirements for systemically risky nonbank financial companies engaged in these activities. We will discuss the Volcker Rule's prohibitions, limitations, and requirements in more detail in the next section.

The motive behind the Volcker Rule is straightforward: Banking entities and certain other financial companies are crucial for the U.S. economy, and are supported and insured by the U.S. government in various ways. But this backing can lead these entities to engage in activities without guarding sufficiently against the associated risks. Effectively, the entity engaging in the risky activities will benefit if the activities prove profitable while the U.S. Government bears the costs should the risky activities lead to distress, a situation referred to as "moral hazard." In a statement to the U.S. Senate's Committee on Banking, Housing, and Urban Affairs before the passage of the Dodd-Frank Act, Paul Volcker described the challenge as follows:[2]

> *The basic point is that there has been, and remains, a strong public interest in providing a "safety net"—in particular, deposit insurance and the provision of liquidity in emergencies—for commercial banks carrying out essential services. There is not, however, a similar rationale for public funds—taxpayer funds—protecting and supporting essentially proprietary and speculative activities. Hedge funds, private equity funds, and trading activities unrelated to customer needs and continuing banking relationships should stand on their own, without the subsidies implied by public support for depository institutions.*

The purposes of the Volcker Rule are threefold, as noted in an implementation study performed in 2011 by the Financial Stability Oversight Council (FSOC):[3]

1. To separate federal support for the banking system from a banking entity's speculative trading activity
2. To reduce potential conflicts of interest between a banking entity and its customers
3. To reduce risk to banking entities and nonbank financial companies that are regulated by the Federal Reserve

It is useful to recognize that the Volcker Rule is the latest evolution in the approach of U.S. policymakers in response to moral hazard concerns and concerns about how the activities of banking entities can threaten financial stability. The Banking Act of 1933, commonly known as the Glass-Steagall Act, separated commercial banks and investment banks and created the Federal Deposit Insurance Corporation (FDIC), which provides deposit insurance. The Glass-Steagall Act was a response to the stock market crash of 1929, the Great Depression, and extensive bank failures. Through separating commercial bank activities from investment bank activities, the Glass-Steagall Act hoped to protect commercial banks, and the U.S. economy, from losses driven by investment bank activities. Over the subsequent decades, interpretations and administrative rulings relaxed the separation of activities. This culminated in the Financial Services Modernization Act of 1999, known as the Gramm-Leach-Bliley Act, which repealed the separation of commercial banks and investment banks.

The Volcker Rule's approach is aligned to the approach of the Glass-Steagall Act. Senator Jeff Merkley noted in a statement that the Volcker Rule:[4]

> ...embraces the spirit of the Glass-Steagall Act's separation of "commercial" from 'investment" banking by restoring a protective barrier around our critical financial infrastructure. It covers not simply securities, but also derivatives and other financial products. It applies not only to banks, but also to nonbank financial firms whose size and function render them systemically significant.
>
> While the intent of section 619 is to restore the purpose of the Glass-Steagall barrier between commercial and investment banks, we also update that barrier to reflect the modern financial world and permit a broad array of low-risk, client-oriented financial services. As a result, the barrier constructed in section 619 will not restrict most financial firms.

THE VOLCKER RULE: DETAILS

The Volcker Rule prohibits banking entities from engaging in proprietary trading; prohibits banking entities from owning or sponsoring hedge funds and private equity funds; and sets limits and requirements for systemically risky nonbank financial companies engaged in these activities. In this section we will first explore these prohibitions, limitations, and requirements. We will then turn to activities that are permitted despite the Volcker Rule's prohibitions, requirements, and limitations.

Prohibition of Proprietary Trading

The Volcker Rule prohibits banking entities from engaging in proprietary trading. Proprietary trading occurs when an entity acts as a principal in transactions for its own trading account. A *trading account* is an account used to generate short-term profits. Hence, the Volcker Rule prohibits the banking entity from trading for its own account to generate short-term profits. A *banking entity* is an insured depository institution; a company that controls an insured depository institution, a bank holding company; or any such entity's affiliate or subsidiary.

Prohibition of Ownership or Sponsorship of Hedge Funds and Private Equity Funds

Hedge funds and private equity funds are *private funds* that are lightly regulated and do not face the same registration requirements that, for example, mutual funds or exchange-traded funds face. The Volcker Rule prohibits banking entities from owning or sponsoring hedge funds and private equity funds, as well as similar funds as determined by the regulators. Sponsorship refers to serving as a general partner, managing member, or trustee of a fund; controlling a majority of directors, trustees, or management of a fund; or to share names with a fund. The FSOC's 2011 study notes that the purposes of these prohibitions are:

1. To ensure that banking entities do not use ownership or sponsorship of hedge fund and private equity funds to circumvent the proprietary trading prohibition
2. To limit the private fund activities of banking entities to providing customer-related services
3. To eliminate the incentive and opportunity of banking entities to bail out a private fund that they own or sponsor

The Volcker Rule and Systemically Risky Nonbank Financial Companies

As discussed in Chapter 9, under the Dodd-Frank Act the FSOC can decide whether to designate a nonbank financial company as systemically important based on a number of factors such as its extent of leverage and the amount and nature of its assets, among many other factors. An entity that receives such a designation is referred to as a nonbank systemically important financial institution (nonbank SIFI), is subject to supervision by the U.S. Federal Reserve, and is subject to heightened prudential standards.

While the Volcker Rule does not prohibit systemically risky nonbank financial companies from engaging in proprietary trading and from owning or sponsoring private funds, it sets limits and requirements for systemically risky nonbank financial companies that engage in such activities. These include additional capital requirements and quantitative limits to their proprietary trading and private fund activities.

Activities That Are Permitted Despite the Volcker Rule

There are proprietary trading and private ownership and sponsorship activities that the Volcker Rule permits despite its prohibitions:

- Trading of the securities listed in Table 10.1 is permitted.
- Trading is permitted in connection with underwriting, market making, risk-mitigating hedging, and for clients.
- Investments are permitted in small business investment companies, investments designed primarily to promote the public welfare, and investments that are qualified rehabilitation expenditures (e.g., in relation to a historic structure).
- Trading by a regulated insurance company directly engaged in the business of insurance is permitted.
- Bona fide (i.e., in good faith) trust, fiduciary, or investment advisory services may be provided to a hedge fund or private equity fund, without ownership beyond a *de minimis* initial funding investment and subject to a number of conditions.
- Proprietary trading outside of the United States by banking entities not controlled by a U.S. banking entity.
- Ownership and sponsorship of a hedge fund or private equity fund outside of the United States by banking entities not controlled by a U.S. banking entity, as long as ownership interest is not offered or held to a U.S. resident.

TABLE 10.1 Securities for which Proprietary Trading Is Permitted Despite the Volcker Rule

U.S. Treasury securities
Federal National Mortgage Association (Fannie Mae) securities
Federal Home Loan Mortgage Corporation (Freddie Mac) securities
Government National Mortgage Association (Ginnie Mae) securities
Federal Home Loan Bank securities
Federal Agricultural Mortgage Corporation securities
A security issued by a Farm Credit System institution
Municipal securities

■ Regulator can permit other activities that are deemed to promote and protect the safety and soundness of the banking entity and U.S. financial stability.

We see that while the Volcker rule sets prohibitions and limitations, it proceeds to permit many activities despite the prohibitions. This may seem complex, but in actuality the complexity of the Volcker rule is much deeper: There are limitations on the permitted activities! For example, no transaction or activity is permitted if it contains a conflict of interest between the banking entity and clients, customers, or counterparties; if it exposes the banking entity to high-risk assets or strategies; if it threatens the banking entities' safety and soundness; or if threatens U.S. financial stability.

IMPLEMENTATION OF THE VOLCKER RULE

The Volcker Rule instructed the FSOC to engage in a study and the formation of recommendations in relation to the Volcker Rule. The FSOC study, which was noted earlier in this chapter, was completed in January 2011. The FSOC made 10 recommendations, presented in Table 10.2.

TABLE 10.2 Financial Stability Oversight Council Volcker Rule Recommendations[5]

1. Require banking entities to sell or wind down all impermissible proprietary trading desks.
2. Require banking entities to implement a robust compliance regime, including public attestation by the CEO of the regime's effectiveness.
3. Require banking entities to perform quantitative analysis to detect potentially impermissible proprietary trading without provisions for safe harbors.
4. Perform supervisory review of trading activity to distinguish permitted activities from impermissible proprietary trading.
5. Require banking entities to implement a mechanism that identifies to Agencies which trades are customer-initiated.
6. Require divestiture of impermissible proprietary trading positions and impose penalties when warranted.
7. Prohibit banking entities from investing in or sponsoring any hedge fund or private equity fund, except to bona fide trust, fiduciary, or investment advisory customers.
8. Prohibit banking entities from engaging in transactions that would allow them to bail out a hedge fund or private equity fund.
9. Identify similar funds that should be brought within the scope of the Volcker Rule prohibitions in order to prevent evasion of the intent of the rule.
10. Require banking entities to publicly disclose permitted exposure to hedge funds and private equity funds.

The Volcker Rule also mandated that various financial regulators should engage in coordinated rulemaking to facilitate implementation. This resulted in the joint issuance on December 10, 2013, of the "final rules" implementing the Volcker Rule by the OCC, the FDIC, the Fed, the SEC, and the CFTC. The final rules, which consist of four subparts and two appendices, are extensive and complex, and include a rigorous compliance regime and reporting of quantitative measures for certain banking entities engaged in proprietary trading. For example, the final rules include careful definitions of *proprietary trading, trading accounts,* and *financial instrument* and clarify whether certain activities, such as repurchase agreements, are deemed proprietary trading. They also carefully define exempted activities and set the compliance and reporting requirements to take advantage of the exemption. The Volcker Rule took effect in July 2015.

VOLCKER RULE: CRITICISM

As explored extensively in this chapter, supporters of the Volcker Rule argue that it is necessary to reduce the risks to which trading activities expose banks and systemically risky nonbank financial companies, as well as financial stability. Yet many others argue that there is reason to question whether the Volcker Rule will succeed. Let's explore some examples of criticism of the Volcker Rule.

Cornell Law School Professor Charles Whitehead argues in a *Harvard Business Law Review* article that the Volcker Rule fails to sufficiently take account of change in financial markets.[6] Specifically, he argues that while the Volcker Rule prohibits risky trading by banks, it does not prohibit hedge funds from engaging in risky trading; hence, hedge funds may take over much of the activity from which banking entities are prohibited. But hedge fund activities can harm financial stability and banks that are exposed to the activities of hedge funds. Whitehead asserts:

> By causing proprietary trading to move to the hedge fund industry, banks continue to be exposed to the same risks—perhaps less directly than before, but now in an industry also subject to less regulation.... If the regulatory concern is with proprietary trading, the question should not be whether banks are engaged in proprietary trading, but rather, whether banks and banking activities are exposed to the risks of proprietary trading. Today, the location of those risks extends beyond the banking industry, reflecting an evolving financial system and change in who is conducting bank-like activities. By failing to take that change into account, the

Volcker Rule potentially results in new and costly regulation that increases risk-taking among less-regulated entities but may still affect banking activities.

Others criticize the Volcker Rule for other reasons as well. In a hard-hitting analysis prepared for the U.S. Chamber of Congress' Center for Capital Markets Competitiveness, finance professor Anjan Thakor argues the Volcker Rule will adversely impact bank customers and banks for four reasons. These include the Volcker Rule's negative impact on market making and liquidity provision; the harm to market-maker networks due to the retrenchment of banks in market making; higher cost of capital to borrowers due to reduced liquidity and regulatory uncertainty; and the damage to bank risk management due to the Volcker Rule's constraints on the types of securities that banks can hold.

There is no immediate resolution of the debate as to whether the Volcker Rule meets its objectives, has no impact, or is harmful. The Volcker Rule's complexity, the wide range of stakeholders, and the usefulness of arguments for and against the Volcker Rule by politicians wishing to take populist positions means that the debate is likely to continue. More broadly, the Volcker Rule is the latest chapter in the evolving approach of U.S. policymakers in response to moral hazard concerns and concerns about how the activities of banking entities can threaten financial stability, and it is unlikely to be the final chapter.

KEY POINTS

- The Volcker Rule prohibits banking entities from engaging in proprietary trading and from owning or sponsoring hedge funds and private equity funds. The Volcker Rule also sets additional capital requirements and quantitative limits for systemically risky nonbank financial companies engaged in these activities.
- Proprietary trading occurs when an entity acts as a principal in transactions for its own trading account. A "trading account" refers to an account used to generate short-term profits.
- The purposes of the Volcker Rule are to separate federal support for the banking system from a banking entity's speculative trading activity; to reduce potential conflicts of interest between a banking entity and its customers; and to reduce risk to banking entities and nonbank financial companies that are regulated by the Federal Reserve.
- The Volcker Rule is the latest evolution in the approach of U.S. policymakers in response to moral hazard concerns and concerns about how

the activities of banking entities can threaten financial stability, and is aligned with the approach of the Glass-Steagall Act, which separated commercial bank and investment bank activities.

■ The purposes of the Volcker Rule's prohibition on banking entities from owning or sponsoring hedge funds and private equity funds are to ensure that banking entities do not use ownership or sponsorship of hedge funds and private equity funds to circumvent the proprietary trading prohibition; to limit the private fund activities of banking entities to providing customer-related services; and to eliminate the incentive and opportunity of banking entities to bail out a private fund that they own or sponsor.

■ Activities that the Volcker Rule permits despite its prohibitions include trading of certain securities; trading in connection with underwriting, market making, risk-mitigating hedging, and for clients; certain investments; trading by a regulated insurance company directly engaged in the business of insurance; bona fide trust, fiduciary, or investment advisory services; proprietary trading outside of the United States by banking entities not controlled by a U.S. banking entity; ownership and sponsorship of a private fund outside of the United States by banking entities not controlled by a U.S. banking entity; and other activities as deemed by regulators to promote and protect the safety and soundness of the banking entity and U.S. financial stability.

■ The Volcker Rule instructed the FSOC to engage in a study and the formation of recommendations in relation to the Volcker Rule. The FSOC completed the study in January 2011. This was followed by the joint issuance in December 2013 of the final rules implementing the Volcker Rule by the OCC, the FDIC, the Fed, the SEC and the CFTC.

■ While supporters of the Volcker Rule argue that it is necessary to reduce the risks to which trading activities expose banks and systemically risky nonbank financial companies, as well as financial stability, others criticize it as being non-helpful and potentially harmful.

KNOWLEDGE CHECK

Q10.1: What is the Volcker Rule?

Q10.2: What are the purposes of the Volcker Rule?

Q10.3: To which legislation is the Volcker Rule's approach aligned?

Q10.4: What is "proprietary trading," a "trading account," and a "banking entity"?

Q10.5: What are the purposes of the Volcker Rule's prohibition on banking entities from owning or sponsoring hedge funds and private equity funds?

Q10.6: What activities does the Volcker Rule permit despite its prohibitions?

Q10.7: For which securities is proprietary trading permitted despite the Volcker Rule?

Q10.8: Which government agencies jointly issued the final rule?

Q10.9: What are criticisms of the Volcker Rule?

NOTES

1. Group of Thirty, "Financial Reform A Framework for Financial Stability," Jan. 2009. Statement that the report was largely authored by Volcker is from a statement by Senator Jeff Merkley, 156 CONG. REC. S5894 (daily ed.), July 15, 2010.
2. *Source:* Statement of Paul A. Volcker before the Committee on Banking, Housing, and Urban Affairs of the United States Senate, Feb. 2, 2010.
3. *Source:* Financial Stability Oversight Council, "Study & Recommendations on Prohibitions on Proprietary Trading & Certain Relationships with Hedge Funds & Private Equity Funds," Jan. 2011.
4. *Source:* 156 CONG. REC. S5894 (daily ed.), July 15, 2010.
5. *Source:* Financial Stability Oversight Council, 2011.
6. *Source:* Charles K. Whitehead, 2011, "The Volcker Rule and Evolving Financial Markets," *Harvard Business Law Review*, 1.

CHAPTER 11

Counterparty Credit Risk

INTRODUCTION

This chapter explores counterparty credit risk in depth. We first learn about OTC derivatives and why they are a source of counterparty credit risk. We then learn how counterparty credit risk is managed through collateral, netting, and central counterparties. This chapter also explores counterparty credit risk as a source of systemic risk.

After you read this chapter you will be able to:

- Describe derivative securities, including forwards, futures, options, and swaps.
- Understand the counterparty exposure associated with a derivative security.
- Explain the concepts of gross assets and net assets.
- Understand how collateral, netting, and central counterparties are used to manage counterparty credit risk.
- Distinguish between bilateral netting and multilateral netting.
- Understand why counterparty credit risk is perceived as a source of systemic risk.

OVERVIEW OF DERIVATIVE SECURITIES

A derivative security is an agreement between two counterparties to transact in the future in which the counterparties' profit or loss is a function of the value of an underlying asset. Derivative securities may trade on a derivatives exchange or through an over-the-counter (OTC) derivatives market. An OTC derivatives market is a market where trading takes place through networks of dealers that are employed by financial institutions, and does not take place on an exchange.

Broadly, there are three varieties of derivative securities:

- Forwards/futures
- Options
- Swaps

Let's briefly explore characteristics of each.[1]

Forward/futures contracts: A forward contract or a futures contract is an agreement in which two counterparties agree to transact an underlying asset in the future for a price that is agreed upon at initiation. The "long" counterparty is obligated to purchase the underlying asset for a fixed price in the future from the "short" counterparty, which is obligated to sell. The expression "forward contract" is used when it trades OTC, and the expression "futures contract" is used when it trades on an exchange.

For example, two counterparties may enter into a futures contract in which the long counterparty agrees to purchase a share of IBM from the short counterparty for $160 in three months. If the value of a share of IBM is greater than $160 in three months, the long counterparty will profit as the long counterparty will pay only $160 for a stock worth more than $160. The short counterparty will suffer a loss as it is selling a stock worth more than $160 for only $160. However, if the value of a share of IBM is less than $160 in three months, the long counterparty will suffer a loss and the short counterparty will profit.

Option contracts: Like a forward/futures contract, an option contract is an agreement in which two counterparties agree to transact an underlying asset in the future for a price that is agreed upon at initiation. However, unlike a forward or futures contract, by an option contract one of the counterparties has the *right* and not the *obligation* to transact in the future. There are two varieties of option contract: call options and put options.

- By a call option, the long counterparty has the right—but not an obligation—to *purchase* the underlying asset for a fixed price in the future from the short counterparty. The short counterparty is obligated to sell. The long counterparty will only choose to exercise its right when it is in its best interest to do so. This ability to choose is valuable; hence the long counterparty must pay a premium at initiation to the short counterparty in order to obtain the right.
- By a put option, the long counterparty has the right—but not an obligation—to *sell* the underlying asset for a fixed price in the future to the short counterparty. The short counterparty is obligated to purchase. The long counterparty will only choose to exercise its right when it is in its best interest to do so. The long counterparty to a put option must pay a premium at initiation to the short counterparty in order to obtain its right.

For example, two counterparties may enter into a call option contract in which the long call has the right but not an obligation to purchase a share of IBM from the short call for $160 in three months. The long call pays the short call a premium of $25 in order to obtain this right. If the value of a share of IBM is greater than $160 in three months, the long call will choose to exercise their right to purchase, as they have the right to pay only $160 for a stock worth more than $160. However, if the value of a share of IBM is less than $160 in three months, the long call will not exercise its right.

The expression "OTC option contract" is used when an option trades OTC, and the expression "exchange-traded option contract" is used when an option trades on an exchange.

Swaps: A swap is an agreement between two counterparties to exchange cash flows over a number of periods of time in the future. While a wide variety of swaps are traded, the most commonly traded swaps are interest rate swaps, cross-currency swaps, and credit default swaps. Here's a brief description of each:

- *Interest rate swap:* Two counterparties agree to exchange a fixed rate of interest for a floating rate of interest over a number of periods of time. For example, the counterparties may agree to periodically exchange a fixed 3% for LIBOR over a five-year period of time.[2]
- *Cross-currency swap:* Two counterparties agree to exchange cash flows in distinct currencies over a number of periods of time. For example, the counterparties may agree to periodically exchange 3% of a specified amount of USD for 3.25% of a specified amount of euros over a five-year period of time.
- *Credit default swap:* One of the counterparties agrees to make periodic payments. In return, the second counterparty agrees to make a large payment to the first counterparty should a specified reference asset issued by a specified reference entity experience a credit event, such as a bankruptcy or a default. For example, one of the counterparties agrees to pay $10,000 per quarter for the next three years. In return, the second counterparty agrees to make a large payment should a specified IBM bond experience a credit event.

There are also swaps in which the counterparties agree to exchange cash flows based on the levels of equity indexes, commodity values, inflation levels, and volatility, among other varieties. Typically, both counterparties to a swap are obligated to make payments of cash flows. However, in some swaps, such as caps, floors, and swaptions, one of the counterparties has a right while the other counterparty has an obligation, similar to an option. Swaps trade through OTC derivative markets.

As we've seen, swap agreements typically specify a rate that is exchanged over a number of periods in the future, yet the actual transactions are exchanges of *cashflows*, not *rates*. To translate the rate specification into a dollar amount, each swap agreement will include a *notional principal*. Hence, the cashflows that are transacted are identified through multiplying the rates by the specified notional principal. For example, if a given rate is 3%, and the notional principal is $1 million, then the cashflow is 3% × $1,000,000 = $30,000. Typically, the notional principal is not exchanged, either at initiation or termination; hence its typical role is to translate rates into cashflows.[3]

COUNTERPARTY EXPOSURE

In the previous section we explored forwards, futures, options, and swaps. While these contracts vary widely, in all of them transactions will take place in the future at a price or a rate that is fixed today. Inevitably, this will be beneficial to one of the counterparties and detrimental to the other. For example, an interest rate swap counterparty that is paying a fixed rate of 3% and receiving LIBOR in return will profit if LIBOR rises above 3% and will suffer a loss if the reverse occurs.

Valuation techniques are used to value positions in derivative securities. Using these techniques, counterparties record the value of a given derivative security as either an asset or a liability. A position will be recorded as an asset if the present value of the cash inflows that it is expected to generate is greater than the present value of the cash outflows that it is expected to generate, and will be recorded as a liability if the reverse is true. Derivative securities are "zero-sum games" in which the value of the asset that one of the counterparties holds in relation to a given derivative security is exactly equal to the size of the liability that the other counterparty holds.

The counterparty to a given derivative security whose position is an asset—which we will refer to as the *asset counterparty*—faces counterparty exposure. After all, the value of derivative position that is an asset is only valuable if the other counterparty—the *liability counterparty*—satisfies its obligations per the agreement. Should the liability counterparty experience financial distress and be unable to satisfy its obligations, the asset counterparty will have to write down the value of its asset to reflect whatever recovery it expects to obtain from the financially distressed liability counterparty.

To explore further the nature of the assets and liabilities associated with derivatives, we can make a broad distinction between two types of agreements: those in which both counterparties are obligated to transact in the future, and those in which one of the counterparties has the right to transact in the future and the other counterparty has an obligation. Let's explore each in more detail.

Derivative security in which both counterparties are obligated to transact in the future: Forward contracts, futures contracts, interest rate swaps, cross-currency swaps, and credit default swaps are examples of derivative securities in which both counterparties are obligated to transact in the future. For all of these, the contract is structured at initiation such that the value of each of the counterparties' positions is neither an asset nor a liability. This is implemented through setting transaction prices or rates at a level designed to ensure the position is valued at zero, given the counterparties' expectations of drivers of the derivative security's value, such as the underlying asset's future prices or rates. Once the agreement is executed, the drivers of value will change and the position will become an asset for one of the counterparties and a liability to the other counterparty.

Derivative security in which one of the counterparties has the right to transact in the future and the other counterparty has an obligation: Call options, put options, and caps, floors, and swaptions are examples of derivative securities in which one of the counterparties has the right to transact in the future and the other counterparty has an obligation. Having the right—and not the obligation—to transact is valuable as the counterparty can transact when it is beneficial to do so and not transact when doing so is detrimental. Hence, the derivative security is always an asset for the counterparty with the right and is never a liability. Conversely, the other counterparty—the one that is obligated to transact should the counterparty with the right choose to exercise—will only find itself transacting when doing so benefits the counterparty with the right and, inevitably, is detrimental to the counterparty with the obligation. Hence, the derivative security is always a liability for the counterparty with the obligation and is never an asset.

We see that the derivative security is always an asset for the counterparty with the right and is always a liability for the counterparty with the obligation. So why does the counterparty with the obligation agree to participate? The answer is that the counterparty with the obligation receives a premium. The premium compensates the counterparty for accepting the obligation and is reflective of the value of the liability. Once the agreement is executed, the drivers of value will change and the position will become an increasingly larger or smaller asset for the counterparty with the right and an increasingly larger or smaller liability for the counterparty with the obligation.

Table 11.1 summarizes the two types of agreements and the associated assets and liabilities. Both counterparties to a derivative security in which both counterparties are obligated to transact in the future face potential counterparty credit risk, as both are potentially asset counterparties.

TABLE 11.1 Types of Derivative Security Agreements and the Associated Assets and Liabilities

Type of Agreement	Derivative Security in which Both Counterparties Are Obligated to Transact in the Future		Derivative Security in which One of the Counterparties Has the Right to Transact in the Future and the Other Counterparty Has an Obligation	
Examples	Forward contracts, futures contracts, interest rate swaps, cross-currency swaps, and credit default swaps		Call options, put options, caps, floors, and swaptions	
Counterparties	Counterparty A	Counterparty B	Counterparty A	Counterparty B
Right or obligation?	Obligation	Obligation	Right	Obligation
Asset or liability at initiation?	Neither an asset nor a liability: valued at zero	Neither an asset nor a liability: valued at zero	Asset: as receives a right and has no obligation	Liability: as provides a right to the other counterparty
Pays or receives a premium?	No premium	No premium	Pays a premium	Receives a premium
Asset or liability during life of the agreement?	Asset or liability, depending on the level of the drivers of value	Asset or liability, depending on the level of the drivers of value	Asset: larger or smaller depending on the level of the drivers of value	Liability: larger or smaller depending on the level of the drivers of value
Potential source of counterparty risk?	Yes, as position may be a liability	Yes, as position may be a liability	No, as position can never be a liability	Yes, as position is always a liability
Potentially faces counterparty risk?	Yes, as position may be an asset	Yes, as position may be an asset	Yes, as position is always an asset	No, as position is never an asset

Positions that hold rights also face potential counterparty credit risk, as they are always an asset counterparty. Conversely, counterparties with an obligation that is conditional on the other counterparty exercising a right do not face counterparty credit risk as they are exclusively a liability counterparty.

HOW COUNTERPARTY CREDIT RISK IS MANAGED

We've seen that counterparties to derivative securities face counterparty credit risk exposure. This exposure is managed in a number of ways, key among which are the following:

- Collateral
- Netting
- Central counterparties

Collateral

Many of us are deeply familiar with the concept of collateral: Collateral refers to property that the counterparties to an agreement pledge to each other, which they agree to forfeit if they do not satisfy their obligations per the agreement. The concepts of netting and central counterparties are less well-known. It will therefore be useful to explore the concepts of netting and central counterparties in more detail.

Netting

Netting refers to the offsetting of positions. There are two types of netting: payment netting and closeout netting. Payment netting is the netting that occurs when two counterparties plan to transact cashflows with each other at a specific point in time: Rather than each counterparty making the agreed payment, the two payments are netted out and only a single payment is made. The benefit of payment netting is that it avoids situations whereby one of the counterparties to a deal satisfies its payment obligation while the other fails to do so.

For example, consider a swap in which counterparty A is required to make a $40,000 payment to counterparty B on December 15 while counterparty B is required to make a $30,000 payment to counterparty A on the same date as well. Instead of each of the two counterparties making the required payments, the two payments are netted out and the only payment that occurs is a $10,000 payment from counterparty A to counterparty B.

Closeout netting is a more sophisticated netting concept that occurs when one of the counterparties to an agreement experiences a termination event such as a bankruptcy. Upon the termination event, the gross assets and gross liabilities are identified across all agreements that the counterparties have entered into with each other. Then, the gross assets and gross liabilities across all of the agreements are netted out, resulting in net positions that are smaller than the gross positions. The smaller net positions mean that the counterparty has less counterparty credit risk exposure than the gross asset position might suggest.

For example, consider two counterparties, A and B, which have entered into four derivative securities agreements with each other. Table 11.2 lists the asset and liability positions for each of the counterparties. Counterparty A's gross assets are $80,000 while counterparty B's gross assets are $90,000. However, due to closeout netting, these gross asset amounts are not the two counterparties' counterparty exposure. Instead, through closeout netting each counterparty's gross assets are offset by their gross liabilities, and the net exposure is much lower. Counterparty A has $10,000 in net liabilities, and therefore is not exposed to counterparty B at all. Counterparty B has $10,000 in net assets. Should counterparty A experience financial distress, counterparty B's exposure is its $10,000 in net assets and not its $90,000 in gross assets. We see from this example that closeout netting can greatly reduce counterparty exposure.

To further explore, consider another example. A marketplace consists of four counterparties: A, B, C, and D. Each of these counterparties holds multiple derivative securities against each other, and their gross assets against each of their counterparties are illustrated in Figure 11.1. In this figure, an arrow pointing toward an entity refers to the gross assets it holds against the given counterparty. For example, counterparty A holds 30 of gross assets against B, while counterparty B holds 20 of gross assets against A. Figure 11.2 illustrates the same example, this time from the perspective of net assets.

Table 11.3 lists the gross assets and liabilities positions for each of the counterparties. For example, counterparty A has gross assets against

TABLE 11.2 Counterparty Credit Risk Following Closeout Netting

Derivative Security Agreement	Counterparty A	Counterparty B
#1	$20,000 Asset	$20,000 Liability
#2	$60,000 Asset	$60,000 Liability
#3	$80,000 Liability	$80,000 Asset
#4	$10,000 Liability	$10,000 Asset
Gross assets	$80,000 Gross Assets	$90,000 Gross Assets
Gross liabilities	$90,000 Gross Liabilities	$80,000 Gross Liabilities
Net assets or liabilities	$10,000 Net Liabilities	$10,000 Net Assets

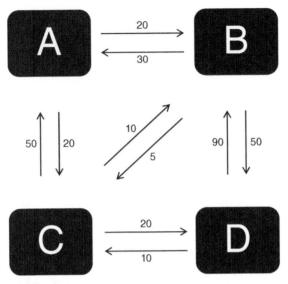

FIGURE 11.1 Gross assets, market consisting of four counterparties

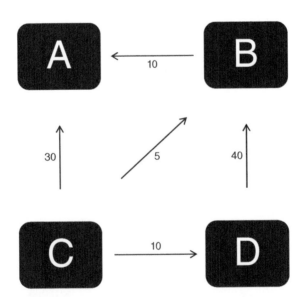

FIGURE 11.2 Net assets, market consisting of four counterparties

TABLE 11.3 Gross Assets, Market Consisting of Four Counterparties

	Counter-party A	Counter-party B	Counter-party C	Counter-party D	Market
Gross assets against A	NA	20	20	0	40
Gross assets against B	30	NA	5	50	80
Gross assets against C	50	10	NA	20	80
Gross assets against D	0	90	10	NA	100
Gross assets against all counterparties	80	120	35	70	300

TABLE 11.4 Net Assets, Market Consisting of Four Counterparties

	Counter-party A	Counter-party B	Counter-party C	Counter-party D	Market
Net assets against A	NA	0	0	0	0
Net assets against B	10	NA	0	0	10
Net assets against C	30	5	NA	10	45
Net assets against D	0	40	0	NA	40
Net assets against all counterparties	40	45	0	10	95

all counterparties of 80, and this represents A's exposure should all of A's counterparties experience financial distress. Conversely, the market has gross assets of 40 against A, and this represents the overall market's exposure to A's financial distress. Notably, the total gross assets across all counterparties across the entire market is 300.

Table 11.4 lists the net assets positions for each of the counterparties. For example, counterparty A has net assets against all counterparties of 50, and, assuming the market facilitates closeout netting, this represents A's exposure should all of A's counterparties experience financial distress. Conversely, all counterparties have zero net assets against A, indicating that no counterparty is exposed to A's financial distress. Most noteworthy is that the total net assets across all counterparties across the entire market is 95, less than one third of the 300 in exposure identified in Table 11.3. This reduction of counterparty exposure demonstrates the usefulness of closeout netting in reducing counterparty exposure.

Central Counterparties

Our previous discussion of netting implicitly assumes that each agreement is a bilateral agreement between two counterparties. In a bilateral agreement, counterparties remain obligated to each other during the life of the agreement, and bilateral netting takes place across the agreements between the two counterparties. An alternative mechanism exists that permits multilateral netting. This mechanism is facilitated by an entity called a *central counterparty clearinghouse* (CCP). In a market that utilizes a CCP, counterparties enter into agreements with each other to transact in the future. Then, once the agreement is executed, through a process called *novation*, the counterparties switch from being counterparties with each other to being counterparties with the CCP. Hence, the original counterparties are no longer exposed to each other's counterparty credit risk but face counterparty exposure against the CCP.

The existence of CCPs and the novation mechanism works to reduce counterparty exposure in two ways. First, the CCP works to maintain high credit ratings, through objective and conservative margin requirements and careful monitoring of margin levels, among other means. Hence, the CCP is likely a safer counterparty than one's original counterparty. Second, the existence of CCPs allows for multilateral netting rather than bilateral netting. Since the CCP is one's counterparty for all agreements, netting can occur against the CCP instead of netting against each of one's counterparties on a bilateral basis. This allows for more extensive netting and therefore less exposure.

To demonstrate the usefulness of multilateral netting, let's return to the example explored in the previous section and previously illustrated in Figures 11.1 and 11.2 and Tables 11.3 and 11.4. As illustrated in Figure 11.3, counterparties A, B, C, and D no longer hold gross assets against each other. Instead, they all hold gross assets against the CCP. Figure 11.4 and Table 11.5 show the impact of netting when there is a CCP. Most noteworthy is that the total net assets across all counterparties across the entire market is 75, less than the 95 of exposure identified in Table 11.4.

TABLE 11.5 Net Assets, Market Consisting of Four Counterparties and a CCP

	Counter-party A	Counter-party B	Counter-party C	Counter-party D	CCP
Net assets against A	NA	0	0	0	0
Net assets against B	0	NA	0	0	0
Net assets against C	0	0	NA	0	45
Net assets against D	0	0	0	NA	30
Net assets against the CCP	40	40	0	0	NA
Net assets against all counterparties	40	35	0	0	75

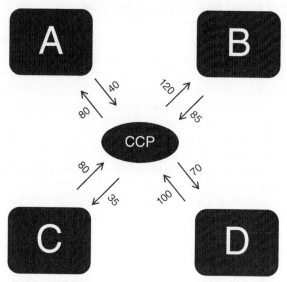

FIGURE 11.3 Gross assets, market consisting of four counterparties and a CCP

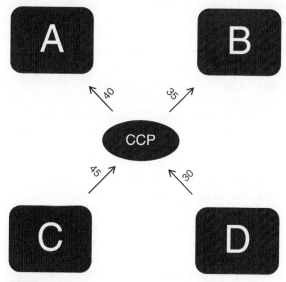

FIGURE 11.4 Net assets, market consisting of four counterparties and a CCP

COUNTERPARTY CREDIT RISK AND SYSTEMIC RISK

The Credit Crisis of 2007–2009 has led to intense scrutiny of the willingness and ability of financial institutions to manage counterparty credit risk. Indeed, counterparty credit risk is perceived as a source of systemic risk. A financial institution that has built up a large asset position against a counterparty will be forced to write down the value of the assets should the counterparty experience financial distress, which can lead to the financial institution's insolvency. Hence, counterparty credit risk can lead to a cascade of write-downs and financial distress. To illustrate, consider a market in which there are three agreements: between counterparties A and B, counterparties B and C, and counterparties C and D. The financial distress of A requires counterparty B to write down the value of its assets against A. But this can lead to financial distress for counterparty B, which requires counterparty C to write down the value of its assets against B. But this can lead to financial distress for counterparty C, which requires counterparty D to write down the value of its assets against C. While this is a simplistic example, it does illustrate the key concern: The failure of one counterparty can lead to a cascade of failures and, ultimately, be a source of systemic risk. Several factors made the concerns regarding systemic risk during the Credit Crisis of 2007–2009 particularly acute.

First, while CCPs were available pre-Crisis for some varieties of OTC derivatives, most OTC derivatives agreements were privately negotiated bilateral agreements between counterparties that did not utilize CCPs; hence, counterparties were able to build up large asset positions against each other without the benefits of multilateral netting. This was unlike exchange-traded derivatives, which mandated the use of CCPs and thereby facilitated multilateral netting.

Second, as these were private bilateral agreements, there was limited understanding on the part of regulators of the nature of exposure that counterparties faced.

Third, counterparties to transactions were often financial institutions. Should a financial institution fail, its value drops precipitously—much more precipitously than, for example, the value of an auto manufacturer following a bankruptcy. Hence, there is little recovery value associated with financial institutions upon insolvency; and, therefore, the write-downs are significant.

Fourth, the products and strategies that were the source of counterparty exposure were often poorly understood, and there was often difficulty in accurately evaluating the counterparty exposure. Notably, during the period before the financial crisis, there was significant growth in exposure to credit default swaps and various structured credit vehicles such as collateralized debt obligations. Certain positions and strategies exposed counterparties to credit risk, market risk, liquidity risk, and counterparty credit risk in ways that were neither fully understood nor measured.

Fifth, while many products and strategies were a significant source of exposure, when initially executed they were off-balance-sheet exposures. For example, as noted earlier, for a derivative security in which both counterparties are obligated to transact in the future, the contract is structured at initiation such that the value of each of the counterparties' positions is neither an asset nor a liability. This off-balance-sheet nature meant that the traditional methods of reporting and evaluating exposure were not useful.

While the financial crisis has led to intense scrutiny of the willingness and ability of financial institutions to manage counterparty credit risk, it is less than clear that counterparty credit risk led to the crisis or is even a source of systemic risk. In the next chapter, we will explore methods of measuring counterparty exposure and look at data to evaluate the degree of exposure. We will also explore Title VII of the Dodd-Frank Act, which works to address the counterparty credit risk exposure associated with OTC derivatives.

KEY POINTS

- A derivative security is an agreement between two counterparties to transact in the future in which the counterparties' profit or loss is a function of the value of an underlying asset.
- Derivative securities may trade on a derivatives exchange or through an over-the-counter (OTC) derivatives market.
- A forward contract is an OTC derivatives agreement in which two counterparties agree to transact an underlying asset in the future for a price that is agreed upon at initiation. A futures contract is an exchange-traded version of a forward contract.
- An option contract is an agreement in which two counterparties agree to transact an underlying asset in the future for a price that is agreed upon at initiation, in which one of the counterparties has the *right* and not the *obligation* to transact in the future. Options trade both OTC and through exchanges.
- By a call option, the long counterparty has the right to purchase the underlying asset for a fixed price in the future from the short counterparty. By a put option, the long counterparty has the right to sell the underlying asset for a fixed price in the future to the short counterparty.

- A swap is an agreement between two counterparties to exchange cashflows over a number of periods of time in the future. By an interest rate swap, two counterparties agree to exchange a fixed rate of interest for a floating rate of interest over a number of periods of time. By a cross-currency swap, two counterparties agree to exchange cashflows in distinct currencies over a number of periods of time. By a credit default swap, one of the counterparties agrees to make periodic payments and the second counterparty agrees to make a large payment to the first counterparty should a specified reference asset issued by a specified reference entity experience a credit event. The notional principal translates the rates associated with swaps into cashflows.

- Typically, both counterparties to a swap are obligated to make payments of cashflows. However, in some swaps, such as caps, floors, and swaptions, one of the counterparties has a right while the other counterparty has an obligation, similar to an option. Swaps trade through OTC derivative markets.

- The counterparty to a given derivative security whose position is an asset faces counterparty exposure. Should the liability counterparty experience financial distress and be unable to satisfy its obligations, the asset counterparty will have to write down the value of its asset to reflect whatever recovery it expects to obtain from the financially distressed liability counterparty.

- By derivative security in which both counterparties are obligated to transact in the future, the contract is structured at initiation such that the value of each of the counterparties' positions is neither an asset nor a liability. Once the agreement is executed, the drivers of value will change and the position will become an asset for one of the counterparties and a liability to the other counterparty.

- By a derivative security in which one of the counterparties has the right to transact in the future and the other counterparty has an obligation, the derivative security is always an asset for the counterparty with the right and always a liability for the counterparty with an obligation.

- Counterparty credit risk exposure is managed through the use of collateral, netting, and central counterparties. Collateral refers to property that the counterparties to an agreement pledge to each other, which they agree to forfeit if they do not satisfy their obligations per the agreement. Netting refers to the offsetting of positions.

- Payment netting is the netting that occurs when payments are netted out and only a single payment is made. Closeout netting occurs when one of the counterparties to an agreement experiences a termination event, at which time the gross assets and gross liabilities across all of the agreements are netted out.

- In a market that utilizes a central counterparty clearinghouse (CCP), counterparties enter into agreements with each other to transact in the future. Once executed, through a process called "novation," the counterparties switch from being counterparties with each other to being counterparties with the CCP.
- One benefit associated with a CCP is that a CCP is likely a safer counterparty than the original counterparties. Another benefit is that CCPs allow for multilateral netting, whereby netting occurs against the CCP instead of counterparties netting against each other on a bilateral basis.
- The Credit Crisis of 2007–2009 has led to intense scrutiny of the willingness and ability of financial institutions to manage counterparty credit risk and has led counterparty credit risk to be perceived as a source of systemic risk. Several factors driving this perception include the private bilateral nature of most OTC derivatives agreements pre-Crisis; limited understanding on the part of regulators of the nature of exposures; the low recovery values associated with insolvent financial institutions; poorly understood and difficult-to-evaluate products and strategies; and the off-balance-sheet nature of exposures.

KNOWLEDGE CHECK

Q11.1: What is a derivative security?
Q11.2: What is a forward contract?
Q11.3: What is a futures contract?
Q11.4: What is an option contract?
Q11.5: What is a call option?
Q11.6: What is a put option?
Q11.7: What is a swap?
Q11.8: What is an interest rate swap?
Q11.9: What is a cross-currency swap?
Q11.10: What is a credit default swap?
Q11.11: What is the typical role of notional principal?
Q11.12: Why does the asset counterparty to a derivative security face counterparty credit risk exposure?
Q11.13: How is counterparty credit risk managed?
Q11.14: What are the two types of netting?
Q11.15: What is a CCP?
Q11.16: What are the benefits of a CCP?
Q11.17: What factors drove the perception that counterparty credit risk was problematic during the Credit Crisis of 2007–2009?

NOTES

1. For a more extensive introduction to derivative securities, please see Gottesman, Aron, *Derivatives Essentials: An Introduction to Forwards, Futures, and Swaps.* Hoboken, NJ: Wiley, 2016.
2. LIBOR is a commonly used index of interest rates that changes over time.
3. In some swaps, such as cross-currency swaps, the notional principal is exchanged both at initiation and termination.

CHAPTER 12

The Dodd-Frank Act and Counterparty Credit Risk

INTRODUCTION

This chapter explores Title VII of the Dodd-Frank Act, which heavily regulates over-the-counter (OTC) derivatives markets. We will develop an understanding of the level of counterparty exposure through looking at historical data of the notional outstanding, gross market value, gross credit exposure, and collateral associated with OTC derivatives markets. We will then explore how Title VII of the Dodd-Frank Act works to reduce the counterparty exposure faced by participants in the OTC derivatives market through setting mandatory clearing and other requirements.

After you read this chapter you will be able to:

- Distinguish between notional outstanding, gross market value, gross credit exposure, and collateral.
- Show the degree to which OTC derivatives markets are characterized by counterparty exposure.
- Explain the evolution of the U.S. regulatory approach toward OTC derivatives.
- Describe key provisions of Title VII of the Dodd-Frank Act.
- Discuss criticism of Title VII.

MEASURING COUNTERPARTY EXPOSURE IN THE OTC DERIVATIVES MARKET

In this chapter we explore how Title VII of the Dodd-Frank Act works to reduce the counterparty exposure faced by participants in the OTC derivatives market. Before doing so, it will be useful to understand the various ways that counterparty exposure can be measured and to look at historical data to explore the degree to which the OTC derivatives market is characterized by counterparty exposure. We explore the following four measures, which were introduced in the previous chapter.

Notional outstanding: Each swap agreement specifies a dollar amount of notional principal, which is used to translate the rates associated with swaps into cashflows. Typically, notional principal is not exchanged either at initiation or at termination. Notional outstanding is the aggregate of the notional principal of all OTC derivatives securities.

Notional outstanding provides a crude metric of counterparty exposure insofar as it provides observers a sense of market size. However, notional outstanding is not a true metric of counterparty exposure. After all, typically notional principal is not exchanged. Hence any write-down that occurs upon the failure of a counterparty is not based on the notional principal. Indeed, the actual cashflows associated with an OTC derivative security are often a small proportion of the notional principal.

Gross market value: Counterparties record the value of a given derivative security as either an asset or a liability. Gross market value refers to the aggregate of the gross assets of all OTC derivative securities. Hence, gross market value does not take into account the ability of the counterparties to engage in closeout netting should there be a termination event. Because derivative securities are zero-sum games, the gross market value is exactly equal to the aggregate of gross liabilities associated with all OTC derivatives.

Gross market value provides a more realistic metric of counterparty exposure insofar as it reflects the assets that entities have built up against counterparties. Gross market value can ostensibly be used as an indication of the write-downs that will occur should these counterparties experience financial distress. However, gross market value is also not a true metric of counterparty exposure, as it fails to take into account closeout netting, which mitigates the actual exposure.

Gross credit exposure: Closeout netting occurs when one of the counterparties to an agreement experiences a termination event, at which time the gross assets and gross liabilities across all of the agreements are netted out. The smaller net positions means that the counterparty has less counterparty credit risk exposure than the gross asset position might suggest. Gross credit exposure refers to the aggregate of the net asset positions held by all participants in OTC derivative securities. Gross credit exposure is a superior metric of counterparty exposure, as it reflects the actual write-downs that will occur should a given entity's counterparties experience financial distress. However, one limitation of gross credit exposure is that it does not take into account the collateral that market participants hold, which they receive if their counterparties do not satisfy their obligations per the agreement.

Collateral: Collateral refers to property that the counterparties to an agreement pledge to each other, which they agree to forfeit if they do not satisfy their obligations per the agreement. Collateral, when compared to gross credit exposure, can provide a strong sense of the OTC derivatives markets' actual counterparty exposure.

OVERVIEW OF HISTORICAL DATA

To explore the counterparty exposure faced by participants in the OTC derivatives market, let's look at the historical data for notional outstanding, gross market value, gross credit exposure, and collateral. The sources of the data we will explore are the semiannual OTC derivative statistics provided by the BIS and the annual ISDA margin survey.

Figure 12.1 presents the notional outstanding for OTC derivatives from June 1998 through June 2016. The notional outstanding over this time period increased tremendously. The change in notional outstanding can be best understood through looking at two separate time periods: June 1998–June 2008 and June 2008–June 2016. From June 1998 through June 2008, the notional outstanding increased tenfold, from approximately 72 USD trillion to 672 USD trillion. During June 2008–June 2016 the notional outstanding did not increase dramatically, and in fact dropped from approximately 672 USD trillion to 544 USD trillion, with increases and decreases in the notional outstanding across various semiannual periods.

An individual measuring counterparty exposure using notional outstanding would be very alarmed: 600–700 USD trillion is a tremendous amount of exposure. However, an individual measuring counterparty exposure on this basis would be engaging in a superficial exercise: as noted, notional outstanding is not a true metric of counterparty exposure as any write-down that occurs upon the failure of a counterparty is not based on the notional principal, which is, after all, typically not exchanged between the counterparties.

Figure 12.2 presents the gross market value and the gross credit exposure for OTC derivatives from June 1998 through June 2016. For every semi-annual period, gross market value is only a small fraction of the notional outstanding. For example, in December 2008, when gross market value reached its highest level of approximately 35 USD trillion, it was only 6% of the approximately 598 USD trillion notional outstanding at that time. Further, as noted, gross market value is also not a true metric of counterparty exposure as it fails to take into account closeout netting, which mitigates the actual exposure. The gross credit exposure, also presented in Figure 12.2, is a small fraction of the gross market value. For example, in December 2008,

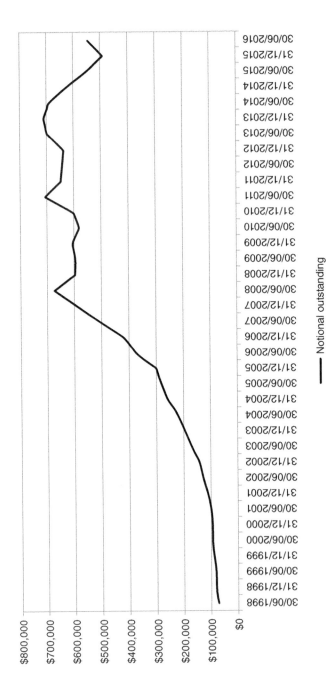

FIGURE 12.1 OTC derivatives notional outstanding, USD billions[1]

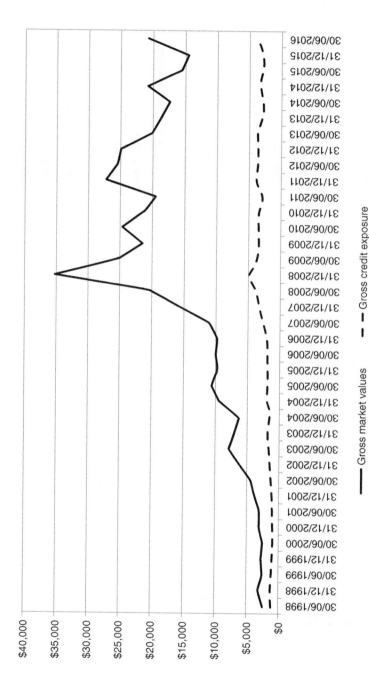

FIGURE 12.2 OTC derivatives gross market value and gross credit exposure, USD billions[2]

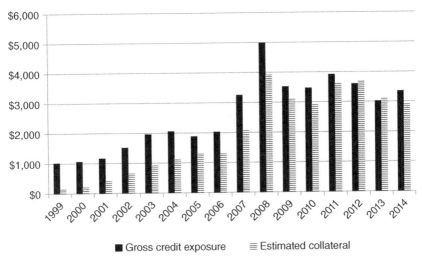

FIGURE 12.3   OTC derivatives gross credit exposure and estimated collateral, USD billions[3]

the gross credit exposure was approximately 5 USD trillion, approximately 14% of the gross market value and less than 1% of the notional outstanding.

We see that from the perspective of gross credit exposure, counterparty exposure is much smaller than one would perceive when looking at notional outstanding or gross market value. Further, as noted, gross credit exposure does not take into account the collateral that market participants hold. Figure 12.3 presents the gross credit exposure and the estimated collateral for each year from 1999 through 2014. We see from this figure that the estimated collateral is a large proportion of the gross credit exposure, particularly following the 2007–2008 crisis. For example, in December 2008, the estimated collateral is approximately 4 USD trillion, which is 80% of the 5 USD trillion in gross credit exposure. Further, Figure 12.3 demonstrates that the estimated collateral closely tracks the level of gross credit exposure. Indeed, the correlation across the two is approximately 96%.

THE EVOLUTION OF THE U.S. REGULATORY APPROACH TOWARD OTC DERIVATIVES

The previous section illustrates that OTC derivatives' counterparty exposure during the runup to the Credit Crisis of 2007–2009 was offset by both closeout netting and the use of collateral. Regardless, the financial crisis led to intense scrutiny of the willingness and ability of financial institutions to manage the counterparty exposure of participants in OTC derivatives markets. As noted in the previous chapter, factors driving this perception included the private bilateral nature of most OTC derivatives agreements pre-Crisis; limited understanding on the part of regulators of the nature of exposures; the low recovery values associated with insolvent financial institutions; poorly understood and difficult-to-evaluate products and strategies; and the off-balance-sheet nature of exposures.

As a result of the perceived flaws in the ability of financial institutions to manage the counterparty exposure associated with OTC derivatives, the Dodd-Frank Act extensively transformed the nature of the OTC derivatives market. So as to reduce counterparty exposure, Title VII of the Dodd-Frank Act, formally titled "Wall Street Transparency and Accountability Act of 2010," mandated changes to the OTC derivatives markets that effectively forced them to be similar to derivatives exchanges, a change known as the "futurization of OTC derivatives."

We will explore key aspects of Title VII in the next section. Before doing so, note that Title VII represents the most recent evolution of the approach of regulators and politicians toward the regulation of OTC derivatives. Previously, the Commodities Exchange Act of 1936 prohibited "off-exchange futures." This prohibition was loosened through notable rule changes such as the Swap Exemption of 1993 that exempted OTC swaps from the Commodities Exchange Act. It was eventually overturned by the Commodities Futures Modernization Act of 2000, which provided legal certainty to OTC derivatives trading. Title VII's key objective is to reverse course through forcing OTC derivatives to trade in a way that is similar to how exchange-traded derivatives trade.

KEY PROVISIONS OF TITLE VII OF THE DODD-FRANK ACT

This section will explore key provisions of Title VII of the Dodd-Frank Act. Throughout, we will make reference to OTC derivatives that trade through networks of dealers that are employed by financial institutions, and not through an exchange. Title VII refers to OTC derivatives as either "swaps," "security-based swaps," or "mixed swaps." While the definition of each is detailed, the expression "swaps" refers to OTC derivatives based on broad-based indexes, interest rates, and currencies, among other underlying assets. A security-based swap refers to OTC derivatives based on a single security or a narrowly defined index, while a mixed swap refers to an OTC derivative with characteristics of both swaps and security-based swaps. While the key provisions that we explore in this section broadly apply to all OTC derivatives, the distinction between swaps, security-based swaps, and mixed swaps is noteworthy insofar as swaps are regulated by the Commodities Futures Trading Commission (CFTC), security-based swaps are regulated by the Securities and Exchange Commission (SEC), and mixed swaps are jointly regulated by the CFTC and the SEC.

The key provisions that we will explore are the following:

- Mandatory clearing
- Execution platforms and data repositories
- Registration requirements
- The push-out rule
- The end user exemption

Mandatory Clearing

As discussed in the previous chapter, a derivative security may be a bilateral agreement in which counterparties remain obligated to each other during the life of the agreement and bilateral netting takes place across the agreements between the two counterparties. Alternatively, the derivative security can be cleared through a central counterparty clearinghouse (CCP), whereby, following the agreement to transact in the future, through novation counterparties switch from being counterparties with each other to being counterparties with the CCP. One advantage of a CCP is that it is a low-risk counterparty. Another advantage is that it facilitates multilateral netting, which permits more extensive netting and therefore less counterparty exposure.

Before Title VII of the Dodd-Frank Act, there was no mandatory clearing requirement for OTC derivatives. While CCPs were available pre-Crisis for some varieties of OTC derivatives, many OTC derivatives agreements were privately negotiated bilateral agreements. The key contribution of Title VII is that it makes the clearing of OTC derivatives through a CCP mandatory, similar to how exchange-traded derivatives require mandatory clearing.

Execution Platforms and Data Repositories

Before Title VII of the Dodd-Frank Act, OTC derivatives were privately negotiated and, upon execution, represented private bilateral agreements, which meant that regulators had limited understanding of the nature of exposure that counterparties faced. Title VII of the Dodd-Frank Act mandates that OTC derivatives trade through formal platforms, such as a designated contract market, a national securities exchange, or an execution facility that can accept quotes from multiple participants. It also mandates that data related to OTC derivatives agreements be reported to, and maintained by, a registered data repository.

Registration Requirements

Title VII of the Dodd-Frank Act sets registration requirements for certain participants in OTC derivatives markets, including dealers, major participants, CCPs, execution platforms, and data repositories. These registration requirements place a significant compliance burden on OTC derivatives markets participants. Further, given the role of both the CFTC and the SEC in regulating OTC derivatives, the requirements can be complex and challenging to satisfy.

The Push-Out Rule

The *push-out rule* is a provision of Title VII of the Dodd-Frank Act that prohibits the U.S. federal government from bailing out, or providing any other financial assistance to, financial institutions that participate in an OTC derivatives market. This provision is referred to as the "push-out rule" as it forces financial institutions that wish to participate in OTC derivatives market to push out their OTC derivatives activities to an affiliate. The push-out rule is also known as the "Lincoln Amendment" due to the role of Senator Blanche Lincoln in encouraging its inclusion in Title VII of the Dodd-Frank Act.

The End User Exemption

While the Dodd-Frank Act requires mandatory clearing of OTC derivatives, it also provides an exemption through which "end user" entities transact an OTC derivative with clearing. This exemption is limited to nonfinancial entities that are using the OTC derivative for risk-mitigating or hedging purposes. The transaction must still be reported to a data repository.

CRITICISM OF TITLE VII OF THE DODD-FRANK ACT

Among the objectives of the Dodd-Frank Act is the promotion of financial stability, the ending of "too big to fail," and the ending of bailouts. Proponents of Title VII will argue that its mandatory clearing requirement and the transparency associated with its execution platform and reporting requirements work to reduce the perceived counterparty exposure and opaqueness that characterized the OTC derivatives markets during the period of time preceding the Credit Crisis of 2007–2009.

Yet others criticize Title VII. They argue that the complexity of Title VII and the costs associated with complying with its provisions will make it more difficult to transact OTC derivatives. This can have the effect of making OTC derivatives markets less liquid and OTC derivatives more difficult to use for hedging and risk-mitigating purposes. They also argue that Title VII has not ended "too big to fail" but instead has created a new type of too-big-to-fail entity—namely the CCPs, which facilitate multilateral clearing in OTC derivatives markets. The concentration of counterparty exposure against CCPs means that their failures would require extensive write-downs on the part of their many counterparties. These counterparties include systemically important financial institutions; hence, the failures of CCPs would represent a threat to financial stability.

As explored in Chapter 9, the Dodd-Frank Act requires that the Financial Stability Oversight Council identify Systemically Important Financial Market Utilities (SIFMUs), such as CCPs, and subject them to standards of risk management and conduct, enhanced supervision, and liquidity requirements. Broadly, however, given the concentration of exposure associated with CCPs there is concern whether they are sufficiently protected. Indeed, as recently as Summer 2016, the Financial Stability Board was seeking comment on resolution planning for CCPs.[4]

KEY POINTS

- Notional outstanding provides a crude metric of counterparty exposure insofar as it provides observers a sense of market size. However, notional outstanding is not a true metric of counterparty exposure as the actual cashflows associated with an OTC derivative security are often a small proportion of the notional principal.
- Gross market value provides a more realistic metric of counterparty exposure insofar as it reflects the assets that entities have built up against counterparties. However, it fails to take into account closeout netting, which mitigates the actual exposure.
- Gross credit exposure refers to the aggregate of the net asset positions held by all participants in OTC derivative securities. Gross credit exposure is a superior metric of counterparty exposure, as it reflects the actual write-downs that will occur should a given entity's counterparties experience financial distress. However, it does not take into account the collateral that market participants hold.
- Historically, notional outstanding has been hundreds of trillions in USD terms. Gross market value has been in the tens of trillions and gross credit exposure is less than five trillion. Estimated collateral is equal to a significant proportion of gross credit exposure.

- Title VII of the Dodd-Frank Act mandated changes to the OTC derivatives markets that effectively forced them to be similar to derivatives exchanges. Previous approaches include the Commodities Exchange Act of 1936's prohibition of "off-exchange futures," the Swap Exemption of 1993, and the Commodities Futures Modernization Act of 2000, which provided legal certainty to OTC derivatives trading.
- Key provisions of Title VII of the Dodd-Frank Act include mandatory clearing of OTC derivatives through a CCP; mandatory trading through formal platforms; requirements to report to a registered data repositories; and registration requirements.
- The push-out rule of Title VII prohibits the U.S. federal government from bailing out, or providing any other financial assistance to, financial institutions that participate in an OTC derivatives market, effectively forcing financial institutions that wish to participate in OTC derivatives market to push out their OTC derivatives activities to an affiliate. There is also an end-user exemption to the mandatory clearing requirement for nonfinancial entities that are using the OTC derivative for risk-mitigating or hedging purposes.
- Criticism of Title VII includes its complexity and the costs associated with complying with its provisions, as well as the concentration of counterparty exposure against CCPs, effectively creating a new type of too-big-to-fail entity.

KNOWLEDGE CHECK

Q12.1: What is the limitation associated with using notional outstanding as a measure of counterparty exposure?

Q12.2: What is the limitation associated with using gross market value as a measure of counterparty exposure?

Q12.3: What is the limitation associated with using gross credit exposure to measure counterparty exposure?

Q12.4: What were some of the key approaches to regulating OTC derivatives pre-Title VII of the Dodd-Frank Act?

Q12.5: What is the difference between a swap, a security-based swap, and a mixed swap?

Q12.6: What is the mandatory clearing requirement of Title VII?

Q12.7: What is the execution platform requirement of Title VII?

Q12.8: What is the data repository requirement of Title VII?

Q12.9: What is the push-out rule?

Q12.10: What are criticisms of Title VII?

NOTES

1. www.bis.org/statistics/derstats.htm. Extracted Nov. 2016.
2. www.bis.org/statistics/derstats.htm. Extracted Nov. 2016.
3. www.bis.org/statistics/derstats.htm. Extracted Nov. 2016; and "ISDA Margin Survey 2015," Aug. 2015, ISDA.
4. FSB press release, "FSB Publishes Discussion Note on Essential Aspects of CCP Resolution Planning and Progress Report on CCP Workplan," Aug. 16, 2016.

CHAPTER 13

The Basel Accords

INTRODUCTION

The Basel Accords are multinational accords that set minimum capital requirements for banks. The Basel Accords were established by the BIS's Basel Committee on Banking Supervision in order to strengthen the soundness and stability of the international banking system. In this chapter we explore the Basel Accords, including Basel I, II, and III.

After you read this chapter you will be able to:

- Describe the Basel Accords' approach.
- Explain the importance of capital.
- Understand credit risk, market risk, operational risk, and liquidity risk.
- Describe Basel I, II, and III.

WHAT ARE THE BASEL ACCORDS?

The Basel Accords are multinational accords that set minimum capital requirements for banks. The Basel Accords were established by the BIS's Basel Committee on Banking Supervision, otherwise known as the "Basel Committee."[1]

The Basel Accords have evolved over time.[2] Basel I, the first of the Basel Accords, set the original minimum capital adequacy ratio requirements. Basel I was published in 1988 and implemented by the end of 1992. Basel I was amended several times. Basel II, which was proposed in 1999 and published in June 2004, revised Basel I's capital framework. Basel III, which was published in 2011, set additional revisions to the capital framework, which were agreed to following the financial crisis. Basel III's revisions to the capital framework added additional capital buffers, standards in relation to liquidity, and other new requirements.

THE APPROACH OF THE BASEL ACCORDS

The objectives of the Basel Accords are twofold:

- To strengthen the soundness and stability of the international banking system
- To do so in a manner that is both fair and consistent so as to reduce competitive inequality

Like any corporation, a bank consists of a portfolio of assets. A commercial bank's most important assets are the loans that it makes. A bank's assets are funded through accepting liabilities (i.e., through borrowing) and through capital. Capital consists of paid-in capital that is generated through issuing equity and retained earnings that are generated over time.

A bank will become insolvent if its assets drop below its liabilities. For example, consider a bank that has funded $10 billion in loans through borrowing $7 billion and raising capital of $3 billion. Should the loans decline in value to $6 billion, then the value of the bank's assets are less than its liabilities of $7 billion and the bank is insolvent. Assets can decline in value for one of a number of reasons. Three sources of risk to the value of a bank's assets that are addressed are as follows:

1. *Credit risk:* The risk that a borrower will face financial distress, thereby lowering the value of the loan asset.
2. *Market risk:* The risk that changes in market factors will lower the value of the bank's assets. For example, a bank's assets may be negatively impacted by changes in the risk-free rate of interest or in changes in exchange rates.
3. *Operational risk:* The risk that a failure or inadequacy in the bank's processes, people, or systems will lower the value of the bank's assets. For example, a bank may face losses due to a lawsuit or a technology failure.

To address the fear that a bank will face insolvency should its assets fall below its liabilities, the Basel Accords specify minimum capital adequacy ratios that banks must maintain. Broadly, these are ratios of capital to assets. Capital is the difference between a bank's assets and liabilities. By definition, a bank with positive capital has assets that are greater than its liabilities. Hence, a minimum ratio of capital to assets acts as a "capital cushion" against the possibility of the bank's assets falling below its liabilities. Central to setting capital requirements is the specification of how capital and assets are measured. As we will explore in this chapter, the approach that is used by the Basel Accords to form capital adequacy ratios is a complex one, in which there are different tiers of capital and in which a bank's assets are risk-weighted so as to require a larger capital cushion for riskier assets than for less-risky assets.

Another type of risk that threatens the solvency of a bank is liquidity risk. Liquidity risk is the risk that a bank will not have sufficient liquidity to make the payments associated with its obligations. As we will explore in this chapter, the Basel Accords require that banks satisfy ratios to ensure sufficient liquidity.

BASEL I

Basel I set the original minimum capital adequacy ratio requirements. To understand the requirements, we first have to explore how three concepts are defined by the Basel Accords:

1. *Tier 1 capital:* Tier 1 capital refers to the highest quality capital. It consists of permanent shareholders' equity (e.g., common shares) and disclosed reserves (e.g., retained earnings).
2. *Tier 2 capital:* Tier 2 capital refers to other capital. It consists of undisclosed reserves that are not reported on the bank's balance sheet; revaluation reserves that are held against revaluations; general provisions or loan loss reserves that are held against presently unidentified future losses; and hybrid capital instruments that combine characteristics of debt and equity.
3. *Risk-weighted assets:* A bank's assets can be risk-weighted so as to require a larger capital cushion for riskier assets than for less-risky assets. The weightings given to various asset classes are provided in Table 13.1.

Basel I requires that the ratio of a bank's Tier 1 capital to its risk-weighted assets be no less than 4% while the ratio of the combination of Tier 1 and Tier 2 capital be no less than 8%.

Originally, Basel I only focused on credit risk. In 1996, Basel I was amended to incorporate market risk as well. Markets risk incorporates risk of loss due to interest rate risk, equity position risk, foreign exchange risk, and commodities risk. The amendment requires banks to measure their market risk, multiply the resulting amount by 12.5, and add this amount to the bank's risk-weighted assets when calculating the capital adequacy ratios.

The 1996 amendment also introduces Tier 3 capital, which consists of short-term subordinated debt. Under the amendment, the use of Tier 3 capital is subject to a number of conditions. For example, Tier 3 capital can only

TABLE 13.1 Basel I Risk Weights by Category of On-Balance-Sheet Asset[3]

Category	Risk Weight
Cash	0
Claims on central governments and central banks denominated in national currency and funded in that currency	0
Other claims on OECD central governments and central banks	0
Claims collateralized by cash of OECD central-government securities or guaranteed by OECD central governments	0
Claims on domestic public-sector entities, excluding central government, and loans guaranteed by such entities	0, 10, 20, or 50% (at national discretion)
Claims on multilateral development banks and claims guaranteed by, or collateralized by, securities issued by such banks	20%
Claims on banks incorporated in the OECD and loans guaranteed by OECD-incorporated banks	20%
Claims on banks incorporated in countries outside the OECD with a residual maturity of up to one year and loans with a residual maturity of up to one year guaranteed by banks incorporated in countries outside the OECD	20%
Claims on nondomestic OECD public-sector entities, excluding central government, and loans guaranteed[4] by such entities	20%
Cash items in process of collection	20%
Loans fully secured by mortgage on residential property that is or will be occupied by the borrower or that is rented	50%
Claims on the private sector	100%
Claims on banks incorporated outside the OECD with a residual maturity of over one year	100%
Claims on central governments outside the OECD (unless denominated in national currency and funded in that currency)	100%
Claims on commercial companies owned by the public sector	100%
Premises, plant, and equipment and other fixed assets	100%
Real estate and other investments (including nonconsolidated investment participations in other companies)	100%
Capital instruments issued by other banks (unless deducted from capital)	100%
All other assets	100%

be used in relation to market risk; hence, the Tier 1 capital and Tier 2 capital requirement for credit risk remained unchanged following the amendment.

BASEL II

Basel II revised Basel I's capital framework. Basel II is organized around three pillars as follows:

- Pillar I: Minimum capital requirements
- Pillar II: Supervisory review
- Pillar III: Market discipline

Basel II is extensive. In this section we explore some—among many—of its features.

Pillar 1: Minimum Capital Requirements

Pillar 1 of Basel II strengthens the minimum capital requirements in a number of ways. For example, to make risk-weighting more reflective of the credit risk that banks face, Basel II permits banks to choose between either a standardized approach or an internal ratings-based approach. Under the standardized approach, risk-weightings are determined based on external credit assessments. Tables 13.2 and 13.3 present the risk-weightings for claims on sovereigns and their central banks, and corporates. Under the internal ratings-based approach, banks are permitted to determine risk-weightings based on internal measurement of credit risk, subject to supervisory approval.

Another example of Basel II's strengthening of minimum capital requirements is its requirement that banks measure their operational risk and, similar to the requirement in relation to market risk, multiply the resulting

TABLE 13.2 Basel II Standardized Approach Risk Weights for Sovereigns and Their Central Banks[4]

Rating	Claims on Sovereigns and Their Central Banks
AAA to AA–	0%
A+ to A–	20%
BBB+ to BBB–	50%
BB+ to B–	100%
Below B–	150%
Unrated	100%

TABLE 13.3   Basel II Standardized Approach Risk Weights for Corporates[5]

Rating	Claims on Sovereigns and Their Central Banks
AAA to AA–	20%
A+ to A	50%
BBB+ to BB–	100%
Below BB–	150%
Unrated	100%

amount by 12.5 and add this amount to the bank's risk-weighted assets when calculating the capital adequacy ratios. Basel II also specifies various methods through which a bank can measure operational risk and market risk.

Pillar 2: Supervisory Review

Pillar 2 is supervisory review of the bank's internal assessment of its capital adequacy. Pillar 2 allows supervisors to address sources of risk not captured by Pillar 1. Basel II indicates that three main areas not captured by Pillar 1: factors not captured such as credit concentration risk; factors not taken into account such as business and strategic risk; and external factors such as the business cycle.[6] Table 13.4 presents four key principles of supervisory review as detailed in Basel II.

Pillar 2 recognizes that supervision is not an exact science and that supervisions will reflect discretionary decision making. The supervisors must act

TABLE 13.4   Basel II Key Principles of Supervisory Review[7]

Principle 1: Banks should have a process for assessing their overall capital adequacy in relation to their risk profile and a strategy for maintaining their capital levels.

Principle 2: Supervisors should review and evaluate banks' internal capital adequacy assessments and strategies, as well as their ability to monitor and ensure their compliance with regulatory capital ratios. Supervisors should take appropriate supervisory action if they are not satisfied with the result of this process.

Principle 3: Supervisors should expect banks to operate above the minimum regulatory capital ratios and should have the ability to require banks to hold capital in excess of the minimum.

Principle 4: Supervisors should seek to intervene at an early stage to prevent capital from falling below the minimum levels required to support the risk characteristics of a particular bank and should require rapid remedial action if capital is not maintained or restored.

in transparent and accountable fashion through making publicly available their criteria and through making public factors used to require capital above the regulatory minimum either across the banking sector or for an individual bank.

Pillar 3: Market Discipline

Pillar 3 encourages market discipline through setting minimum disclosures requirements. Pillar 3 details extensive qualitative and quantitative disclosures in relation to the corporate entity, capital structure, capital adequacy, credit risk, credit risk mitigation, counterparty credit risk, securitization, market risk, and operational risk, among other disclosures.

Basel II.5

Following the 2007–2008 financial crisis, the Basel Committee implemented additional revisions to the Basel Accords, known as Basel II.5. Basel II.5 includes changes in how banks keep positions in their "trading book" versus their "banking book"; changes to the measurement of market risk; changes to the supervisor review process and disclosure requirements for market risk; and changes in the treatment of illiquid assets.

BASEL III

Basel III provided extensive further revisions to the capital framework. In this section we explore some—among many—of its key features.

Under Basel III, the minimum capital ratios are strengthened. Basel III increases the ratio of a bank's Tier 1 capital to its risk-weighted assets from 4% to 6%; 4.5% of this 6% must be common equity. Basel III also sets a leverage ratio that does not risk-weight the bank's assets. The leverage ratio requires a minimum ratio of Tier 1 capital to assets of 3%. The leverage ratio is intended to provide a simple non-risk-based measure that can constrain the buildup of leverage, which can lead to destabilization when deleveraging occurs. Further, Basel III eliminates Tier 3 as acceptable capital when determining minimum ratios.

Basel III creates two additional buffers, the capital conservation buffer and the countercyclical buffer. The capital conservation buffer is an additional buffer of 2.5% common equity. Should a bank fail to meet this additional buffer, they are constrained in their distributions (such as dividends) but can continue to operate. The countercyclical buffer is an additional buffer that supervisors can demand to avoid the buildup of debt.

Basel III addresses liquidity risk through introducing two new liquidity ratios: the liquidity coverage ratio and the net stable funding ratio. The liquidity coverage ratio requires that the ratio of high-quality liquid assets to total net cashflows over the next 30 calendar days be greater than 100%. The net stable funding ratio requires that the ratio of available amount of stable funding to required amount of stable funding is greater than 100%.

Basel III also reforms risk coverage to ensure that all material risks are captured. These reforms are driven by the recognition that the 2007–2008 financial crisis was the failure to capture certain balance sheet risks, off-balance-sheet risks, and derivatives exposures.

THE CONTINUING EVOLUTION OF THE BASEL ACCORDS

The Basel Accords are far from perfect, as is demonstrated by their evolution over time. This is unsurprising. The challenges that the Basel Accords work to address are complex and impact many stakeholders across multiple jurisdictions. New risks and challenges arise over time, revealing gaps in regulation that were not previously addressed.

Yet some argue that the overall approach of the Basel Accords may be flawed. For example, academics Christopher Kobrak and Michael Troege note that the capital requirements mandated by the Basel Accords are less useful than is commonly perceived, as losses due to bank failures typically cannot be absorbed by even reasonably high capital requirements.[8] They present data from the FDIC that shows that the average loss due to a bank failure in the United States during 1986 to 2000 was 24% of the bank's assets while the median loss was 19%. Further, Kobrak and Troege argue that banks can manipulate their capital adequacy ratios. They note that during the 1990s, Japanese banks used techniques through which to make their capital adequacy ratios satisfactory though they were in fact insolvent.

We will certainly see additional revisions to the capital framework in the future. Indeed, there is already talk of "Basel IV."[9]

KEY POINTS

- The Basel Accords are multinational accords that set minimum capital requirements for banks that were established by the BIS's Basel Committee on Banking Supervision.
- The objectives of the Basel Accords are to strengthen the soundness and stability of the international banking system and to do so in a fair and consistent manner.

- A bank will become insolvent if its assets drop below its liabilities. Three sources of risk to the value of a bank's assets are credit risk, market risk, and operational risk. The Basel Accords address these risks. A bank will also become insolvent if it does not have sufficient liquidity to make the payments associated with its obligations. The Basel Accords address liquidity risk as well.
- Basel I requires that the ratio of a bank's Tier 1 capital to its risk-weighted assets be no less than 4% while the ratio of the combination of Tier 1 and Tier 2 capital be no less than 8%. It also requires banks to measure their market risk, multiply the resulting amount by 12.5, and add this amount to the bank's risk-weighted assets when calculating the capital adequacy ratios.
- The three pillars of Basel II are minimum capital requirements; supervisory review; and market discipline. Pillar 1 strengthens the minimum capital requirements and includes a requirement related to operational risk. Pillar 2 requires supervisory review of the bank's internal assessment of its capital adequacy. Pillar 3 encourages market discipline through minimum disclosures requirements.
- Basel III provided extensive further revisions to the capital framework, including strengthened minimum capital requirements; the introduction of a leverage ratio; the creation of the capital conservation buffer and the countercyclical buffer; the introduction of the liquidity coverage ratio and the net stable funding ratio; reformation of risk coverage, and other revisions.
- The Basel Accords are far from perfect, as is demonstrated by their evolution over time. We will certainly see additional revisions to the capital framework in the future.

KNOWLEDGE CHECK

Q13.1: Which committee created the Basel Accords?
Q13.2: What are the objectives of the Basel Accords?
Q13.3: When will a bank become insolvent?
Q13.4: What risks does the Basel Accords address?
Q13.5: What is Tier 1 capital?
Q13.6: What is the purpose of risk-weighting assets?
Q13.7: What are the three pillars of Basel II?
Q13.8: What are the two additional buffers created by Basel III?
Q13.9: What is the leverage ratio?
Q13.10: How does Basel III address liquidity risk?

NOTES

1. The Basel Committee was established by the G10 central banks governors in 1974, and was originally known as the "Committee on Banking Regulations and Supervisory Practices."
2. *Source of historic information:* "A brief history of the Basel Committee," Basel Committee on Banking Supervision, Oct. 2015.
3. *Source:* Annex 2, "International Convergence of Capital Measurement and Capital Standards," Basel Committee on Banking Supervision, July 1988.
4. *Source:* "International Convergence of Capital Measurement and Capital Standards: A Revised Framework, Comprehensive Version," Basel Committee on Banking Supervision, June 2006.
5. *Source:* Basel Committee, June 2006.
6. *Source:* Basel Committee, June 2006.
7. *Source:* Basel Committee, June 2006.
8. Kobrak, Christopher, and Troege, Michael, 2015, "From Basel to bailouts: Forty Years of International Attempts to Bolster Bank Safety," *Financial History Review*, 22(2).
9. For example, see Heltman, John, "Ready or Not, Here Comes Basel IV," *American Banker*, Dec. 4, 2014.

CHAPTER 14

Lender of Last Resort

INTRODUCTION

A lender of last resort is ready to lend money to banks and other financial institutions when others are not. In this chapter we delve into the concept of a lender of last resort, including its benefits and risks. We further delve into various views of the function of the lender of last resort and its application. This chapter concludes through exploring the role of the U.S. Federal Reserve during the Great Depression and the Credit Crisis of 2007–2009.

After you read this chapter you will be able to:

- Define the role of a lender of last resort.
- Understand why a lender of last resort is important.
- Understand the risks associated with a lender of last resort.
- Learn about the classical view and alternative views of the function of the lender of last resort.
- Learn about the Great Depression and U.S. Federal Reserve's response.
- Learn about the Credit Crisis of 2007–2009 and U.S. Federal Reserve's response.

LENDER OF LAST RESORT CONCEPT

A central bank such as the U.S. Federal Reserve is described as "lender of last resort" as it is ready to lend money to banks and other financial institutions when others are not. In a review published in *Financial Stability Review*, Freixas et al. (1999) define the role of a lender of last resort:[1]

> *The discretionary provision of liquidity to a financial institution (or the market as a whole) by the central bank in reaction to an adverse shock which causes an abnormal increase in demand for liquidity which cannot be met from an alternative source.*

The adverse shock can be caused by internal factors, such as poor management decisions, or external factors, such as a market crisis. The existence of this safety net enhances the confidence that others have when lending to financial institutions. A lender of last resort has no other lender to turn to should it face stress. Hence, a crucial characteristic of a lender of last resort is its responsibility to avoid drains of its resources that could erode confidence in its ability to act as a lender of last resort.

Freixas et al. (1999) note the distinction between emergency lending that occurs when a financial institution is illiquid but solvent, versus risk capital support for insolvent financial institutions. Illiquidity can occur due to a bank run, where depositors demand the withdrawal of their deposits from financial institutions whose assets are illiquid. Illiquidity can also occur due to the failure of the interbank market, making it difficult for a financial institution to use interbank borrowing to source liquidity. The lender of last resort can provide the financial institution liquidity in exchange for illiquid assets, increasing its liquidity without altering its balance sheet. Emergency lending may also occur in the form of risk capital support for insolvent institutions. Such support can avoid the instability caused by insolvency.

While the benefits to financial stability associated with a lender of last resort are straightforward, the cost is moral hazard. A financial institution will be more willing to engage in activities that expose it to liquidity risks and insolvency risks if it knows that the lender of last resort is willing to engage in emergency lending should these activities lead to crisis. Further, counterparties to a given financial institution will not monitor its creditworthiness as carefully if they know that emergency lending is available should the financial institution face a crisis. An important way to address moral hazard is ambiguity surrounding the willingness of the lender of last resort to provide emergency lending. With such ambiguity, financial institutions will be less willing to engage in activities that may require such lending, and counterparties will more carefully monitor the creditworthiness of financial institutions, as they do not know what will actually happen should a crisis occur.

HENRY THORNTON, WALTER BAGEHOT, AND ALTERNATIVE VIEWS

Reference to the concept of lender of last resort has been identified as early as 1797 when Francis Baring used the expression *dernier resort* (last resort) to describe the role of the Bank of England.[2] However, historians attribute the development of the concept to Henry Thornton and Walter Bagehot: Thornton in his 1802 text, "An Inquiry Into the Nature and Effects of the

Paper Credit of Great Britain," and Bagehot in his 1873 text, "Lombard Street." While academics have highlighted differences in their approaches, the commonalities across their approaches represent the classical view of the purpose of the lender of last resort—to provide the funds necessary should a panic occur. Thomas M. Humphrey summarizes the commonality of the approaches of Thornton and Bagehot:[3]

> *Thornton and Bagehot believed the LLR had the duty (1) to protect the money stock, (2) to support the whole financial system rather than individual institutions, (3) to behave consistently with the longer-run objective of stable money growth, and (4) to preannounce its policy in advance of crises so as to remove uncertainty. They also advised the LLR to let insolvent institutions fail, to lend to creditworthy institutions only, to charge penalty rates, and to require good collateral. Such rules they thought would minimize problems of moral hazard and remove bankers' incentives to take undue risks.*

Michael D. Bordo notes three alternatives to the classical view.[4] One alternative is for the lender of last resort function to be implemented exclusively using open market operations, as proposed by Marvin Goodfriend and Robert King,[5] rather than through sterilized discount window lending. A second alternative is that of Charles Goodhart, which advocates for central banks to provide temporary assistance to insolvent banks.[6] A third alternative is the free banking approach, which takes the view that there is no need for a government authority to act as the lender of last resort—instead, the removal of legal restrictions on the banking system would allow free-market mechanisms to panic-proof the banking system.

In a 1993 speech, Eddie George, the governor of the Bank of England at the time, details five principles of last resort assistance.[7] These principles are indicative of how the varying views of the function of the lender of last resort are applied in practice:

1. *"We will explore every option for a commercial solution before committing our own funds."*
2. *"Central banks are not in the business of providing public subsidy to private shareholders."*
3. *"We aim to provide liquidity; we will not, in normal circumstances, support a bank that we know at the time to be insolvent."*
4. *"We look for a clear exit."*
5. *"We usually try to keep the fact that we are providing systemic support secret at the time."*

THE FED'S ROLE IN THE GREAT DEPRESSION

The Great Depression formally occurred between 1929 and 1934, but its effects lingered on for many years afterwards. The Great Depression was accelerated by the stock market crash of 1929, which led to enormous uncertainty, which led to a drop in consumption.[8] While centered in the United States, the Great Depression also significantly impacted nearly all countries.

In the United States, the Great Depression was characterized by a 36.21% Real GDP decline peak to trough.[9] It was also characterized by CPI decline peak to trough of 27.17% and severe unemployment, reaching a maximum value of 25.36%.[10]

The stock market crash of 1929 played an important role toward the beginning of the Great Depression. The continued decline, however, is attributable to banking panics. Friedman and Schwartz identify four banking crises during the Great Depression, including banking panics in fall 1930, spring 1931, fall 1931, and winter 1933.[11] While Friedman and Schwartz allow for the possibility that the first crisis was due to poor loans and investments on the part of banks during the 1920s, they attribute the subsequent crises to runs on banks in which depositors withdrew their deposits. As a result:[12]

> Banks had to dump their assets on the market, which inevitably forced a decline on the market value of those assets and hence of the remaining assets they held. The impairment in the market value of the assets held by banks, particularly in their bond portfolios, was the most important source of the impairment of capital leading to bank suspensions, rather than the default of specific loans or of specific bond issues.

The banking failures impacted the economy in a number of ways, economics professor Christina Romer has noted. These include a direct decline of the money supply, which resulted in an increase in real interest rates; depression of consumer spending and investment due to the resulting pessimism; and disruption of the intermediation function of banks.

Friedman and Schwartz note a paradox: Assets for which there was an active market were perceived by bank examiners as the most impaired, due to clear decline in the obtainable market value. Conversely, assets for which there was no active market were typically carried at face value, and therefore were not perceived as impaired. This meant that the threat to bank solvency came from its most liquid assets!

The response of the Federal Reserve was limited, focused on more liberal valuation of assets by bank examiners. Friedman and Schwartz attribute the Fed's failures to address the crises in a comprehensive fashion to a number of factors. These include the Fed's "limited understanding of the connection between bank failures, runs on banks, contraction of deposits, and weakness of the bond markets" as well as four additional circumstances:[13]

1. *"Federal Reserve officials had no feeling of responsibility for nonmember banks. In 1921–29 and the first ten months of 1930, most failed banks were nonmembers, and nonmembers held a high percentage of the deposits involved."*
2. *"The failures for that period were concentrated among smaller banks and, since the most influential figures in the System were big-city bankers who deplored the existence of smaller banks, their disappearance may have been viewed with complacency."*
3. *"Even in November and December 1930, when the number of failures increased sharply, over 80 percent were nonmembers."*
4. *"The relatively few large member banks that failed at the end of 1930 were regarded by many Reserve officials as unfortunate cases of bad management and therefore not subject to correction by central bank action."*

THE CREDIT CRISIS OF 2007–2009

The Credit Crisis of 2007–2009—sometimes referred to as the "Great Recession"—was the worst financial crisis in the United States since the Great Depression.[14] While significant, most would argue that it was nowhere near as severe as the Great Depression. While it is difficult to easily compare two separate crises, the different outcome may be due to the fact that unlike the Fed's response to the Great Depression, the Fed responded vigorously to the Credit Crisis of 2007–2009.

The Credit Crisis was driven by problematic mortgage products and practices, such as interest-only adjustable-rate mortgages, no-documentation loans, and others. These mortgages experienced a significant decline in value, which left financial institutions vulnerable and triggered a panic and the withdrawal of funding by short-term lenders. The decline in the value of mortgage products took place in an environment characterized by private-sector and public-sector vulnerabilities. According to Ben Bernanke private-sector vulnerabilities included excessive leverage, excessive use of short-term funding, poor monitoring by banks, and extensive use of exotic instruments, while public-sector vulnerabilities included gaps in the regulatory system, failures of regulation and supervision, and inadequate capital.[15]

Three broad types of tools were used in the Fed's response to the Credit Crisis:[16]

1. Provision of liquidity to financial institutions
2. Provision of liquidity directly to participants in key credit markets
3. Expansion of open market operations

The provision of liquidity to financial institutions, the classic lender of last resort response, took place through the discount window through which financial institutions traditionally borrow from the Fed, as well as various facilities that were created in response to the crisis, including the Term Auction Facility, the Primary Dealer Auction Facility, and the Term Securities Lending Facility. The provision of liquidity directly to participants in key credit markets included the Commercial Paper Funding Facility, the Asset-Backed Commercial Paper Money Market Mutual Fund Liquidity Facility, the Money Market Investor Funding Facility, and the Term Asset-Backed Securities Loan Facility. The expansion of open market operations included the monthly purchase of tens of billions of mortgage-backed securities and Treasury securities, which kept long-term interest rates low.

KEY POINTS

- A lender of last resort is ready to lend money to banks and other financial institutions when others are not, which enhances the confidence that others have when lending to financial institutions.
- The lender of last resort can provide the financial institution liquidity in exchange for illiquid assets, or risk capital support for insolvent institutions.
- A cost associated with a lender of last resort is moral hazard, as financial institution will be more willing to engage in risky activities and counterparties will not monitor creditworthiness as carefully. Ambiguity surrounding the willingness of the lender of last resort to provide emergency lending can reduce moral hazard.
- Historians attribute the development of the classical view of the lender of last resort concept to Henry Thornton and Walter Bagehot. While their approaches differ somewhat, among the commonalities in their views is that the duty of the lender of last resort is to protect the money stock, provide support to the entire financial system rather than individual institutions, to behave consistently, and pre-announce policy.

- Alternative views of the function of the lender of last resort focus exclusively on open market operations; provision of temporary assistance to insolvent banks; and a free banking approach that takes the view that there is no need for a government authority to act as the lender of last resort and instead advocates the removal of legal restrictions.
- While the stock market crash of 1929 played an important role toward the beginning of the Great Depression of 1929–1934, the continued decline is attributable to banking panics, including banking panics in fall 1930, spring 1931, fall 1931, and winter 1933. The response of the Federal Reserve was limited, focused on more liberal valuation of assets by bank examiners.
- While the Credit Crisis of 2007–2009 was the worst post–World War II financial crisis in the United States, it was less severe than the Great Depression. The different outcome may be due to the fact that unlike the Fed's response to the Great Depression, the Fed responded vigorously to the Credit Crisis of 2007–2009.
- Three broad types of tools were used in the Fed's response to the Credit Crisis of 2007–2009: provision of liquidity to financial institutions; provision of liquidity directly to participants in key credit markets; and expansion of open market operations.

KNOWLEDGE CHECK

Q14.1: What is the role of a lender of last resort?

Q14.2: Why is the lender of last resort important?

Q14.3: What are two types of emergency lending?

Q14.4: Why can the existence of a lender of last resort lead to moral hazard?

Q14.5: What can reduce the moral hazard associated with a lender of last resort?

Q14.6: What are the duties of the lender of last resort according to the approaches of Henry Thornton and Walter Bagehot?

Q14.7: What are alternatives to the classical view of the lender of last resort function?

Q14.8: To what is the continued decline during the Great Depression attributed?

Q14.9: Did the Fed address the Great Depression in a comprehensive fashion?

Q14.10: What were three types of tools that were used in the Fed's response to the Credit Crisis of 2007–2009?

NOTES

1. Freixas, Xavier, Giannini, Curzio, Hoggarth, Glenn, Sossa, Farouk, 1999, "Lender of Last Resort: A Review of the Literature," *Financial Stability Review*, Nov.
2. Baring, Francis, 1797, *Observations on the Establishment of the Bank of England*, printed at the Minerva Press for Sewell, Cornhill, and Debrett.
3. Humphrey, Thomas M., 1989, "The Lender of Last Resort: The Concept in History," *Federal Reserve Bank of Richmond Economic Review*, Mar./Apr., pp. 8–16.
4. Bordo, Michael D., 1990, "The Lender of Last Resort: Alternative Views and Historical Experience," *Economic Review, Federal Reserve Bank of Richmond Economic Review*, Jan./Feb., pp. 18–29.
5. Goodfriend, Marvin, and Robert A. King, 1989, "Financial Deregulation, Monetary Policy, and Central Banking," in *Restructuring Banking and Financial Services in America*, Haraf, W.S. and Kushmeider, R.M. (eds.). Washington: American Enterprise Institute.
6. Goodhart, Charles A.E., 1987, "Why Do Banks Need a Central Bank?" *Oxford Economic Papers* (Mar.), 39, pp. 75–89.
7. George, Edward Alan John, 1994, "The Pursuit of Financial Stability," *Bank of England Quarterly Bulletin*, Feb., pp. 60–66.
8. Romer, Christina, 2002, "The Nation in Depression," *Journal of Economic Perspectives*, 2(2): 19–39.
9. *Source: Table 1*, Wheelock, David C., 2010, "Lessons Learned? Comparing the Federal Reserve's Responses to the Crises of 1929–1933 and 2007–2009," *Federal Reserve Bank of St. Louis Review*, Mar./Apr., pp. 89–108.
10. Ibid.
11. Friedman, Milton, and Schwartz, Anna J., 1963, *A Monetary History of the United States 1867–1960*. Princeton University Press.
12. Ibid., p. 355.
13. Ibid., pp. 358–359.
14. The aftermath of the credit crisis is described in detail in Chapter 3.
15. Bernanke, Ben S., 2012, "Lecture 3: The Federal Reserve's Response to the Financial Crisis," Chairman Bernanke's College Lecture Series, presented March 27, 2012, at the George Washington University School of Business.
16. Federal Reserve, "The Federal Reserve's Response to the Financial Crisis and Actions to Foster Maximum Employment and Price Stability," www.federalreserve.gov/monetarypolicy/bst_crisisresponse.htm. Extracted Dec. 2016.

CHAPTER 15

Interconnectedness Risk

INTRODUCTION

The impact of systemic risk depends very much on the collective behavior of financial institutions and their interconnectedness as well as on the interaction between financial markets and the macro-economy. Elements of interconnectedness can generally be measured by consideration of counterparty risks related to a financial institution's activities. Knowing the interconnectedness of a financial institution could enable a systemic risk regulator to determine how many additional failures could be caused by the failure of an individual firm.[1]

The theme of *interconnectedness* is still in its nascent stages, having garnered broad attention by the financial industry, regulators, and academia only since the Credit Crisis. The reason for the latter is attributable largely to lessons learned from the failure and/or government bailout of financial firms such as Lehman Brothers Inc. and American International Group in 2008.

As interested parties analyzed the risks posed by these firms during the Credit Crisis, it became very clear that the real risks posed to the global financial system did not only originate from the stand-alone size or direct counterparty exposures posed by such firms. Instead, it was only after the massive size and complexity of the direct and indirect financial, operational, and legal connections of Lehman and AIG became more clear that the true systemic impact of these firms became evident. As discussed in detail in Chapter 2, Lehman's bankruptcy impacted 8,000 subsidiaries and affiliates worldwide, approximately 100,000 creditors, and its 26,000 employees worldwide.[2]

Time and time again, from the Spring of 2007 on, policymakers and regulators were caught off guard as the contagion spread, responding on an ad-hoc basis with specific programs to put fingers in the dike. There was no comprehensive and strategic plan for containment, because they lacked a full understanding of the risks and interconnections of the financial markets. Some regulators have conceded this error. We had allowed the system to race ahead of our ability to protect it.[3]

Interconnections among financial firms can also lead to systemic risk under crisis conditions. Financial institutions are interconnected in a variety of networks in bilateral and multilateral relationships and contracts, as well as through markets.[4]

After reading this chapter you will be able to:

- Provide a definition of *interconnectedness risk* as it relates to the financial industry.
- Understand how interconnectedness likely played a role in bailout decisions of the U.S. government during the Credit Crisis.
- Give examples of *direct, indirect,* and *operational interconnectedness.*
- List the five components that make up the classification of Globally Systemically Important Banks (G-SIBs) by the Bank for International Settlements.
- Explain the various measures employed by the Office of Financial Research to measure and monitor the interconnectedness associated with G-SIBs on an ongoing basis.
- Describe the eight steps that comprise a suggested roadmap for implementing a new interconnectedness risk program for financial institutions.

A CASE STUDY OF INTERCONNECTEDNESS

As mentioned earlier, the Credit Crisis illustrated that future risk analysis and monitoring by financial market participants and supervisors needs to go well beyond assessing the impact of a firm on a stand-alone basis. Analysis and monitoring must become more sophisticated and consider the interconnections that firms have around the globe. When a large, highly interconnected firm fails, that could lead to a significant risk of global contagion by spreading losses to hundreds, if not thousands, of counterparties.

For example, when two Bear Stearns hedge funds fell into distress in 2007, due largely to leveraged exposure to mortgage-backed securities, this propagated risk across the financial system. Due to continued losses at the two hedge funds in 2006 and 2007, investors began to steadily withdraw money. During 2007, the funds were forced to sell assets at distressed prices given that the prices and demand for mortgage-related securities both fell dramatically during this time. As this occurred, firms that had lent the funds money against this mortgage collateral began to demand higher margin terms while others refused to renew maturing secured financing trades, known as *repos*. For example, one of the fund's largest repo lenders, Merrill Lynch, seized $850 million of collateral that the funds had posted against their loans.[5]

Although ultimate parent Bear Stearns was not legally obligated to support the funds, the firm decided to take out repo lenders to the *Bear Stearns High-Grade Structured Credit Enhanced Leveraged Fund* by assuming about $1.8 billion of subprime assets onto its books, contributing to a write-down of nearly $2 billion of mortgage-related collateral by Bear in November 2007. This led investors, creditors, and rating agencies to more closely scrutinize Bear's leverage, asset quality, and liquidity. At that time, Bear was the second largest *prime broker*[6] in the industry and was a top-three underwriter of private-label mortgage-backed securities. Over the subsequent months and into early 2008, lenders began demanding more collateral from Bear and rumors swirled of their diminishing capital and liquidity.

On Thursday, March 13, Bear's CEO informed the SEC that the firm would be "unable to operate normally" the next day. On Sunday, March 16, J.P. Morgan informed the Fed and Treasury that it was interested in a deal to buy Bear contingent on financial support from the Fed. The Fed, under section 13(3) of the Federal Reserve Act, agreed to purchase $29.97 billion of Bear's assets to get them off the firm's books through a newly created entity called *Maiden Lane LLC*.[7] J.P Morgan financed the first $1.15 billion through a subordinated loan while the Fed bore the risk of the remaining $28.8 billion of assets. On the evening of March 16, J.P. Morgan announced a deal to buy Bear for $2 share, which was subsequently increased to $10 share on March 24.

Fed Chairman Ben Bernanke justified the Fed's saving of Bear by citing the beginnings of a "breakdown" in the $2.8 trillion tri-party repo market and their view that Bear " ... was so essentially involved in this critical repo financing market, that its failure would have brought down that market, which would have had implications for other firms."[8]

The Financial Crisis Inquiry Commission (FCIC) concluded that Bear experienced runs by repo lenders, hedge fund customers, and derivatives counterparties and was rescued by a government-assisted purchase by J.P. Morgan because the government considered it too interconnected to fail.

INTERCONNECTEDNESS CATEGORIES

It's important to note that there is no single, universally accepted definition of *interconnectedness* within the financial industry, particularly since it's a relatively new concept. Moreover, the term can cover an extremely broad array of financial, operational, and legal relationships, contracts, or dependencies. As one real-life example, as previously referenced with respect to some of the failed financial firms during the Credit Crisis, such firms were party to hundreds of thousands of derivatives and collateral contracts across the globe. One can think of Lehman Brothers as the central node or hub in a complex web of connections with its losses spreading across this web and affecting, to different degrees, any entity that maintained a relationship with it.

The Depository Trust & Clearing Corporation

Given this inherent complexity in defining interconnectedness, we begin by providing readers a broad taxonomy of categories according to research by The Depository Trust & Clearing Corporation ("DTCC") that may assist firms in applying interconnectedness analysis to their respective organizations or other analytical endeavors.

Direct and Indirect Financial Connections:[9]
- Lending relationship between two firms
- Derivatives contract between two firms
- Trading relationships between firms and financial market infrastructures
- Links between various financial market infrastructures
- Liquidity providers
- Exposure to common assets/securities
- Investment counterparties
- Mark-to-market losses
- Margin calls and haircuts on collateral
- Intra-financial system liabilities
- Intra-financial system assets
- Shadow banking activities

Operational Connections:
- Vendors and other critical third-party suppliers
- Settling banks
- Clearing banks
- Custodians
- Data providers

POST-CRISIS REGULATORY VIEW OF INTERCONNECTEDNESS

Basel Committee on Banking Supervision

Global regulators such as the Basel Committee on Banking Supervision have agreed on five categories (listed in the following Table 15.1) for measuring the systemic importance of Global Systemically Important Banks (G-SIBs). Subsequently, the Fed adopted this methodology to determine which U.S. banks are G-SIBs. The methodology gives an equal weight of 20% to each of the five categories of systemic importance, which are: size, cross-jurisdictional activity, interconnectedness, substitutability/financial institution infrastructure, and complexity. For purposes of this chapter, we focus primarily on two of these five categories: (i) *interconnectedness*, which attempts to measure a G-SIB's financial interconnectedness; and (ii) *substitutability*, which focuses on critical services provided by the G-SIBs to the industry. See Chapter 9 for details and a listing of current G-SIBs.

1. *Size:* Measured through total exposures. This is a more comprehensive measure than total assets, and it is measured consistently across jurisdictions, whereas the measurement of assets varies with national accounting standards.

TABLE 15.1 The G-SIB Assessment Methodology

Category (and Weighting)	Individual Indicator	Indicator Weighting
Interconnectedness (20%)	Intra-financial system liabilities	6.67%
	Intra-financial system assets	6.67%
	Wholesale funding ratio	6.67%
Substitutability/ financial institution infrastructure (20%)	Assets under custody	6.67%
	Payments cleared and settled through payment systems	6.67%
	Values of underwritten transactions in debt and equity markets	
Cross-jurisdictional activity (20%)	Cross-jurisdictional claims	10%
	Cross-jurisdictional liabilities	10%
Size (20%)	Total exposures as defined for use in the Basel III leverage ratio	20%
Complexity (20%)	OTC derivatives notional value	6.67%
	Level 3 assets	6.67%
	Held for trading and available for sale value	6.67%

2. *Interconnectedness:* Measured through a bank's intra-financial system assets, intra-financial system liabilities, and total securities outstanding.
3. *Substitutability:* The extent to which a bank provides important financial infrastructure that would be difficult to replace if the bank were to fail. It is measured through payments activity, assets under custody, and underwriting activity.
4. *Complexity:* Measured through a bank's over-the-counter derivatives activity, trading and available-for-sale assets, and holdings of less liquid assets.
5. *Cross-jurisdictional activity:* Measured through a bank's foreign claims and total cross-jurisdictional liabilities.

According to a detailed systemic risk survey conducted jointly by Deloitte and SIFMA (June 2010), the factors identified by Basel are largely in line with the views of the broader market. The survey found that factors typically included in a definition of systemic risk include: size (of an individual financial institution or a combination of smaller firms); interconnectedness; and the potential for underlying issues, such as complexity and leverage, exposure concentrations, erosion of market practices, marketplace bubbles, and the potential of a failure (of a systemically important firm or group of firms) to serve as a trigger event that may impact the broader real economy. When considering the complexity of the global financial system, it is essential that key drivers of systemic risk are identified. Knowing these drivers will enable a systemic risk regulator to identify, measure, and monitor systemic risk events across the entire financial services system.

Office of Financial Research

The OFR describes interconnectedness as the failure of a bank to meet payment obligations to other banks, which can accelerate the spread of a financial system shock if the bank is highly interconnected. The OFR has adopted Basel's five-part methodology for assessing a bank's degree of systemic importance.

One of the OFR's many different measures of the systemic risks posed by large banks includes a bank's total claims on the financial system, its total liabilities to the financial system, and the total value of debt and equity securities issued by a bank. For the first two of these indicators, the financial system includes banks, securities dealers, insurance companies, mutual funds, hedge funds, pension funds, investment banks, and central counterparties.

TABLE 15.2 Global Systemically Important Banks

Bank Holding Company	G-SIB Bucket[10]
JP Morgan Chase & Co.	4
HSBC	4
Citigroup	3
BNP Paribas	3
Deutsche Bank	3
Barclays	3
Bank America	2
Credit Suisse	2
Goldman Sachs	2
Mitsubishi	2
Morgan Stanley	2
Industrial & Commercial Bank of China	1
Royal Bank of Canada	1
Société Générale	1
Bank of China	1
Banco Santander	1
Wells Fargo	1
UBS	1
Credit Agricole	1
China Construction Bank	1
Unicredit	1
Agricultural Bank of China	1
Mizuho	1
Groupe BCPE	1
Bank of New York Mellon	1
State Street	1
Sumitomo Mitsui	1
Standard Chartered	1
ING Group	1
Nordea Bank	1

Table 15.2 illustrates the OFR's annual ranking of G-SIBs' systemic importance based upon the five equally weighted measures described earlier.[11]

Another measure of a bank's systemic risk performed by the OFR includes analysis conducted of the public sections of the eight U.S. G-SIBs' living wills. To minimize the risk of costly bank bailouts in the future, the Dodd-Frank Wall Street Reform and Consumer Protection Act (Dodd-Frank Act) requires every bank holding company with $50 billion or more in assets to prepare a resolution plan, or living will. Living wills describe how a failing bank would wind down. Each of the individual living wills for the eight U.S. G-SIBs differs somewhat in terms of format and content. However, most contain enough standardized information to allow the OFR to conduct analysis across banks and across time. One such category is called "complexity" and measures the number of core business lines, material legal entities, and critical operations of each bank, which can serve as measures of complexity and provide an indication of the ease by which each bank could be resolved.

The next category of complexity measured by the OFR is a study of the layers of corporate structure within the U.S. G-SIBs. According to the OFR, multiple layers of corporate structure can make orderly resolution of a bank more difficult. In this study, the average subsidiary is 4 to 6 layers below the parent and in some cases 20 layers below.

Another measure employed by the OFR is called *intra-firm interconnectedness*, which quantifies the total number of internal connections with other material legal entities within each organization. It also measures the total number of membership each G-SIB maintains in *financial market utilities* (FMUs), which provide payment, clearance, and settlement services to banks. This is deemed important as FMUs require G-SIBs to post collateral to them on a regular basis, and they also maintain certain early termination rights, both of which can complicate the resolution process.

CPMI IOSCO Principles

As covered in Chapter 8 of this book, CPMI IOSCO publishes a set of 24 principles for financial market infrastructures which recognizes that interconnectedness among FMIs may foster *knock-on* effects throughout the financial system in a stress event, thereby impacting participants and markets across the FMIs. Specific examples include:

- *Principle 3: Framework for the comprehensive management of risks* directs FMIs to regularly review the material risks they bear from and pose to other entities because of interdependencies (such as other FMIs, settlement banks, liquidity providers, and service providers) and develop appropriate risk management tools to address these risks.
- *Principle 20: FMI links* directs FMIs to identify, monitor, and manage sources of risk arising from the links it has established with other FMIs. An example of an FMI link is a connection established between central securities depositories (CSDs) for purposes of enabling participants of one CSD to access the services of and securities maintained in another CSD.

AN APPROACH TO ANALYZING INTERCONNECTEDNESS RISK

The Depository Trust & Clearing Corporation

In this section, we will explore an approach proposed by DTCC that financial firms may employ to initiate their own *risk analysis*, consisting of the following elements:[12]

- Make a comprehensive inventory of external entities on which your firm relies.
- Determine which interconnections are critical to your business.
- Quantify your critical interconnections, if practical.
- Assess in detail how an impaired interconnection could affect specific areas of the firm.
- Identify highly interconnected entities and assess the potential impact of their failure on your business entity.
- Manage exposures to interconnected entities holistically.
- Cooperate across departments.
- Take a gradual approach.

Let's explore each of these elements.

Make a comprehensive inventory of external entities on which your firm relies: Most financial institutions rely on adequate funding and liquidity, credit, access to markets and market infrastructures, as well as the provision of reliable and timely data—among many other processes. External entities that provide or support these services represent external interconnections to your firm. Given that insolvencies occur at a legal entity level, intragroup dependencies between distinct legal entities should also be represented as external interconnections.

Determine which interconnections are critical to your business: Use the following criteria to assess the level of criticality of your interconnections:

- *Severity:* How severely might an impaired or failed interconnection impact your firm, its clients, shareholders, regulators, or other stakeholders?
- *Time sensitivity:* How long would it take for a failed interconnection to have a considerable impact?
- *Substitutability:* How easily and quickly could you switch to a suitable replacement?

Quantify your critical interconnections if practical: Quantifying interconnections can be useful as a straightforward and objective way to aggregate, rank, and assess the related risks. It may also help prioritize risks and monitor their evolution over time. That said, operational interconnections with providers of data and other financial services may be harder to quantify than those with borrowers/lenders, trade counterparties, and funding providers. Therefore, interconnections should be quantified as appropriate depending on the circumstances and the effort involved in doing so.

Assess in detail how an impaired interconnection could affect specific areas: Depending on the circumstances, the failure of an interconnected entity may cause a credit or trading loss, but it may also cause a loss of revenue, affect funding, or have a different type of impact altogether. In assessing the effect of an impaired or failing interconnection, it may be more appropriate to consider peak volumes and associated risks, rather than average values.

Identify highly interconnected entities and assess the potential impact of their failure on your business entity: While the analysis described earlier is valuable, its real power lies in the aggregation of risks across areas that may be simultaneously affected by a single failure. The failure of a highly interconnected entity may have a combined effect—for instance, by simultaneously causing credit losses while affecting your firm's funding as well as your access to other financial services. While each of these impacts may be manageable individually, their combined effect may not be.

Manage exposures to interconnected entities holistically: Given the potential combined effect of the failure of a highly interconnected entity, it is important to manage the associated risks holistically. Among other things, that means that concentration risk should be managed not only by assessing the relative exposures to funding, trading, credit, and other counterparties in isolation, but also in its entirety across these various areas. Stress tests and scenario analyses can be very valuable in this respect, provided they explicitly incorporate these forms of interconnectedness.

Cooperate across departments: Organize cross-functional risk reviews and discussions to make interconnectedness awareness an integral part of your organization's risk management culture. Interconnectedness analysis should complement other disciplines, not replace them.

Take a gradual approach: As is the case for other risk management disciplines, interconnectedness analysis is an iterative process—start small and expand gradually. Periodically assess in which areas you may need to become more sophisticated.

KEY POINTS

- The theme of *interconnectedness* is still in its nascent stages, having garnered broad attention by the financial industry, regulators, and academia only since the Credit Crisis.
- The Financial Crisis Inquiry Commission found that policymakers and regulators were caught off guard as the contagion spread during the

Credit Crisis and they lacked a full understanding of the risks and inter-connections of the financial markets.

- The Credit Crisis illustrated that future risk analysis and monitoring by financial market participants and supervisors need to go well beyond assessing the impact of a firm on a stand-alone basis. Analysis and monitoring must become more sophisticated and consider the interconnections that firms have around the globe.
- As discussed in detail in Chapter 2, Lehman Brothers' bankruptcy impacted 8,000 subsidiaries and affiliates worldwide, approximately 100,000 creditors, and its 26,000 employees worldwide.
- Although interconnectedness can represent an extremely broad range of categories, we have provided a partial listing of the more common and critical types of interconnections and divided these into two broad categories: direct and indirect financial connections and operational connections.
- The Basel Committee on Banking Supervision have created 5 categories to statistically measure the systemic risk posed by G-SIBs, which encompass 12 distinct factors: size, interconnectedness, substitutability, complexity, and cross-jurisdictional activity
- In addition to Basel, other regulatory bodies have adopted intercon-nectedness as a key area of focus, research, and monitoring, including the Federal Reserve Board, the Office of Financial Research, and CPMI IOSCO.
- Suggested best practices that financial firms might consider when initi-ating efforts to identify and monitor their key interconnectedness risks include making a comprehensive inventory of external entities on which you rely; determining which interconnections are critical to your busi-ness; quantifying your critical interconnections, if practical, by assessing in detail how an impaired interconnection could affect specific areas; identifying highly interconnected entities and assessing the potential impact of their failure on your business entity; managing exposures to interconnected entities holistically; cooperating across departments; and taking a gradual approach.

KNOWLEDGE CHECK

Q15.1: Which event in the financial industry brought the concept of inter-connectedness into the forefront for the first time?

Q15.2: Provide some examples of how interconnectedness risk manifested itself with respect to failed financial firms such as Lehman Brothers, AIG, and Bear Stearns during 2008?

Q15.3: What is the primary difference between interconnectedness risk and the way in which G-SIBs were analyzed prior to the Credit Crisis by risk managers and financial regulators?

Q15.4: Which regulatory institution was the first to create a formal methodology for quantifying the relative systemic risk introduced by G-SIBs?

Q15.5: What are the five primary categories that comprise the methodology used today by several regulatory bodies to assess the degree of systemic risk for G-SIBs?

Q15.6: Of the five categories referenced earlier, which two are most relevant for interconnectedness risk analysis and why?

Q15.7: What are the two broad categories of interconnectedness as detailed in this chapter? Please name three of the subcategories of each.

Q15.8: What three financial measures does the Office of Financial Research apply to G-SIBs to calculate each bank's total interconnectedness?

Q15.9: What three criteria does the Office of Financial Research apply to G-SIBs to calculate each bank's total substitutability risk?

Q15.10: What is the first step that firms should take when attempting to initiate a new analysis of the level of interconnectedness risk their firm is exposed to?

NOTES

1. Deloitte and SIFMA, 2010, "Systemic Risk Information Study," June, pp. 19–23.
2. Financial Crisis Inquiry Report (2011) p. 339.
3. Financial Crisis Inquiry Report, 2011.
4. Acharya, V.V., Pedersen, L.H., Philippon, T., and Richardson, M., 2010, "Measuring Systemic Risk," working paper, New York University Stern School of Business.
5. Financial Crisis Inquiry Report, 2011, p. 240.
6. *Prime brokerage* is the generic name for a bundled package of services offered by investment banks and securities firms to hedge funds and other professional investors needing the ability to borrow securities and cash to be able to invest on a netted basis and achieve an absolute return.
7. To facilitate a prompt acquisition of Bear Stearns by JPMC, the FRBNY created a limited liability company, Maiden Lane LLC, to acquire that set of assets of Bear Stearns.
8. Financial Crisis Inquiry Report, 2011, p. 291.
9. "Understanding Interconnectedness Risks to Build a More Resilient Financial System," White Paper, The Depository Trust & Clearing Corporation, Oct. 2015, pp. 5–6.
10. See Basel Committee on Banking Supervision, "Global Systemically Important Banks: Updated Assessment Methodology and the Higher Loss Absorbency Requirement," consultative document, July 2013 (available at www.bis.org/

publ/bcbs255.pdf, accessed Mar. 1, 2016). Capital surcharges: Bucket 4 = 2.5%, Bucket 3 = 2.0%, Bucket 2 = 1.5%, Bucket 1 = 1.0%.

11. Loudis, Bert, and Allahrakha, Meraj, 2016, "Systemic Importance Data Shed Light on Banking Risks Global Banking Risks," Office of Financial Research, Brief Series, Apr.

12. "Understanding Interconnectedness Risks to Build a More Resilient Financial System," White Paper, The Depository Trust & Clearing Corporation, Oct. 2015, pp. 26-27.

CHAPTER 16

Conclusion: Looking Ahead

In this book, we have presented a detailed history of some of the numerous financial crises that have occurred over many centuries. For example, we discussed one of the first well-documented events from the early 1600s, referred to as the Dutch Tulip Crisis, as well as the South Street Sea Bubble, which gripped Europe in the 1700s. These events were only precursors to the Great Depression in the late 1920s and 1930s and the Credit Crisis of 2007–2009, arguably the two worst global financial crises ever. In Chapters 1 and 2 we discussed in detail some of the key drivers that fueled the Credit Crisis, as well as many of the crises in modern history. For example, while bank failures have occurred for centuries, the volume of bank failures during the past 40 years or so has been considerably higher than in previous decades. Between 1970 and 2011 there were 147 episodes of banking crises around the globe, and the costs to society have been substantial. In addition to banking-related crises, we highlighted some of the other common drivers of systemic events throughout history:

- Bursting of asset bubbles
- Speculative manias
- Sovereign defaults
- International contagion

To better understand and hopefully avoid or minimize the impact of future crises, in Chapter 4 we discussed several longstanding economic and behavior theories. Regarding the former, there are many theories that point to a so-called "easy credit" environment that often persists in the years leading up to financial crisis. The basic premise is that loose monetary conditions lead consumers and businesses to overleverage, and take excessive business risks, which in turn leads to unsustainable asset bubbles that eventually burst. Furthermore, there are many theories that relate to human behavior, including groupthink, excessive optimism, and the role of fear and greed in contributing to prior crises.

We also learned through the Credit Crisis that future risk analysis and monitoring by financial market participants and supervisors needs to go well beyond assessing the impact of a firm on a stand-alone basis. Analysis and monitoring must become more sophisticated and consider the interconnections that firms have around the globe. When a large, highly interconnected firm such as Lehman Brothers fails, that could lead to a significant risk of global contagion by spreading losses to hundreds, if not thousands of counterparties.

Because of the catastrophic impact of the Credit Crisis on the global financial sector, as well as the economies of the United States and Europe, the response by financial regulators has been dramatic. As outlined in Chapters 7 and 8, in 2010 the United States enacted the Dodd-Frank Act, the most sweeping set of enhanced regulations the financial services sector has experienced since the Great Depression. Meanwhile, internationally the response was also significant. The Financial Stability Board was formed by the G20 following the Credit Crisis to promote international financial stability. In addition, the European Systemic Risk Board was created in 2010 to provide macroprudential oversight of the EU's financial system and work to mitigate systemic risk. The creation of the ESRB was driven by the 2009 de Larosière report, which is a report by a group formed by the EU that was chaired by Jacques de Larosière. The de Larosière report argued that the financial crisis was driven by several failures, including a lack of adequate macroprudential supervision; ineffective early warning mechanisms; failures to challenge supervisory practices on a cross-border basis; and no means for supervisors to take common decisions, among others. To address these failures, the de Larosière report recommended the creation of a new entity at the EU level. The ESRB plays a role in the EU like the role of the Financial Stability Oversight Council (FSOC) in the United States, and both were established in response to the Credit Crisis.

As discussed in Chapter 9, the FSOC implemented two new categories of entities that will be deemed systemically important:

1. Systemically Important Financial Institutions (SIFIs), which include both systemically important banks and systemically important nonbank financial companies.
2. Systemically Important Financial Market Utilities (SIFMUs). Financial market utilities are systemically important multilateral systems that comprise the infrastructure of financial markets.

Furthermore, the Financial Stability Board in conjunction with Basel developed an indicator-based measurement approach through which to identify Globally Systemically Important Banks (G-SIBs) based on the following five equally weighted measures: (i) cross-jurisdictional activity,

(ii) size, (iii) interconnectedness, (iv) substitutability/financial institution infrastructure, and (v) complexity. The list of G-SIBs is updated each year by the FSB and the complete list is covered in Chapter 9.

IT'S NOT A QUESTION OF *IF*, BUT *WHEN*, *WHERE*, AND *HOW*

If history has taught us anything, it's that financial crises are sure to occur again, and likely soon. As mentioned previously, the frequency of financial crises has increased dramatically over the past few decades. At least some of these events may be attributed to common themes that have emerged through several centuries, such as reckless speculation by investors, loose monetary policies of certain central banks, and excessive leverage, to name just a few. However, financial markets have become potentially more susceptible to new crises for several reasons. First, as discussed in Chapter 15, financial markets and financial institutions have become more interconnected than ever before. This increases the likelihood that should a single, systemically important institution fail, risk can spread throughout global markets, impacting multiple institutions and/or economies. Second, new and more challenging risks have emerged in recent years with more frequency and impact, such as cybersecurity attacks and geopolitical events. Both risks are extremely difficult to anticipate and defend against for different reasons and have the potential to cause massive financial losses or operational failures. Furthermore, market structure and regulatory changes have led to heightened risks associated with market liquidity and shadow banking activities.

It is an understatement to say that it is a challenge to predict from where and when the next systemic event might emerge. That said, perhaps because of lessons learned from the Credit Crisis, there are several organizations that monitor the landscape of potential systemic threats to the global financial system that are widely disseminated publicly. A few examples include annual systemic risk surveys conducted by ISOCO, the Bank of England, and the Depository Trust & Clearing Corporation.

A SUMMARY OF GLOBAL SURVEYS

As part of the heightened focus in recent years on the early identification of emerging systemic threats, several organizations have launched periodic surveys of financial industry participants. While these surveys all differ to varying degrees in terms of their respective scope and intended use of the data, most share the common goal of gauging the overall climate of systemic risk facing the global financial services industry and identifying those risks that are deemed most likely to occur and to have a systemic impact on the markets or a region. Following are some of the key findings from a select group of surveys conducted in 2016:

Overall Outlook for Potential Systemic Events:

- A *Bank of England* survey[1] finds the perceived probability of a high-impact event in the U.K. financial system over the short term has fallen, but the perceived probability of such an event in the medium term (1–3 years) has increased significantly (+26%) to 63%. The report shows that medium-term risks are building, driven by continued slowdown in global growth, low inflation expectations, low interest rates, and an uncertain political climate in many countries.
- The OFR's 2016 *Financial Stability Report* represents its annual assessment of potential threats to U.S. financial stability, weighed against an evaluation of financial system resilience. The report finds that financial stability risk remains in a medium range overall.
- The results of the 3Q 2016 *Systemic Risk Barometer Survey* conducted by the Depository Trust & Clearing Corporation revealed that respondents felt the probability of a systemic event occurring in the next 12 months increased 42% over the past six months.

Sources of Systemic Risk

Listed here are the top risks cited in several surveys conducted by financial regulators and other institutions involved in the monitoring of global financial stability in the financial markets:

- Respondents to the 2016 H2 *Bank of England Survey* cited the following top five risks:
  1. U.K. political risk (86% of respondents)
  2. Risks surrounding the low-interest-rate environment (47%)
  3. Risks of a global/overseas economic downturn (37%)
  4. Geopolitical risks (36%)
  5. Cyberattack (34%)
- Respondents to the 2016 *EY/IIF Bank Risk Management Survey*[2] revealed the following as the top-five risks requiring most attention by chief risk officers in the next 12 months:
  1. New regulatory rules and expectations (68%)
  2. Cybersecurity (51%)
  3. Credit risk (44%)
  4. Risk appetite (37%)
  5. Operational risk (37%)

- Among respondents to the Oct. 2016 *IMF* report, the top risks cited were:
  1. Emerging markets risks
  2. Credit risks
  3. Market and liquidity risks
  4. Macroeconomic risks
  5. Monetary policy
- The top risks cited by the IOSCO *Securities Markets Risk Outlook 2016* include:
  1. Corporate bond market liquidity
  2. The use of collateral in financial transactions
  3. Harmful conduct in relation to retail financial products and services
  4. Cyber-threats
  5. Risks associated with asset management activity
- Per the *Two Sigma Street View 2016* survey,[3] the top-five macro risks cited by its respondents include:
  1. Loss of central bank credibility or ability to influence economic growth and market prices (65%)
  2. Risk of a market liquidity event (49%)
  3. The bursting of an asset bubble (46%)
  4. China hard landing (27%)
  5. Breakup of the European Union (25%)
- The *OFR's 2016 Financial Stability Report* finds the following themes to represent the greatest threats to financial stability in the United States:
  1. Disruptions in the global economy, such as the uncertainties related to the U.K.'s exit from the European Union
  2. Risks facing U.S. financial institutions, such as cyber-risk and weakness in the banks' resolution plans
  3. Challenges to improving data
  4. Central counterparties (CCPs) as contagion channels
- The DTCC *Systemic Risk Barometer Survey* 3Q 2016 revealed the following risks selected as their top-five concerns:
  1. Cyber-risk (56%)
  2. U.S. presidential election (50%)
  3. Geopolitical risk (38%)
  4. Impact of new regulations (35%)
  5. Britain's exit from EU (33%)

PREPARING FOR THE NEXT CRISIS

Trying to accurately predict the source and timing of a financial crisis is a daunting if not impossible task. As history has shown, time and time again crises continue to emerge despite the existence of numerous financial regulatory bodies across the world and despite the ever-increasing sophistication of risk management departments of financial institutions and the tools they employ to manage risk.

Nonetheless, since the Credit Crisis of 2007–2009 there has indeed been a paradigm shift in terms of the degree to which both financial regulators and firms operating in the financial services industry attempt to monitor and mitigate emerging systemic threats. This is exemplified in part by the numerous systemic risk surveys now being conducted across the globe by a wide range of institutions and regulators. It is also evidenced by the significantly enhanced rigor of internal stress testing programs employed by financial institutions. Such programs are utilized to estimate the potential losses their firm might suffer should any of a wide range of historical or hypothetical events occur.

In Chapters 7 and 8 we discuss the new regulatory bodies and key new regulatory requirements designed to mitigate systemic risk. In the United States, the enacting of the Dodd-Frank Act, which includes, among other requirements, designations of Systemically Important Financial Institutions and Systemically Important Financial Market Utilities, was the most significant regulatory development to affect the financial services sector since the Great Depression. The primary purpose of the Dodd-Frank Act is to reduce the exposure of both the U.S. financial system and the U.S. government to systemic risk. Internationally, enhanced capital and liquidity standards under the Basel Accords, as well as enhanced Principles for Financial Market Infrastructures, have also contributed to a heightened focus on financial stability versus the pre–Credit Crisis environment.

It should be evident from this book that the topic and scope of systemic risk is extremely broad and complex. We explained how even though financial crises have been occurring for hundreds of years, we continue to witness events that have similar characteristics to those that have taken place many times before. In addition to providing a chronological history of key systemic events dating back to the 1300s in Chapter 2, we group many of these events into key themes or drivers, such as dislocations in global banking sectors, easy monetary conditions that fueled speculative manias and the bursting of asset price bubbles, and sovereign debt crisis, to name a few.

Any broad analysis of systemic risk must also consider the role that human behavior has played throughout history in either fueling or contributing to systemic events. As described in detail in Chapter 3, an entire body of research exists on behavioral finance that includes longstanding theories such as Rational Expectations Theory, Homogeneous Expectations versus Heterogeneity, Risk Aversion Bias, and many others that help to explain investors' behaviors under a variety of circumstances, particularly during periods of market stress.

Another key message from this and other studies of systemic risk should be the tremendous costs that systemic events can have for the financial markets, institutions, and society as a whole. We explain in Chapter 3 the massive number of bailouts provided by the U.S. government following the Credit Crisis of 2007–2009, which exceeded $600 billion, and the failure of more than 300 financial institutions in the United States. The latter included the bankruptcy of Lehman Brothers Holdings Inc., which not only served as a tipping point for the Credit Crisis, but represented the largest bankruptcy in U.S. history. Concerning the Credit Crisis, the recession in the United States officially began in December 2007 and the fallout on the U.S economy was dramatic. In 2008, the United States lost 3.8 million jobs, the greatest annual decline since records were first kept in 1940. With respect to the impact on economic growth, the average downturn in GDP following severe financial crises is 4.8 years. Regarding the Credit Crisis, GDP fell at an annual rate of 4% in the third quarter of 2008 and 6.8% in the fourth quarter, representing the largest decline since 1946. One model used by Fed staff[4] estimates that cumulative loss in output relative to potential over the period was on the order of one quarter of a year's worth of economic output. Overall, in advanced economies, the median cumulative loss in output relative to its pre-Crisis trend has been 33% of GDP. In the European Union, through 2013, GDP remained below pre-Crisis level and is about 13% below its pre-Crisis trend.

What should be very evident from this book is that following the catastrophic impact of the Credit Crisis, systemic risk for the first time is now becoming engrained in the risk management cultures of financial market participants and is clearly the most important focus of global financial regulators. As described earlier this chapter and elsewhere in the book, stakeholders in the financial sector continue to develop new and enhanced tools designed to monitor the buildup of risks in key areas and to attempt to quantify potential risk exposures via stress testing analyses, more sophisticated collateral models, and so forth.

Despite these very encouraging developments concerning the industry's enhanced appreciation for and understanding of systemic risk, the financial industry and global economies may be just as susceptible to future risk events as they were pre–Credit Crisis. A few reasons for this include the fact that the largest banks in the world, despite the improved risk profiles of their individual balance sheets, remain as large, interconnected, and systemically important as ever before. In addition, market structure changes, together with the unintended impact of certain regulations, may lead to reduced market liquidity, a key factor in prior financial crises. Finally, new risks have begun to emerge in recent years, such as cyber-risk, against which the financial industry is struggling to defend itself.

Given the ever-changing landscape and complexity of systemic threats, it is imperative that stakeholders in the financial industry remain vigilant, do not fall prey to complacency, and collaborate very closely going forward. These behaviors are unlikely to prevent all future crises, as history has proven, but these efforts may allow for better preparation for systemic events and hopefully reduce the impact that such events will have on society.

NOTES

1. Bank of England, *Systemic Risk Survey*, 2016, H2. ISSN 2048–7800.
2. Institute for International Finance and Ernst & Young, "A Set of Blueprints for Success," Seventh Annual Global EY/IIF *Bank Risks Management Survey*. Oct. 2016.
3. Saret, J.N., and Sholder, L.M., 2016, *Two Sigma Street View*, https://www.two sigma.com, Oct. 2016.
4. This estimate is from the FRB/US model, which is one model of the U.S. economy used by staff at the Federal Reserve Board. For a description of the model and access to the data, see www.federalreserve.gov/econresdata/frbus/us-models -package.htm.

Systemic Risk Models

INTRODUCTION

In Chapter 5 we discussed the importance of data to allow for the effective monitoring of systemic risk. We provided several examples of existing public indices that may be used as early warning indicators of systemic risk buildup, such as the CBOE Volatility Index, the St. Louis Fed Financial Stress Index, and the Global Financial Stress Index, to name a few.

This appendix provides a taxonomy and literature review of some of the key quantitative models that are used to measure systemic risk in different ways. We begin by introducing how "structural" default models may be used as an analytical tool for assessing default risk in companies. The rest of this chapter consists of a comprehensive survey of several different categories of existing systemic risk models used by a combination of risk management professionals, systemic risk regulators, and academics.

A key goal of this model taxonomy is to provide stakeholders the ability to identify a particular model(s) that is best suited for their specific type of research or goal. For example, systemic risk regulators may find the models covered in the section on macroprudential tools useful, whereas credit risk management professionals may be drawn to the Counterparty Risk models. While certain models may represent a good fit for a given industry participant, many of the models discussed herein will be useful for more than one category of stakeholder.

STRUCTURAL VERSUS REDUCED-FORM CREDIT MODELS

Structural models have been the subject of significant academic research over many years, a large portion of which has centered on the seminal work of Merton (1974) in his classic study on corporate debt valuation [which represents a variation of the Black Scholes (1973) and Merton (1973) models]. This framework introduced a methodology for assessing credit risk of a company by classifying a company's equity as a derivative on its assets. This framework is commonly referred to in academia as the Black-Scholes-Merton Option Pricing Model (BSOP Model).

The difference between *structural* and *reduced-form* models can be characterized in terms of the information assumed known by the modeler. Structural models assume that the modeler has the same information set as the firm's manager (complete knowledge of all the firm's assets and liabilities). In most situations, this knowledge leads to a predictable default time. In contrast, reduced-form models assume that the modeler has the same information set as the market (e.g., incomplete knowledge of the firm's condition). In most cases, this imperfect knowledge leads to an inaccessible default time. As such, the key distinction between structural and reduced-form models is not whether the default time is predictable or inaccessible, but whether the information set is observed by the market.[1]

The BSOP Model was chosen for the initial focus of this chapter primarily because it represents a foundational risk model in academia and because two of the main components of the model (i.e., option pricing theory and the use of accounting balance sheets) can be applied and are relevant to the banking sector and counterparty risk, both major factors in the Credit Crisis. Regarding the latter, the BSOP Model represents a structural model, which relies entirely on the capital structure of the firm (e.g., debt and equity) for modeling credit risk. Many industry experts such as Stern and Feldman (2013) have found that the structural form, versus the reduced-form model, is especially helpful for practitioners involved in the field of credit risk management.

CONTINGENT CLAIMS AND DEFAULT MODELS

Contingent claims analysis (CCA) assumes equity owners of a leveraged firm hold a call option on the firm value net of outstanding debt repayment. The equity holders retain the *option* to default if the value of the firm falls below the present value of the outstanding debt (e.g., *strike*), which represents an obligation to bondholders at maturity. Therefore, bondholders essentially write a European (exercisable at maturity only) put option to equity owners, who in turn maintain the final/residual claim on the firm's asset value assuming a state with no-defaults. Bondholders are compensated for holding risky corporate debt via the credit spread they receive above the risk-free rate. Bondholders bear this potential loss due to the limited liability of equity owners. The put option value is a function of the tenor of the debt claim, the leverage of the firm, and asset-price volatility.

Concerning a structural approach to modeling probability of default, Merton (1973) illustrates that equity can in fact be deemed equivalent to a call option on a firm's assets. Once a stochastic process for the assets value is selected, equity and debt contracts on those assets, and implied default probabilities, can be valued using CCA.[2] This is the approach taken by Capuano (2008), Gray and Jobst (2010), and Huang, Zhou, and Zhu (2009a).

CCA can also be applied to estimating the implied cost of guarantees. For example, Khandani, Lo, and Merton (2009)[3] estimate the amount of aggregate losses absorbed by mortgage lenders through the implied put option that exists in all nonrecourse mortgages. Gray and Jobst (2010)[4] show how systemic CCA allows the determination of the marginal contribution of an individual institution to simultaneous changes of both the severity of systemic risk and the dependence structure across any combination of sample institutions for any level of statistical confidence and at any given point in time. In contrast, CoVaR, CoRisk, and SES examine incremental effects that cover only a portion of available data that could be used to analyze the system-wide sensitivity of contingent liabilities to individual default risk of financial institutions (and the associated cost to governments for potential financial aid).

As detailed in the following pages, since its origin in 1974 the empirical critiques of the BSOP Model have been many with very mixed results. These have spanned the full gamut from conclusions that the model is "not a sufficient statistic for assessing probability of default and that it does not reflect all available market-based information" (Hillegeist, Keating, Cram, and Lundsted, 2002[5]), to the findings of Kealhofer and Kurbat (2002),[6] who, in their comparison of the BSOP Model to Moody's KMV, conclude that "there is no information contained in Moody's ratings that is not already contained in Merton, and Merton has been unfairly characterized as producing too many rejections of firms that do not subsequently default."

Given the vast volume of research conducted about the BSOP Model over the past 40 years, it was impractical to endeavor to analyze or even reference all of them. Instead, a more realistic goal was to provide a thorough and balanced overview of the most noteworthy studies of this landmark model, both supportive and critical. Additionally, following the discussion of Merton-related literature a detailed taxonomy of other categories of systemic risk models is provided. This section starts by reviewing some of the key historical literature that has rejected the BSOP Model, in whole or in part, as an effective measure of probability of default ("PD").

Hillegeist, Keating, Cram, and Lundstedt (2002) analyze whether accounting-based or market-based measures represent a better statistic for estimating potential bankruptcies. To do so, the authors compare the relative and incremental informativeness of the traditional BSOP Model to two other, accounting-based, default predictor models that have significant popularity in the industry (i.e., the Z-Score[7] and O-Score[8]). Using a discrete hazard model, the authors analyze over 20 years of data per firm over the time period of 1979–1993, which includes 561 bankruptcies and nearly 66,000 firm-year observations. The authors find that Black-Scholes-Merton Option Pricing Model is not a sufficient statistic relative to the Z and O Scores, concluding that accounting variables appear to capture different information than the former, perhaps because the two scores contain information about the probability of a firm violating accounting-based debt covenants, consistent with Core and Schrand (1999).[9]

Du and Suo (2004)[10] analyze the extent to which Merton's (1974) default probability measure using a structural approach offers a more accurate way to explain and predict credit ratings versus traditional statistical models. The authors' empirical test outcomes reveal that Merton's default measure "is not a sufficient statistic of equity market information concerning credit quality." The authors find they can improve the predictive ability of the model by incorporating the market value of the firm as an independent variable.

Consequently, the authors determined that structural models don't offer any incremental capacity to capture credit risk. Their results show that rather than using the firm value solely through the debt leverage ratio, as proposed in the structure models, the market value of the firm should be employed as an independent factor impacting probability of default when constructing credit risk models.

According to Allen and Powell (2011)[11] structural models such as the BSOP Model have been criticized because they assume precise information about the point at which a firm theoretically defaults (i.e., the point in which asset values drops below a fixed liability threshold). Some critics consider this to be unrealistic, and instead prefer a reduced-form approach.[12,13] This approach considers default as an unexpected outcome. Additional critiques of structural models have mainly focused on the view of information contained in the model being inadequate to produce meaningful default probabilities. Huang and Huang (2003)[14] determine that structural models produce very modest spreads for investment-grade bonds. Meanwhile, Eom, Helwege, and Huang (2004)[15] find the BSOP Model provides spreads that are too low. The authors also explore several other types of structural models and conclude that they all struggle to predict credit spreads accurately.

Wang (2009)[16] points out some of the key limitations of the BSOP Model, such as (i) the assumption that a company can only default at its maturity date, (ii) that the assumption of constant interest rates is not reliable, (iii) that mapping all debts into a single zero-coupon bond is not always feasible, and (iv) that more sophisticated structural models have been developed since the BSOP Model, some of which provide more accurate results, albeit with a greater degree of analytical complexity.

On the positive side, Wang points to the appealing feature of structural models that connects credit risk to underlying structural variables and allows for the application of option pricing models.

Allen and Powell (2011) determined in their study that structural models underestimated credit risk in the time leading up to the Credit Crisis period, but exaggerated it during the highly volatile times. Moody's KMV calculates distance to default based on the Merton approach. However, to calculate probability of default, KMV uses their own proprietary global database, which has data on thousands of corporate defaults, rather than using a normal distribution to calculate PD.

Gurny, Lozza, and Giacometti (2013)[17] first introduce a structural credit risk model based on the stable Paretian distributions as a representative of subordinated models. Second, they show that it is possible to use this model in the Merton's framework, and propose an empirical comparison of the KMV methodology applied to the BSOP Model. In particular, they show that the basic assumption of the BSOP Model is generally rejected, and thus the log-returns of the company's assets value are not Gaussian distributed and that the probability of default is generally underestimated by the BSOP Model. For this reason, the authors discuss the possibility for using other subordinated processes to approximate the behavior of the log-returns of the company value.

Kulkarni, Mishra, and Thakker (2005)[18] study the effectiveness of the BSOP Model with respect to assessing the credit risk of a portfolio of Indian corporates and overall find mixed results. On the one hand, the authors find that it can accurately distinguish highly rated companies from those in default mode. The authors also demonstrate that the BSOP Model output is in sync with CRISIL's average 1-year default ratings, as well as the Altman Z-score measure.[19] However, the model doesn't produce spreads at the same elevated level as generally seen in the corporate bond market.

Chan-Lau (2011)[20] conclude that the BSOP Model provides insights regarding the potential conflicts of interest between shareholders and bond holders. For example, the payoff of equity is similar to the payoff of a long call option, which benefits from an increase in asset volatility. Meanwhile, the opposite is true for bond holders. Chan-Lau states that the volatility of a firm is determined not just by the volatility of individual projects, but on their mutual dependence (or correlation), which in turn requires the use of a Copula pricing model. The authors view the use of Copula as a natural extension of the contingent claims approach since it accommodates several types of claims and the fact that the firms hold portfolios comprising multiple projects and assets.

Laajimi (2005)[21] conducts a review of existing structural models and finds that they do not possess the necessary accuracy to explain the cross-section of credit spreads as determined by the yield differential on risky corporate bonds and riskless bonds. In addition, structural models under-predict short-term default probabilities (Leland, 1994). Laajimi finds that the BSOP Model contains too-simplistic assumptions with respect to the asset value process (e.g., assumes that the assets of the firm are traded and the market is sufficiently complete), interest rate (e.g., assumes risk-free rate), and capital structure (e.g., single capital structure). That said, the author finds that evidence of contributions in the extensive structural models literature consists primarily of extensions of the original BSOP Model. One of the main assumptions of the latter that has undergone numerous modifications is the assumption regarding the default threshold. Laajimi finds three possible categories of default triggers: (i) the use of a zero-net-worth trigger (e.g., when firm value falls below some exogenous trigger such as nominal value of debt) found in Merton (1974); (ii) that default occurs when firm cash flow is insufficient to satisfy its debt service requirements, found in Kim, Ramaswamy, and Sundaresan (1993),[22] Anderson and Sandaresan (1996),[23] and Ross (2005);[24] and (iii) endogenous default models such as Black and Cox (1976),[25] which calculate the minimum asset level at which shareholders maximize their own claim by ceasing debt service payments.

Elaborating further on Black and Cox (1976), rather than following the approach of the BSOP Model, in which the default is limited only to the maturity of the debt, independent of the change in the firm's asset value before maturity, the authors pioneered the approach of assuming that optimum level of the default barrier is a function of the time of stockholders' willingness to issue new equities to satisfy debt service. To maximize the value of their equities, stockholders choose the optimal default boundary in a way such that the debt value is minimized.

Duffe, Saita, and Wong (2007)[26] modify the original BSOP Model in their test of default predictions associated with a sample of approximately 2,800 industrial firms. The authors state that the main distinction between their model and the BSOP Model are the types of events that trigger default. For example, the authors follow the same assumptions as Merton regarding asset volatility process and distance-to-default process (e.g., a Geometric Brownian Motion[27]). However, regarding default triggers, the author's model varies from structural models, which assume default if asset value falls below some fixed threshold. Under Duffe, Saita, and Wong (2005), default occurs at random, with a probability that depends on the current distance to default and other explanatory variables. The authors refer to findings by Duffie and Lando (2001)[28] that these structural models result in very unrealistically shaped term structures of default probabilities. In particular, the associated default probabilities are very minimal for maturities of about two years or less and even lower for poor-quality firms. The authors' results suggest that enhancing the BSOP Model with additional variables such as macroeconomic variables could lead to an improved prediction for such structural models.

Merton versus Garch

Per Malone, Rodriguez, and Horst (2009),[29] the asset return volatility found using Merton's (1974) calibration method can exhibit significant variation over time for many firms, similar to asset volatilities calculated using the maximum likelihood method of Duan (1994)[30] and those reported by the commercial software of Moody's-KMV. Such shifts can lead to wide swings in risk indicators, such as credit spreads. Therefore, the authors believe that the volatility of firms' asset returns is stochastic, rather than constant. Firms and industries alike go through periods of high levels of uncertainty regarding their future rates of asset growth, as well as periods of relative tranquility. Considering these issues, the BSOP Model's assumption of constant asset return volatility in option pricing has long been deemed too restrictive.

For this reason, academic literature has experienced several methods of pricing options on an underlying asset whose volatility can be time-varying (Engle, 1982;[31] Nicolato and Venardos, 2003;[32] Heston and Nandi, 2000;[33] Duan, 1994). However, in most time-varying volatility models, there exists no closed-form solution for the option price. Thus, one must use Monte Carlo methods instead to calculate option prices (Christoffersen and Jacobs, 1995). To avoid that problem, Heston and Nandi (2000) proposed a closed-form option pricing model in which asset returns follow a GARCH process. The resulting option pricing formula closely resembles the one derived in Black and Scholes (1973) and Merton (1973).

A simulation study performed by Malone, Rodriguez, and Horst (2009) finds that the GARCH Model outperforms the calibrated BSOP Model in all cases, in terms of achieving a lower average error in estimation of assets, asset volatility, and the spread, except for the low business risk, low financial risk case, in which the performance of the three models is similar in their estimation of the asset level and volatility.

Per Engle and Siriwardane (2014),[34] during the financial crisis of 2007–2010 it is widely observed that equity volatilities reached sustained levels not seen since the Great Depression. This was particularly true for the financial sector. Yet it is also observed that the leverage in the financial sector reached extremely high levels. When firm leverage is high, measured by firm asset value divided by equity value, it is not surprising that equities would be highly volatile.

The Structural GARCH Model proposed by the authors is rooted in the classical Merton (1974) structural model of credit, but departs from it in a flexible way. In doing so, they show high-frequency asset return and asset volatility series. Given the unprecedented rise in leverage and equity volatility during the financial crisis of 2007–2010, systemic risk measurement is a natural application of the Structural GARCH Model. For example, in an experiment, following a negative shock to equity value, the financial leverage of the firm mechanically rises. In a simple asymmetric GARCH Model for equity, the rise in volatility following a negative equity return is invariant to the capital structure of the firm. However, in the Structural GARCH Model, the leverage multiplier will be higher following a negative equity return; thus, equity volatility will be even more sensitive to even slight rises in asset volatility. In simulating the model, this mechanism would manifest itself if the firm experiences a sequence of negative asset shocks, which, due to asset volatility asymmetry, increase asset volatility. In turn there will potentially be explosive equity volatility since the leverage multiplier will be large in this case. Observation of equity volatility and leverage during the crisis supports such a sequence of events.

Studies in Support of Merton

On the other end of the spectrum are the findings of Kealhofer and Kurbat (2002), who refute prior conclusions by Stein (2002) that the BSOP Model is deficient in measuring credit risk, that the credit information contained in the BSOP Model can be significantly improved by combining it with Moody's debt ratings and other accounting ratios, and that the theoretical bases of options pricing and BSOP Model are incorrect. The authors find that the BSOP Model not just outperforms Moody's ratings and various accounting measures in predicting defaults, but also already contains information that is found in the latter. They attribute these findings primarily to their view that since the BSOP Model relies heavily on equity prices, such prices should contain the information in accounting ratios such as Return on Assets (ROA).

Hull, Nelken, and White (2004)[35] employed a model similar to BSOP Model that assumes a company has a certain amount of zero-coupon debt that will become due at a future time T and that the firm will default if the value of its assets is less than the required debt repayment at time T. The authors conclude that the BSOP Model can be reliably used to estimate either the risk-neutral probability that the company will default or the credit spread on the debt. However, they also propose a new method of implementing Merton's model using implied volatilities. The traditional approach to implementing Merton's model involves estimating the instantaneous equity volatility and the debt outstanding at a specific future date. The authors present a variation where the inputs to the model are more straightforward. For example, an implied credit spread is the implied equity volatility of the sample firms. The authors find that when implied volatilities are introduced into the BSOP Model the overall performance improves.

In addition to its use as an estimator for probability of default, many others have relied on versions of the BSOP Model to equate the value of U.S. deposit insurance to a one-year put option written by the FDIC.[36] Some examples covered here include Hovakimian, Kane, and Laeven (2012),[37] Marcus and Shaked (1984),[38] Ronn and Verma (1986),[39] and Duan, Moreau, and Sealey (1992).[40]

As background, in its role as insurer of a bank's deposits, the FDIC receives a premium and assumes a liability of actual and potential future cash outflows for surveillance costs and for any "shortfall" between the assets and deposits in the event of the bank's liquidation (Merton, 1978). The FDIC insures guaranteed depositors against such losses, and even uninsured depositors are protected when the FDIC arranges a purchase and assumption transaction. The annual reviews conducted by bank regulators effectively make deposits akin to a debt obligation with an effective tenor equivalent to the frequency of the regulatory reviews (Markus and Shaked, 1984). According to Merton (1977),[41] if the value of a bank's assets follows a diffusion process, then the fair market value of FDIC insurance can be equated to the value of a put option that gives depositors an option to sell their claims on the bank to the FDIC at the face value equal to the level at which deposits will grow if left in the bank until the next examination.[42]

Markus and Shaked (1984) also follow Merton's (1977) suggestion and calculate bank-specific estimates of the proper premium for deposit insurance. For the banks in their sample, they determined that FDIC insurance premiums significantly exceeded estimates of the fair value of the insurance calculated via the BSOP Model. Per Markus and Shaked (1984), the use of option pricing approach to estimate appropriate premium rates offers two advantages. First, CCA analysis permits banks to estimate the correct premium, and second, the estimated premium can be calculated using data collected over relatively short time periods.

Ronn and Verma (1986) developed a model that applied the BSOP Model to the valuation of corporate liabilities. The authors contend that deposit insurance converts debt that is risky to essentially a risk-free obligation and the value of this insurance can be portrayed as a put option on the assets of the bank. Therefore, per Merton (1977), "fair" deposit insurance obtains this put value via the insurance premium. The authors find that the BSOP Model "convincingly argues" that through this relationship, the maturity of the put option is the same as that of the debt issue and that the strike price is equal to maturity value of debt. As such, this model can practically be applied to deposit insurance pricing analysis. This is valid even though the BSOP Model assumption of a single uniform-term debt issue is not completely realistic for banks that issue mainly demand deposits. BSOP Model solves this issue by recasting the tenor of the debt as the time period until the next audit of the bank's assets by the insurer.

Hovakimian, Kane, and Laeven (2012)[43] create measures of stand-alone and systemic bank risk that are derived from the structural model of deposit-insurance benefits developed by Merton (1977). The authors extend this contribution by portraying the value of banking-sector losses from systemic risk as the value of a put option on a portfolio of aggregate bank assets, whose exercise price equates to the face value of aggregate bank debt, and then estimating an individual bank's systemic risk as its contribution to the value of this sector-wide put on the "financial safety net." To track the performance of their model of systemic risk during and leading up to several business-cycle contractions, the authors apply their model to quarterly 1974–2010 data for a portfolio of U.S. commercial banks. The authors' empirical tests conclude that long-period patterns of systemic risk for both individual banks and at the sector levels are consistent with actual historical variations in systemic risk (including the recent Credit Crisis).

Vassalou and Xing (2002)[44] produced a study that utilizes the BSOP Model to compute default measures for individual firms and assess the effect of default risk on equity returns. The authors find that accounting models use information obtained from financial statements, which are not forward looking as financial statements report a firm's past performance. Alternatively, the BSOP Model utilizes the market value of a firm's equity to estimate its risk of default and estimates its MV of debt instead of using book value as is the practice for accounting models. Market prices reflect investors' expectations about a firm's future performance and as such include more forward-looking information, which is better suited for estimating the probability of a firm's future default. In addition, accounting models don't factor in the volatility of a firm's assets in estimating its default risk and simply imply that firms with similar financial ratios will have similar PDs. However, with respect to the BSOP Model, firms may have similar levels of equity and debt, but if the volatility associated with their assets differs, each may have very different PDs.

The volatility of a firm's assets provides important information about the firm's probability of defaulting (Campbell et al., 2001). Furthermore, using data from 1995 to 1999, Campbell and Taksler (2003)[45] show that the volatility of a firm and its credit ratings help explain the cross-sectional variation in corporate bond yields. A firm's volatility is a key input in the BSOP Model.

Gray and Jobst (2010)[46] extend the CCA approach to a systemic risk framework by estimating the magnitude of contingent liabilities from the financial sector under systemic distress assumptions. The authors find a material increase of implied financial sector support because of the widening gap between the risk of default implied by equity and CDS put option values. The authors also find that sudden changes to contingent liabilities and systemic risk were fueled mainly by changes in market capitalization, as explicit or implicit financial sector support didn't have a noticeable impact on slowing the increase of CDS spreads as equity prices of distressed firms fell.

Another model in a similar vein to the BSOP Model and CCA, the *Option-iPoD* model, attempts to obtain a market-based measure of the probability of default implied by the price of equity options. The goal of Capuano's (2008)[47] study is to develop a reliable early warning indicator of future crises in the banking sector. While the Option-iPoD is based on the balance sheet structure utilized by Merton, it is different from existing methodologies in that it doesn't assume any ad-hoc default barrier, which is instead determined endogenously. Capuano states that while equity options aren't well-suited to describe the default state [i.e., state in which the asset value (V) is below the default barrier (D)] because the entire information set used in the model is comprised of stock and option prices, which refer to the non-default state, they do contain information about the cumulative distribution function, the probability of default.

Capuano uses the 2008 collapse of Bear Stearns to test the predictive ability of their Option-iPOD methodology against Moody's EDF. While the EDF for Bear Stearns remained almost constant until March 13 and presented only a small increase on the day Bear Stearns collapsed (March 14), using a put/call option contract expiring 3/22/08 (closest available contract to Bear's collapse), the Option-iPOD started to reveal market nervousness as early as February 21. On February 29, it jumped by a factor of 766, reverted to relative calm the next week, before jumping 4× larger than the first jump. Following the bailout announcement by the Fed, the Option-iPod dropped significantly on March 17. These results appear to indicate that the Option-iPOD may be a useful leading indicator of default.

Giesecke and Kim (2011)[48] find that inadequate capital provisioning by firms that were large players in the CDO market was at the core of the problem that fueled the Credit Crisis. The authors develop, implement, and validate stochastic methods to measure the risk of investment positions in CDOs and related credit derivatives linked to an underlying portfolio of risky securities. The authors suggest a reduced-form statistical model for the estimation of banking defaults that is designed to capture the impacts of direct and indirect systemic interconnections among financial institutions.

The model is developed in terms of a default rate, or "intensity," hence the term *default intensity model* (DIM). The default rate jumps at failure events, reflecting the increased probability of further events due to spillover effects. The magnitude of the jump is a function of the value of the default rate just before the event. The model structure guarantees that the impact of an event increases with the default rate prevailing at the event. The impact of an event tends to be "regime-dependent," meaning that it is often higher during a default clustering episode, when many firms are in a weakened financial condition.

The authors produce 1-year predictions of defaults over rolling quarters and find that the tail of the estimated 1-year distribution became very fat during 2008, exceeding the levels seen during the Internet bubble. The authors conclude that the DIM accurately captures the clustering of the economy-wide default events, supporting the dependability of the model's out-of-sample forecasts.[49]

According to Khandani, Lo, and Merton (2009), some of the key drivers of the Credit Crisis were surging real estate prices, low interest rates, and easy refinancing terms. The authors identify a so-called *ratchet effect* in which the amount of leverage imbedded in consumers' homes is stable or rises during favorable economic environments, but can't be reduced during a weak economy. The authors model the U.S. housing market under the scenarios of both equity withdrawals and no equity withdrawals and calculate the amount of losses sustained by mortgage lenders by estimating the value of the embedded put option that exists in all nonrecourse mortgages. The change in the value of this put option is used as a proxy for systemic risk.

The authors' analysis revealed that the value of their housing market put option rose significantly to a peak of $1.5 billion during the Credit Crisis and since this amount was too much to be covered by the capital of the mortgage lenders, the need for a public bailout became necessary.

Huang, Zhou, and Zhu (2009)[50] create what they call the *distressed insurance premium* (DIP), which is an ex ante indicator of systemic risk. It represents a hypothetical insurance premium against a systemic event, which the authors classify as all losses beyond a fixed threshold, typically a flat percentage of total liabilities. This approach is broad enough that it can be used for any type of company, provided it has publicly traded equity and CDS. The contribution to systemic risk of each company is driven by its probability of default, total size, and asset correlation (e.g., size and correlation estimated via market data).

The authors calculate their DIP indicator starting in 2000, and the results appear to support the DIP as an accurate leading indicator of systemic risk. For example, the per-unit DIP started out at 10 basis points in early 2001, then steadily increased, reaching a peak of 35 basis points in late 2002 during a period of high corporate defaults. The DIP then remained low for several years, hitting a bottom in late 2006 and early 2007. The indicator then increased rapidly, peaking in 2008 and then falling drastically after the Fed bailed out many large banks. The authors also find that most of its movement was impacted by the changing probability of defaults, although the correlation measure also plays a role.

MACROECONOMIC MEASURES

Since many decades have passed since the creation of the FDIC and Fed, the financial system and the types of institutions that comprise it have evolved tremendously. This evolution includes a significant shift away from traditional banking activities. For example, the growth in so-called *shadow banking* firms and activities has prompted significant regulatory concern and focus globally. Some examples include hedge funds, mutual funds, exchange-traded funds (ETFs), and structured investment vehicles (SIVs), to name a few. Because of this growth in nonregulated institutions, when the Credit Crisis originated in late 2007, there were significant segments of the overall industry that didn't have either the FDIC's orderly resolution regime or the Fed's lender-of-last-resort support.

Macro-level indicators usually are centered around overall imbalances in the economy and are meant to serve as early indicators of financial system stress building up. As such, it is very common for those interested in this field to rely on the use of official economic statistics, applied over time series, to perform such analyses. Borio and Drehmann (2009),[51] as an example, try to identify overlapping imbalances in broad indicators of equity, property, and credit markets. Meanwhile, Alfaro and Drehmann (2009)[52] examine CDOs over a time series for signs of weakening ahead of a crisis. Hu, Pan, and Wang (2010)[53] use a metric of illiquidity in the market due to noise in Treasury prices. The *absorption ratio* of Kritzman, Li, Page, and Rigobon (2010) measures the propensity of markets to move in a correlated fashion, suggesting tight coupling.

Borio (2009)[54] states that when a rapid growth in easy credit occurs while asset prices rise substantially, there is a greater likelihood of a systemic event. The author devises an early warning metric to help identify future crises in the banking sector. By extending the approach used by Borio and Lowe (2004),[55] the author creates three indicators: (i) a property price gap, (ii) the (real) equity price gap, and (iii) the credit gap.

Borio finds that with respect to forecasting the recent crisis in the United States, since 2002 the "credit gap" was above 6%, and steadily increased to a peak of 12.5% in 2007. Additionally, the property gap was above 15% since 2001 and reached a peak of 32% in 2005. Therefore, Borio argues that using this methodology the Credit Crisis would have been predicted.

Alfaro and Drehmann (2009) employ a macroeconomic stress test utilizing a basic model[56] of GDP growth, which is assumed to depend only on past behavior. The reason the authors select GDP is they found that GDP growth typically wanes ahead of a banking crisis. Furthermore, they found that once economic stress emerges, output drops significantly in most crises. The authors' main requirement in all scenario construction is that each needs to meet the test of *severe yet plausible*. They find that in many cases (70%), their stress scenarios were less severe than the events themselves. None of the 11 countries that suffered a banking crisis and large GDP dislocation post-2007 would have been predicted by the stress tests.

During 2009–2010, the Fed conducted stress tests of the biggest U.S. bank holding companies under a new program called Supervisory Capital Assessment Program (SCAP). Hirtle, Schuermann, and Stiroh (2009)[57] analyze the results and key features of this program and discuss how they might be used to enhance macro-supervision of banks in the future.

The authors report that the projected losses at the 19 studied banks, assuming the economy followed the worst-case path, could be $600 billion, with approximately 75% of such losses stemming from the banks' residential mortgages and other consumer-related loans. The authors note that estimated two-year cumulative losses on all loans under the adverse scenario would exceed the historical peak banking sector losses from the Great Depression. Finally, trading-related exposures and securities held in investment portfolios amounted to $135 billion under the SCAP analysis.

In Duffie's (2010)[58] proposal, supervisors would obtain and analyze information related to the exposures of a certain number of "important" institutions (identified by the FSB) to predefined stress scenarios. For each scenario, a firm would report its profit or loss in aggregate, and regarding its open trading positions with each of its counterparties. Under Duffie's approach, the joint exposure of the system to individual stress tests and specific institutions (or groups of firms) could be clarified.

PROBABILITY DISTRIBUTION MEASURES

A key measure of systemic risk is the joint distribution of negative outcomes of a group of SIFIs. Examples of literature based on joint distributions of asset returns include the financial turbulence model of Kritzman and Li (2010)[59], the multivariate density (BSMD) function of the banking system by Segoviano and Goodhart (2009),[60] the codependence measures of Adrian and Brunnermeier (2011),[61] (CoVaR), International Monetary Fund (2009), and Acharya, Pedersen, Philippon, and Richardson (2010).[62]

While such approaches are largely theoretical, they can nonetheless offer helpful estimates of correlated losses. Furthermore, the probability distributions on which these measures are based frequently serve as inputs to other measures. For example, Segoviano and Goodhart's (2009) BSMD is used to produce the joint probability of default (JPoD); banking stability index (BSI); distress dependence matrix (DDM); and the probability of cascade effects (PCE).

Kritzman and Li (2010) define *financial turbulence* as a scenario in which asset prices move in an unpredictable manner based on their historical patterns. Examples of such behavior might include large price moves, divergence of correlated assets, and convergence of uncorrelated assets. The authors quantify turbulence via the *mahalanobis distance* (Merton 1973), which measures the statistical irregularities of returns given their historical pattern of behavior. Their measure is very general and can be applied across asset classes for which time-series return data are available.

The authors state that during turbulent time periods returns to risk are substantially lower than during more benign periods, regardless of the source of turbulence. Furthermore, they find that financial turbulence is highly persistent. Although the initial outbreak of financial turbulence cannot be predicted, after it begins it typically continues for a period of weeks as the financial markets react to the events causing the turbulence. The authors also test portfolios containing various combinations of U.S. and international bonds, equities, commodities, and real estate, and find that the turbulence-adjusted VaR is a more accurate predictor of peak portfolio losses during the financial crisis compared to the standard VaR statistic, which significantly understates the riskiness of these portfolios. Note that the turbulence-based approach doesn't provide a more reliable prediction of when an event will occur. However, it provides a more reliable estimate of the impact of such an event.

Segoviano and Goodhart (2009) create a measure of systemic risk based on the banking system's multivariate density (BSMD) function. This method equates the banking system to a portfolio of banks and derives its multivariate density from which the proposed measures are estimated. The authors calculate their model on the U.S. banking system, the EU banking system, and the global banking system. As measured by the JPoD and the BSI, the main findings are that U.S. banks are highly interconnected. Furthermore, the distress dependence across banks increases during times of crisis, indicating that systemic risks increase faster than idiosyncratic risks. Linkages across major U.S. banks rose significantly from 2005 to 2008. On average, if any of the U.S. banks fell into distress, the average probability of the other banks also being distressed rose from 27% on July 1, 2007 to 41% on September 12, 2008.

Acharya, Pedersen, Philippon, and Richardson (2010)[63] posit that each firm's contribution to systemic risk may be estimated as its systemic expected shortfall (SES) or its tendency to be undercapitalized when the system as a whole is undercapitalized. The authors use the following three measures to proxy their SES test: (i) the results of regulatory stress tests (e.g., the recommended capital that a bank was required to raise as of February 2009 test results); (ii) the reduction in equity valuations of large banks during the Credit Crisis (e.g., measured by their cumulative equity return from July 2007 to December 2008); and (iii) the widening of the CDS spreads of large banks (e.g., measured by their cumulative CDS spread increases from July 2007 to December 2008).

The authors conduct regression analyses to assess the predictability of MES and LVG on each of the three metrics of SES. Overall, they find relatively high R-squared values ranging from 20% to 60%. Interesting to note is that despite the systemic risk that AIG clearly presented during the Credit Crisis, insurance firms were considered the least systemically risky. This is in contradiction to other recent empirical findings (see Billio, Getmansky, Lo, and Pelizzon, 2010,[64] and Adrian and Brunnermeier, 2011) and the theoretical role of the insurance industry in the financial system (Sapra, Plantin, and Shin, 2008). The authors also conclude that securities brokers are the riskiest type of firms, likely due to the high leverage with which they typically operate.

Adrian and Brunnermeier's (2011) conditional value at risk (CoVaR) model, and the related Co-Risk measure utilized by the International Monetary Fund (2009), study the co-dependence of firms on each other's financial condition. CoVaR effectively relates two firms, and is defined as the VaR of one institution at a specific probability quantile (e.g., 99%), conditional on the other institution being at its VaR threshold for the same quantile. In other words, a high CoVaR means that if the first institution is in distress, the other one will follow a similar path. From a systemic risk measurement perspective, one treats the financial system as one large firm when applying the CoVaR technique.

The authors conclude that, across institutions, there is only a weak tie between a firm's VaR and its contribution to systemic risk as measured by CoVaR. As such, instituting financial regulation that is based only on the individual risk of an institution in a vacuum might not be sufficient to protect the financial system from systemic risk. The authors run regression analyses to examine what firm characteristics are good predictors of future CoVaR and find that firms with higher leverage, more maturity mismatch, and larger size tend to be associated with larger systemic risk contributions one quarter, one year, and two years later, both at the 1% and the 5% levels.

The Co-Risk measure that studies the codependence between the CDS of various financial firms was first employed by the International Monetary Fund (2009). It is similar to CoVaR except that Co-Risk examines the CDS spread of one firm, conditional on the CDS spread of the other. It is more informative than unconditional risk measures because it provides a market assessment of the impact on a firm's credit risk due to its linkages to other firms.

The authors find that in March 2008, when Citigroup's CDS spreads were at their 95th percentile, this would have led to an increase of 135% in Bear Stearns' CDS spread and 103% in Lehman's CDS spread. Furthermore, the risk of Bear Stearns conditional on the risk of AIG is 248% higher than that corresponding to the 95th percentile of Bear Stearns' empirical distribution. Therefore, these results indicate that AIG, Bear Stearns, and Lehman should have been much more closely monitored in March 2008. The authors also find that in March 2008, the conditional co-risks of AIG and Lehman to the rest of the institutions in the sample were, on average, 11% and 24%, respectively. However, on September 12, 2008, these projections increased to 30% and 36%, respectively, underscoring the systemic importance of these firms at the peak of the crisis.

ILLIQUIDITY MEASURES

Given their role as providers of maturity transformation, banks are highly vulnerable to funding illiquidity. This risk is the driving force behind some of the key policy tools currently available to macroprudential regulators such as FDIC deposit insurance and the Fed's role as potential lender of last resort. These issues appear repeatedly in the literature, including recent papers by Kapadia, Drehmann, Elliott, and Sterne (2009)[65] and Brunnermeier and Pedersen (2009).[66] Ricks (2010)[67] and Pozsar, and Adrian, Ashcraft, and Boesky (2010)[68] point out that liquidity risk can apply to both traditional banks, as well as shadow banks (e.g., finance companies).

With respect to asset liquidity, valuation methods employed for marking positions to market model or to market represent a key consideration. Sapra, Plantin, and Shin (2008)[69] evaluate the pros and cons in the choice between these two valuation approaches. Hu, Pan, and Wang (2010)[70] propose a measure of illiquidity by calculating the variation of market-based yields on Treasury bonds from their model-based yields, which in turn are obtained via a daily estimate of the zero-coupon curve. In doing so, the authors determined that deviations are typically quite low (and liquidity very high), but do spike during crises.

Hu, Pan, and Wang (2010) consider the amount of arbitrage capital in the market and the potential impact on price fluctuations in the market for U.S. Treasuries. During market crises, the authors find that the shortage of market capital leaves the yields to fluctuate more freely relative to the yield curve, resulting in more *noise*. As such, noise in the Treasury market can provide information about liquidity in the broad market because of the criticality of this market and the low level of noise that typically exists (e.g., high liquidity and low credit risk).

COUNTERPARTY RISK MEASURES

Counterparty risk is deemed to represent one of the key potential drivers of systemic events. As discussed in Chapter 3, the outright failure of large global firms such as Lehman Brothers, along with the bailout of AIG and many other institutions, fueled the worst financial crisis since the Great Depression.

An important dimension of counterparty risk involves the contagion risk or interconnectedness risk that can result from the economic distress or failure of a large market counterparty. The latter can cause stress to spread through a counterparty network and cause failure clusters significant enough to destabilize the financial system (Giesecke and Zhu, 2013).[71]

Clearly, the majority of new and proposed regulations introduced in the United States and Europe since the Credit Crisis (e.g., Dodd Frank, Basel III, EMIR, etc.) are aimed at reducing counterparty risk that may arise from large, global financial institutions (e.g., G-SIFIs) and other types of firms such as hedge funds, insurance companies, and so on.

Concerning OTC derivatives, while there are many risk-reducing benefits to financial institutions that regularly utilize these products, including the transfer or distribution of risk across many participants and the ability of firms to hedge certain types of exposures, these same features can have precipitated losses since for every counterparty that has a gain on a derivatives contract, another counterparty must have a loss (Hull, 1989). Using the recent Credit Crisis as an example, it has been well-established that losses generated by derivatives such as CDS were mainly responsible for the failure or bailout of many institutions.

Capponi (2012)[72] states that counterparty risk can be studied primarily from two points of view: risk measurement and pricing. Concerning the former, the focus is on estimating counterparty exposure, computing minimum capital requirements, and trading limits. Concerning pricing, one of the earliest studies in this area was performed by Duffe and Huang (1996), who create a model for valuing claims subject to default by both counterparties. Capponi's focus in this study is on the development of an arbitrage-free valuation framework, referred to as *collateralized credit valuation adjustment* (CCVA).

When counterparty default occurs, the reference name's default-intensity jumps upward due to the positive default correlation. Therefore, the breakeven CDS spread jumps upward, leading to a variation in mark-to-market, which is negative in the case of a receiver CDS and positive for the payer's case. This leads to a positive adjustment for the receiver investor when he is the first to default and results in a negative adjustment for the payer investor in the case when the counterparty is the first to default. Additionally, if reference entity and counterparty are positively correlated, the residual value of the contract becomes out-of-the-money for the receiver investor at the counterparty default time. This is an illustration of *wrong-way risk*, as the reference entity is the riskiest name; the higher the correlation between reference entity and counterparty, the worse the quality of the counterparty.

Jarrow and Yu (2001)[73] state that the business cycle is highly correlated with the number of defaults, the number of credit rating downgrades, and credit spreads. This has led to reduced-form models such as Duffie and Singleton (2003), which assume that the intensity of default is a stochastic process that obtains its randomness from variables such as the short-term interest rates. Per the authors, a default intensity that depends linearly on a set of smoothly varying macroeconomic variables is unlikely to account for the clustering of defaults around an economic recession.

Jarrow and Yu (2001) generalize existing reduced-form models to include default intensities dependent on the default of a counterparty. In this model, firms have correlated defaults due not only to an exposure to common risk factors, but also to firm-specific or counterparty risks. Numerical examples illustrate the effect of counterparty risk on the pricing of defaultable bonds and credit derivatives such as default swaps. The authors provide examples with explicit bond pricing formulas and show that market-wide risk factors and firm-specific counterparty risks interact to generate a variety of shapes for the term structure of credit spreads. The authors also show how credit derivatives are priced within such a framework, and explain how mispricings are produced by models that ignore counterparty relations.

Giescke and Kim (2011)[74] state that the Credit Crisis highlights the need to measure and manage systemic risk and that its measurement involves two problems: the quantification of the systemic risk of the financial sector as a whole, and the allocation of that risk to individual institutions. A significant volume of recent research has focused on measuring the marginal systemic risk of individual institutions (see Acharya et al., 2010; Adrian and

Brunnermeier, 2011; Brownlees and Engle, 2012;[75] Huang et al., 2009, and others). Counterparty risk was discussed in detail in Chapter 11.

BEHAVIORAL MODELS

Asset bubbles or dramatic price increases followed by sharp price drops are not a new phenomenon. Famous bubbles include the *Dutch Tulip Mania* of the 1630s, the *Mississippi Bubble*, and the *South Sea Bubble* of the 1720s (Abreu and Brunnermeier, 2002)[76] and the bursting of the Internet stock bubble in 2000. These events are hard to reconcile with the predictions of traditional economic theory wherein all market participants are assumed to be fully rational and that rational investors will typically eliminate a bubble before it has a chance to develop. Proponents of the Efficient Market Hypothesis, such as Fama (1965), are willing to admit that "behavioral/ boundedly rational traders are active in the marketplace." However, they argue that "the existence of many well-informed and well-financed arbitrageurs guarantees that any potential mispricing induced by behavioral traders will be corrected." Hence, the efficient market theory also rules out the persistence of bubbles. Abreu and Brunnermeier (2002) examine whether asset bubbles can survive in the presence of rational arbitrageurs. The conclusions of Abreu and Brunnermeir (2002) suggest that arbitrage ultimately works, though it might be ineffective over substantial periods. In their setting, a bubble persists even though rational investors know that the bubble must burst eventually.

Hong, Scheinkman, and Xiong (2004)[77] build on early work regarding the formation of speculative bubbles due to the combined effects of heterogeneous beliefs and short-sales constraints (Harrison and Kreps, 1978).[78] The authors follow Scheinkman and Xiong (2003)[79] in assuming that overconfidence (i.e., the belief of an investor that her information is more accurate than it is) is the source of disagreement.

In February 2000, the U.S. technology sector, consisting of about 400 companies, had valuations that represented 6% of the market capitalization and a significant 20% of the publicly traded volume of the U.S. stock market (Ofek and Richardson, 2003). This led many to believe that this sector was in the midst of an asset price bubble. Valuations of these technology companies began to fall shortly thereafter and returned to pre-1998 levels, losing nearly 70% from the peak. Trading volume and return volatility in these stocks also largely dried up in the process. Ofek and Richardson (2003)[80] document that at around the same time, the float of the Internet sector dramatically increased as the lockups of many of these stocks expired.

Hong and Stein (2003)[81] develop a theory of market crashes based on differences of opinion among investors. Due to short-sale constraints, bearish investors do not initially participate in the market and their information is not revealed in the prices. The authors' model explains several facts about crashes and develops a new prediction that returns will be more negatively skewed based on high trading volume. The authors make the following assumptions about crashes: (i) there is an unusually significant change in market prices that occurs independent of any meaningful market news, (ii) the price change must be negative, and (iii) such price declines extend to an entire class or sector of stocks, not just a single stock.

NOTES

1. Jarrow and Protter, 2004, "Structural versus Reduced Form Models: A New Information Based Perspective," *Journal of Investment Management* 2(2), 2004: 1–10.
2. A random or stochastic process is a collection of random variables ordered in time.
3. Khandani, A.E., Lo, A.W., and Merton, R.C., 2009, "Systemic Risk and the Refinancing Ratchet Effect," MIT Sloan School Working Paper, p. 23.
4. Gray, D., and Jobst, A., 2010, "Systemic CCA: A Model Approach to Systemic Risk," working paper, International Monetary Fund. Paper presented at conference sponsored by the Deutsche Bundesbank and Technische Universitaet Dresden, Oct. 2010, pp. 28–29.
5. Hillegeist, S.A., Keating, E.K., Cramald, D.P., and Lundstedt, K.G., 2002, "Assessing the Probability of Bankruptcy," *Review of Accounting Studies* 9(1), March 2004.
6. Kealhofer, S., and Kurbat, M., 2002, "The Default Prediction Power of the Merton Approach, Relative to Debt Ratings and Accounting Variables," KMV LLC, mimeo.
7. Created by Altman, 1968, Z Score is based on five major accounting measures that had the highest predictive power in multivariate discriminant analysis.
8. Created by Ohlson, 1980, O-score is a one-year default predictor model using nine accounting-based measures.
9. Core, J., and Schrand, C., 1999, "The Effect of Accounting-Based Debt Covenants on Equity Valuation," *Journal of Accounting and Economics*, 27(1): 1–34.
10. Du, Y., and Suo, W., 2004, "Assessing Credit Quality from Equity Markets: Is a Structural Approach a Better Approach?," working paper, Queen's University.
11. Allen, D., and Powell, R., 2011, "Customers and Markets: Both Are Essential to Credit Risk Measurement in Australian Banks," *Australasian Accounting Business and Finance Journal*, 5(1): 57–75.

12. Jarrow, R.A., Lando, D., and Turnbull, S.M., 1997, "A Markov Model for the Term Structure of Credit Risk Spreads," *Review of Financial Studies*, 10(2): 481–523.
13. The reduced form of a system of equations is the result of solving the system for the endogenous variables.
14. Huang, J., and Huang, M., 2003, "How Much of the Corporate-Treasury Yield Spread Is Due to Credit Risk?," working paper, Penn State and Stanford.
15. Eom, Y., Helwege, J., and Huang, J.Z., 2004, "Structural Models of Corporate Bond Pricing: An Empirical Analysis," *Review of Financial Studies*, 17, 499–544.
16. Wang, Y., 2009, "Structural Credit Risk Modeling: Merton and Beyond," *Risk Management*, June, 30–33.
17. Gurny, M., Lozza, S.O., and Giacometti, R., 2013, "Structural Credit Risk Models with Subordinated Processes," *Journal of Applied Mathematics. Volume 2013, Article ID 138272* .
18. Kulkarni, A., Mishra, A.J., and Thakker, K., 2005, "How Good Is Black-Scholes-Merton Option Pricing Model at Assessing Credit Risk? Evidence from India," National Institute of Bank Management, India, pp. 1–49.
19. CRISIL is an S&P company that is the largest provider of credit ratings in India.
20. Chan-Lau, A. Jorge, 2011, "Fat Tails and Their (Un)happy Endings: Correlation Bias and Its Implications for Systemic Risk and Prudential Regulation," IMF Working Paper, pp. 1–18.
21. Laajimi, S., 2005, "Structural Credit Risk Models: A Review," Canada Research Chair in Risk Management, HEC Montréal.
22. Kim, I.J., Ramaswamy, K., and Sundaresan, S., 1993, "Does Default Risk in Coupons Affect the Valuation of Corporate Bonds? A Contingent Claims Model," *Financial Management*, special issue on Financial Distress.
23. Anderson, R.W., and Sundaresan, S., 1996, "The Design and Valuation of Debt Contracts," *Review of Financial Studies*, 9, 37–68.
24. Ross, S.A., 2005, "Capital Structure and the Cost of Capital," *Journal of Applied Finance* Vol. 15, No. 1 (2005): 7–25.
25. Black, F., and Cox, J.C., 1976 (May), "Valuing Corporate Securities: Some Effect of Bond Indenture Provisions," *Journal of Finance*, 31(2): 351–367.
26. Duffie, D., Saita, L., and Wang, K., 2007, "Multiperiod Corporate Default Prediction with Stochastic Covariates," *Journal of Financial Economics*, 83: 635–666.
27. A geometric Brownian motion (GBM) (also known as exponential Brownian motion) is a continuous-time stochastic process in which the logarithm of the randomly varying quantity follows a Brownian motion (also called a Wiener process) with drift.
28. Duffie, D., and Lando, D., 2001, "Term Structures of Credit Spreads With Incomplete Accounting Information," *Econometrica*, 69: 633–664.
29. Malone, S., Rodriguez, A., and Ter Horst, E., 2009, "The GARCH Structural Credit Risk Model: Simulation Analysis and Application to the Bank CDS Market During the 2007–2008 Crisis." SSRN.

30. Duan, J.C., 1994, "Maximum Likelihood Estimation Using Price Data of the Derivative Contract," *Mathematical Finance* 4: 155–167.

31. Engle, R., 1982, "Autoagressive Conditional Heteroscedasticity with Estimates of Variance of United Kingdom Inflation," *Econometrica*, 50: 987–1008.

32. Nicolato, E., and Venardos, E., 2003, "Option Pricing in Stochastic Volatility Models of the Orenstein-Uhlenbeck Type," *Mathematical Finance*, 13(4): 445–466.

33. Heston, S.L., and Nandi, S., 2000, "A Closed-Form Garch Option Valuation Model," *Review of Financial Studies*, 13.

34. Engle, Robert, and Siriwardane, E., 2014, "Structural GARCH: The Volatility-Leverage Connection," The Office of Financial Research (OFR) Working Paper Series, pp. 1–65.

35. Hull J., N.I., and White, A., 2004, "Merton's Model, Credit Risk, and Volatility Skews," *Journal of Credit Risk*, 1(1), Winter 2004/2, 005.

36. Duan, J., Moreau, A., and Sealey, C., 1992, "Fixed-Rate Deposit Insurance and Risk-Shifting Behavior at Commercial Banks," *Journal of Banking and Finance*, 16: 715–742.

37. Hovakimian, A., Kane E., and Laeven, L., 2012, "Variation in Systemic Risk at U.S. Banks During 1974–2010," working paper, National Bureau of Economic Research, pp. 1–31.

38. Markus, A., and Shaked, I., 1984, "The Valuation of FDIC Deposit Insurance Using Option-Pricing Estimates," *Journal of Money, Credit and Banking*, 16(4): 446–459.

39. Ronn, E., and Verma, A., 1986 (Sept.), "Pricing Risk-Adjusted Deposit Insurance: An Option Based Model," *Journal of Finance*, 41: 871–895.

40. Duan, J., Moreau, A., and Sealey, C., 1992, "Fixed-Rate Deposit Insurance and Risk-Shifting Behavior at Commercial Banks," *Journal of Banking and Finance*, 16: 715–742.

41. Merton, R.C., 1977, "An Analytical Derivation of the Cost of Deposit Insurance and Loan Guarantees: An Application of Modern Option Pricing Theory," *Journal of Banking and Finance*, 1: 3–11.

42. In probability theory, a diffusion process is a solution to a stochastic differential equation. It is a continuous-time Markov process with almost surely continuous sample paths.

43. Hovakimian, A., Kane E., and Laeven, L., 2012, "Variation in Systemic Risk at U.S. Banks During 1974–2010," working paper, National Bureau of Economic Research, pp. 1–31.

44. Vassalou, M., and Xing, Y., 2002, "Default Risk in Equity Returns," *Journal of Finance*, 49(2), April 2004, 831–868.

45. Campbell, J.T., and Taksler, Glen B., 2003, "Equity Volatility and Corporate Bond Yields," *Journal of Finance*, 58: 2321–2349.

46. Gray, D., and Jobst, A., 2010, "Systemic CCA: A Model Approach to Systemic Risk," working paper, International Monetary Fund. Paper presented at conference sponsored by the Deutsche Bundesbank and Technische Universitaet Dresden, Oct. 2010, pp. 28–29.

47. Capuano, C., 2008, "The Option-iPoD. The Probability of Default Implied by Option Prices Based on Entropy," IMF Working Paper 08/194, International Monetary Fund.
48. Giesecke, K., and Kim, B., 2011, "Systemic Risk: What Defaults Are Telling Us." Department of Management Science and Engineering, Stanford University, Stanford, California 94305.
49. Out-of-sample forecasting experiments are used by forecasters to determine if a proposed leading indicator is potentially useful for forecasting a target variable.
50. Huang, X., Zhou, H., and. Zhu, H., 2009 (Nov.), "A Framework for Assessing the Systemic Risk of Major Financial Institutions," *Journal of Banking & Finance*, 33(11): 2036–2049.
51. Borio, C., and Drehmann, M., 2009 (Mar.), "Assessing the Risk of Banking Crises—Revisited," *BIS Quarterly Review.*
52. Alfaro, R., and Drehmann, M., 2009 (Dec.), "Macro Stress Tests and Crises: What Can We Learn?" *BIS Quarterly Review*, 29–41.
53. Hu, X., Pan, J., and Wang, J., 2010, "Noise as Information for Illiquidity," working paper, Massachusetts Institute of Technology.
54. Borio, C., 2009 (Apr. 14), "The Macroprudential Approach to Regulation and Supervision," BIS Working Paper, VoxEU.org, pp. 1–4.
55. Borio, C., and Lowe, P., 2004, "Securing Sustainable Price Stability: Should Credit Come Back from the Wilderness?" BIS Working Paper 157, Bank for International Settlements.
56. Kritzman, Li, Page, and Rigobon, 2010, propose to measure systemic risk via the Absorption Ratio (AR), which they define as the fraction of the total variance of a set of asset returns explained or "absorbed" by a fixed number of eigenvectors. The absorption ratio captures the extent to which markets are unified or tightly coupled. When markets are tightly coupled, they become more fragile in the sense that negative shocks propagate more quickly and broadly than when markets are loosely linked.
57. Hirtle, B., Schuermann, T., and Stiroh K., 2009, "Macroprudential Supervision of Financial Institutions: Lessons from the SCAP," Staff Report No. 409, Federal Reserve Bank of New York.
58. Duffie, D., 2010, *How Big Banks Fail and What to Do about It*. Princeton, NJ: Princeton University Press.
59. Kritzman, M., and Li, Y., 2010, "Skulls, Financial Turbulence, and Risk Management," *Financial Analysts Journal*, 66(5): 30–41.
60. Segoviano, M.A., and Goodhart, C., 2009. "Banking Stability Measures," Financial Markets Group, Discussion Paper 627, London School of Economics and Political Science.
61. Adrian, T., and Brunnermeier, M., 2011, "*CoVaR*," working paper, Federal Reserve Bank of New York.
62. Acharya, V.V., Pedersen, L.H., Philippon, T., and Richardson, M., 2010, "A Tax on Systemic Risk," in forthcoming NBER publication on *Quantifying Systemic Risk*, Haubrich, J., and Lo, A. (eds.). First draft February 3, 2010.

63. Acharya, V.V., Pedersen, L.H., Philippon, T., and Richardson, M., 2010, "A Tax on Systemic Risk," in *forthcoming NBER publication on Quantifying Systemic Risk*, Haubrich, J., and Lo, A. (eds.). First draft February 3, 2010.
64. Billio, M., Getmansky, M., Lo, A.W., and Pelizzon, L., 2010, "Econometric Measures of Systemic Risk in the Finance and Insurance Sectors," NBER Working Paper No. 16223.
65. Kapadia, S., Drehmann, M., Elliott, J., and Sterne, G., 2009, "Liquidity Risk, Cash Flow Constraints, and Systemic Feedback," working paper, Bank of England.
66. Brunnermeier, M.K., and Pedersen, L.H., 2009, "Market Liquidity and Funding Liquidity," *Review of Financial Studies*, 22(6): 2201–2238.
67. Ricks, M., 2010, "Shadow Banking and Financial Regulation." Columbia Law and Economics Working Paper No. 370.
68. Pozsar, Z., Adrian, T., Ashcraft, A., and Boesky, H., 2010, "Shadow Banking," Federal Reserve Bank of New York Staff Reports No. 458, July 2010, revised February 2012.
69. Sapra, H., Plantin, G., and Shin, H.S., 2008 (Oct.), "Fair Value Accounting and Financial Stability," Banque de France, *Financial Stability Review*, No. 12: Valuation and Financial Stability.
70. Hu, X., Pan, J., and Wang, J., 2010, "Noise as Information for Illiquidity," working paper, Massachusetts Institute of Technology.
71. Giesecke, K., and Zhu, S., 2013, "Transform Analysis for Point Processes and Applications in Credit Risk," *Mathematical Finance*, 23: 742–762.
72. Capponi, A., 2012, "Pricing and Mitigation of Counterparty Credit Exposures," in *Handbook of Systemic Risk*, Fouque, J.-P., and Langsam, J. (eds.). Cambridge University Press.
73. Jarrow, R.A., and Yu, F., 2001 (Oct.), "Counterparty Risk and the Pricing of Defaultable Securities," *Journal of Finance*, 56(5).
74. Giesecke, K., and Kim, B., 2011, "Systemic Risk: What Defaults Are Telling Us." Department of Management Science and Engineering, Stanford University, Stanford, California 94305.
75. Brownlees, C.T., and Engle, R.F., 2012, "Volatility, Correlation and Tails for Systemic Risk Measurement," ssrn.com/abstract=1611229 or dx.doi.org/10.2139/ssrn.1611229.
76. Abreu, D., and Brunnermeier, M.K., 2002 (Jan.), "Bubbles and Crashes," *Econometrics*, 1: 173–204.
77. Hong, H., Scheinkman, J., and Xiong, W., 2004, "Asset Float and Speculative Bubbles," *Journal of Finance*, 61(3).
78. Harrison, M., and Kreps, D.M., 1978, "Speculative Investor Behavior in a Stock-Market with Heterogeneous Expectations," *Quarterly Journal of Economics*, 92: 323–336.
79. Scheinkman, J., and Xiong, W., 2003, "Overconfidence and Speculative Bubbles," *Journal of Political Economy*, 111: 1183–1219.
80. Ofek, E., and Richardson, M., 2003. "DotCom Mania: The Rise and Fall of Internet Stock Prices," *Journal of Finance, American Finance Association*, Vol. 58(3).
81. Hong, H., and Stein, J.C., 2003. "Differences of Opinion, Short-Sales Constraints, and Market Crashes," *Rev. Finance. Stud.*, 16(2): 487–525.

Solutions to the Knowledge Check Questions

Chapter 1

A1.1: The key distinguishing characteristic of a systemic risk event is the fact that the impact of such events spills over into the real economy.

A1.2: No. Systemic events have been occurring since at least the Middle Ages, with the most documented event dating back to the 1600s, called the "Dutch Tulip Crisis," in which many European investors and regular citizens took significant losses, in many cases their life savings, by making concentrated bets on the price of tulip bulbs on the futures market.

A1.3: Inflation spikes; currency crashes; currency debasements; bursting of asset bubbles; banking crisis and sovereign defaults.

A1.4: The insolvency of hundreds of U.S. banks was at the center of both the Great Depression and the Credit Crisis.

A1.5: It is critical that in the future systemic risks are better anticipated and mitigated to minimize the negative costs of such events on both the financial services sector as well as society, which often bears the cost of government bailouts.

Chapter 2

A2.1: An asset bubble can be described as a non-sustainable pattern of price changes or cashflows that eventually suffers a precipitous decline in a short period of time.

A2.2: Although not a precondition for an asset bubble, many popular economic theories hold that "easy credit" conditions provided by Central Banks usually exist in the years leading up to a bubble. These conditions allow investors to speculate on investments, driving up the prices to unsustainable levels.

A2.3: Bubbles in real estate and stock markets represent the most common forms of asset bubbles. The most recent example of the former is the Credit Crisis in which residential home prices rose dramatically in many regions of the United States before crashing over the 2008–2010 time period.

A2.4: In early stages of industrialization, a substantial amount of the stock market valuation consists of real estate companies and construction companies and firms in other industries that are closely associated with real estate, including banks. Individuals whose wealth has increased sharply because of the increase in real estate values want to keep their wealth diversified and so they buy stocks, which in turn often fuels a bubble in stock markets.

A2.5: Inflation and capital flows; exchange rate changes; securities price changes

A2.6: Spain and France have incurred the greatest number of combined defaults (36) on external debt dating back to 1300.

A2.7: (i) Napoleonic wars; (ii) 1820s–1840s; (iii) 1870s–1890s; (iv) Great Depression era: 1930s–early 1950s; (v) Emerging markets: 1980s–1990s.

A2.8: The gold standard refers to a monetary system in which the standard unit of currency is freely convertible into gold at a fixed rate.

Chapter 3

A3.1: Although there is no official timeframe designated for the Credit Crisis, much of research and analysis post-Crisis use 2008–2009 as representing the peak years of this event, with most high-profile financial failures or takeovers occurring during 2008.

A3.2: While there are many underlying causes of the Credit Crisis that range from questionable U.S. policy toward homeownership, to lax regulatory oversight, the aggressive use of financial innovation by Wall Street, and so on, the growth and eventual bursting of the residential real estate sector and securities derived from this sector was the primary driver of the failure of hundreds of financial firms and the associated economic fallout that followed.

A3.3: Subprime mortgages were a sub-segment of residential mortgages that differentiated between the credit quality of individual mortgage loans and mortgage-backed securities with *subprime* referring to borrowers with below-average individual credit scores.

A3.4: There have been many theories put forward since the Credit Crisis about what fueled the so-called asset bubble in U.S. residential real estate. Some of these theories include (i) the so-called "easy credit" monetary policy that existed in the early 2000s, in which the Fed Funds target rate declined from 6.5% to 1% between 2000 and 2003, making mortgages much more accessible to millions of additional Americans, (ii) the introduction, starting back in the 1990s, of looser mortgage underwriting standards and riskier mortgage products that required little or no down payment by borrowers, and (iii) the incentives that both the GSEs and many Wall Street firms had to generate greater and greater volumes of mortgages to fuel what was a tremendously profitable mortgage securitization business.

A3.5: Synthetic CDOs represent structured investment vehicles created and sold by Wall Street firms that often used subprime mortgage loans as underlying collateral or reference securities. Many of these structures defaulted when the loss rates on such collateral far exceeded the tolerance levels set by the investment banks for each "tranche" of the CDO. Following the Credit Crisis both investment banks and the large U.S. rating agencies suffered great criticism for the reckless way many of these investments were structured, rated, and marketed.

A3.6: While it's widely believed that no single factor caused the Credit Crisis, one area that has been the subject of significant debate is the extent to which U.S. public policy toward homeownership helped plant the seeds of the crisis dating as far back as the mid-1990s. In 1995, President Bill Clinton announced an initiative to boost U.S. homeownership from 65.1% to 67.5% of families by 2000. Also in 1995, Clinton loosened housing rules by rewriting the Community Reinvestment Act, which put added pressure on banks to lend in low-income neighborhoods.

A3.7: Fannie Mae and Freddie Mac, the two largest U.S. GSEs, were major players in the Credit Crisis. While the GSEs did not originate any individual mortgage loans, the GSEs set the standards in the United States for what constituted a Fannie- or Freddie-eligible or conforming mortgage. The GSEs also were allowed to build up real estate portfolios and offer guarantees on RMBS securities that could not be supported by their extremely thin capitalization, ultimately leading to the need for the U.S. government to seize control of both entities to minimize further dislocations in the functioning of the U.S. mortgage market.

A3.8: Although the views expressed during the months leading up to the failure of Lehman Brothers by senior U.S. government officials such as Ben Bernanke and Henry Paulson, among others, revealed that they were fully aware of the potential systemic impact Lehman's failure would likely have on global markets and economies, they decided not to provide any extraordinary support to Lehman. This decision has come under significant scrutiny since 2008 for several reasons, one of which was an accusation of inconsistency given that the government assisted with the bailout of Bear Stearns, AIG, the GSEs, and other entities.

A3.9: Among many devastating and historic impacts, the Credit Crisis sent both the United States and Europe into deep recessions, and led to >30% average decline in U.S. home prices, a similar decline in U.S. equity markets, a spike in U.S. unemployment to over 10%, and a tremendous loss in personal household net worth.

A3.10: While the economic impact of the Credit Crisis was significant, the primary government bailout program, TARP, was eventually fully repaid by its recipients so individual taxpayers incurred no losses.

Chapter 4

A4.1: A hedge borrower, who is able to service debt payments from current cash flows from investments; speculative borrowers, for whom cash flow from investments can service interest payments on debt but require refinancing to repay principle; Ponzi borrowers who rely solely on appreciation of the underlying asset value to avoid default.

A4.2: The Theory of Benign Neglect posits that crises should be left to work themselves out.

A4.3: The concept of Moral Hazard is that the speculative behavior that fueled many historical systemic events will only be further encouraged in the future if investors feel it is likely that they will be bailed out by the government.

A4.4: Under the Efficient Market Hypothesis market prices should fully reflect all available information about a particular asset or company up to that point in time, and informed investors and traders identify any deviations between current prices and fundamental value and achieve quick arbitrage profits.

A4.5: Behavioral theory challenges these EMH assumptions, including the idea that EMH cannot adequately explain the frequent market anomalies that occur and that the influence of arbitrage on keeping markets efficient is limited.

A4.6: Investors tend to anchor their views to their initial values or judgments and, therefore, even when presented with overwhelming evidence supporting a particular adjustment to such judgments, refuse to take rational actions.

A4.7: Under the Prospect Theory, investors tend to feel the negative impact of a loss more acutely than the pleasure of an equal-sized gain, and research shows that decision makers' reaction to changes in wealth are approximately twice as sensitive to perceived losses than gains. This theory may help explain why most investors did not take advantage of significantly lower asset prices during prior crises, despite unique opportunities to buy assets at historically low prices.

A4.8: Heterogeneous beliefs represents a theory whereby investors do not agree on the basic value or expected return of an asset; meanwhile, under most asset pricing models there is an assumption that all investors will have the same expectations and make the same choices given a set of circumstances.

A4.9: The amygdala region of the brain is the final place where the neuropathway for fear response circumvents the brain's higher capabilities, including those associated with rationality. This may help explain why so many investors have made seemingly irrational and speculative decisions throughout history related to investment and borrowing.

Chapter 5

A5.1: Following the Credit Crisis it became clear that there were large gaps related to information about interconnections large U.S. financial firms had across the global financial system with thousands of other counterparties in numerous geographic jurisdictions.

A5.2: Macroprudential supervision is associated with monitoring of data on broad economic and financial data to identify the buildup of potential systemic threats, whereas microprudential supervision represents the oversight of individual firms.

A5.3: The Office of Financial Research was created by the Financial Stability Oversight Council, which in turn was created under the powers of Title 1—Financial Stability of the Dodd-Frank Act.

A5.4: Based on public annual reports of the 10 largest global banks, these institutions have on average 3,500 subsidiaries located in 80 countries. Additionally, in some cases the greatest systemic risk within a global institution may be located within its non–home country subsidiary. An example of the latter would be the significant deterioration in the financial condition of the U.S. branches of European banks during the Credit Crisis because of their substantial involvement in subprime real estate activities.

A5.5: The VIX Index is a key measure of market expectations of near-term volatility conveyed by S&P 500 stock index option prices. Since its introduction in 1993, the VIX Index has been considered by many to be the world's premier barometer of investor sentiment and market volatility.

A5.6: Four of the 20 recommendations made in a joint report by the IMF and FSB on reducing financial data gaps include development of measures of system-wide macroprudential risk, such as aggregate leverage and maturity mismatches; development of a common data template for systemically important global financial institutions; enhancement of BIS-consolidated banking statistics; and development of a standardized template covering the international exposure of large non-bank financial institutions.

A5.7: Three of the top remaining data-related priorities cited by the Office of Financial Research include: (i) bilateral repo, (ii) securities lending, and (iii) swap and other derivatives data.

A5.8: The bankruptcy of Lehman Brothers Inc. is often cited as the main lesson learned in terms of the lack of transparency that existed before the Credit Crisis into the size and global scope of exposures many banks and investment banks maintained.

Chapter 6

A6.1: Prior to the Credit Crisis many supervisory tools fell in the category of microprudential regulation or regulation at the individual firm level.

A6.2: A key lesson learned from the Credit Crisis is that regulators need new and better tools to provide early warnings of risk buildup across the financial system that can lead to systemic events, not just a focus on individual firms.

A6.3: Microprudential regulations tend to target individual institutions or components of the system on a stand-alone basis, regardless of the institution's impact on the financial system as a whole.

A6.4: Macroprudential policies are concerned with aggregate levels of capital and economic cycles, with the main goal of avoiding systemic risks from building up.

A6.5: While macroprudential policies are distinct from day-to-day risk management, many macroprudential tools are in effect microprudential instruments deployed with a systemic perspective in mind.

A6.6: Examples of commonly used categories of regulatory tools through-out most of modern financial history include underwriting standards, stock margin requirements, and reserve requirements.

A6.7: The four stages of macroprudential policy implementation are risk identification and assessment, instrument selection and calibration, policy implementation, and policy evaluation.

Chapter 7

A7.1: See Table 7.1.

A7.2: The safety and soundness of financial institutions, mitigation of systemic risk, fairness and efficiency of markets, and the protection of customers and investors.

A7.3: Institutional approach, functional approach, integrated approach, and twin peaks approach.

A7.4: Three European Union supervisory authorities are the European Banking Authority (EBA), the European Securities and Market Authority (ESMA), and the European Insurance and Occupational Pensions Authority (EIOPA). The European Systemic Risk Board (ESRB) oversees the EU's financial system and works to mitigate systemic risk. The European System of Financial Supervision (ESFS) is a decentralized system consisting of European and national supervisors.

A7.5: See Table 7.3.

A7.6: To promote financial stability; to end "too big to fail"; to end bailouts; and to protect consumers from abusive financial services practices.

A7.7: See Table 7.4.

A7.8: See Table 7.5.

Chapter 8

A8.1: An organization that works to promote international financial stability.

A8.2: The Standing Committee on Assessment of Vulnerabilities identifies financial systemic risks. The Standing Committee on Supervisory and Regulatory Cooperation generates policy responses. The Standing Committee on Standards Implementation monitors the execution of responses.

A8.3: See Table 8.1.

A8.4: Periodic peer reviews and the implementation of key standards for sound financial systems.

A8.5: Multinational accords that set minimum capital requirements for banks that were established by the Basel Committee.

A8.6: An EU entity that provides macroprudential oversight of the EU's financial system and works to mitigate systemic risk.

A8.7: See Table 8.3.

A8.8: Excessive credit growth and leverage, addressed through capital buffers and minimum loan-to-value and loan-to-income requirements; excessive maturity mismatch and market illiquidity, addressed through stable funding restrictions and liquidity charges; direct and indirect exposure concentration, addressed through large exposure restrictions; and misaligned incentives and moral hazard, addressed through capital surcharges for systemically risky institutions as well as a systemic risk buffer.

A8.9: Entities that facilitate the clearing, settlement, and recording of financial transactions.

A8.10: International standards for the management of financial market infrastructures.

A8.11: As 24 principles and five responsibilities, organized as general organization principles; credit and liquidity risk management principles; settlement principles; central securities depositories and exchange-of-value settlement systems principles; default management principles; general business and operational risk management principles; access principles; efficiency principles; and transparency principles; and responsibilities of central banks, market regulators, and other relevant authorities for financial market infrastructures.

Chapter 9

A9.1: An entity whose failure would cause financial instability that would threaten the economy.

A9.2: Size, contagion, correlation, concentration, and conditions.

A9.3: To identify systemically important banks and nonbank financial companies and make recommendations regarding heightened prudential standards for such entities, and to identify systemically important financial market utilities and payment, clearing, and settlement activities.

A9.4: If the bank has at least $50 billion in assets.

A9.5: Extent of leverage; extent and nature of off-balance-sheet exposure; extent and nature of transactions and relationships with other significant entities; its importance as a source of credit and liquidity for the U.S. financial system; its importance as a source of credit for low-income, minority, or underserved communities; the extent to which assets are managed rather than owned and the diffusion of ownership of assets under management; the nature, scope, size, scale, concentration, interconnectedness, and mix of activities; the degree to which the company is already regulated; the amount and nature of the entity's assets; the amount and type of the entity's liabilities; and other risk-related factors.

A9.6: Monetary value of transactions; exposure to counterparties; relationships, interdependencies, or other interactions with other financial market utilities; the effect of the financial market utility's failure or disruption; other factors that the FSOC deem appropriate.

A9.7: A bank whose distress or failure would threaten the global financial system and harm the economies of multiple countries.

A9.8: Cross-jurisdictional activity, size, interconnectedness, substitutability/ financial institution infrastructure, and complexity.

A9.9: According to the Financial Stability Board, " ... to ensure that G-SIBs have the loss-absorbing and recapitalisation capacity necessary to help ensure that, in and immediately following a resolution, critical functions can be continued without taxpayers' funds (public funds) or financial stability being put at risk."

Chapter 10

A10.1: Section 619 of the Dodd-Frank Act, which prohibits banking entities from engaging in proprietary trading and from owning or sponsoring hedge funds and private equity funds, and sets limits and requirements for systemically risky nonbank financial companies engaged in these activities.

A10.2: To separate federal support for the banking system from a banking entity's speculative trading activity; to reduce potential conflicts of interest between a banking entity and its customers; and to reduce risk to banking entities and nonbank financial companies that are regulated by the Federal Reserve.

A10.3: The Glass-Steagall Act.

A10.4: Proprietary trading is when an entity acts as a principal in transactions for its own trading account. A "trading account" is an account used to generate short-term profits. A "banking entity" is an insured depository institution; a company that controls an insured depository institution, a bank holding company; or any such entity's affiliate or subsidiary.

A10.5: To ensure that banking entities do not use ownership or sponsorship of hedge funds and private equity funds to circumvent the proprietary trading prohibition; to limit the private fund activities of banking entities to providing customer-related services; and to eliminate the incentive and opportunity of banking entities to bail out a private fund that they own or sponsor.

A10.6: Trading of certain securities; trading in connection with underwriting, market making, risk-mitigating hedging, and for clients; certain investments; trading by a regulated insurance company directly engaged in the business of insurance; bona fide trust, fiduciary, or investment advisory services; proprietary trading outside of the United States by banking entities not controlled by a U.S. banking entity; ownership and sponsorship of a private fund outside of the United States by banking entities not controlled by a U.S. banking entity; and other activities as deemed by regulators to promote and protect the safety and soundness of the banking entity and U.S. financial stability.

A10.7: U.S. Treasury securities; Federal National Mortgage Association (Fannie Mae) securities; Federal Home Loan Mortgage Corporation (Freddie Mac) securities; Government National Mortgage Association (Ginnie Mae) securities; Federal Home Loan Bank securities; Federal Agricultural Mortgage Corporation securities; a security issued by a Farm Credit System institution; and Municipal securities.

A10.8: The OCC, the FDIC, the Fed, the SEC, and the CFTC.

A10.9: It fails to sufficiently take account of change in financial markets, as hedge funds may take over much of the activity from which banking entities are prohibited, and their activities can harm financial stability and banks that are exposed to the activities of hedge funds. The Volcker Rule may have a negative impact on market making and liquidity provision; may harm market-maker networks; may increase the cost of capital to borrowers; and may damage bank risk management.

Chapter 11

A11.1: An agreement between two counterparties to transact in the future in which the counterparties' profit or loss is a function of the value of an underlying asset.

A11.2: An OTC derivatives agreement in which two counterparties agree to transact an underlying asset in the future for a price that is agreed upon at initiation.

A11.3: An exchange-traded version of a forward contract.

A11.4: An agreement in which two counterparties agree to transact an underlying asset in the future for a price that is agreed upon at initiation, in which one of the counterparties has the right and not the obligation to transact in the future.

A11.5: An option contract in which the long counterparty has the right to purchase the underlying asset for a fixed price in the future from the short counterparty.

A11.6: An option contract in which the long counterparty has the right to sell the underlying asset for a fixed price in the future to the short counterparty.

A11.7: An agreement between two counterparties to exchange cash flows over a number of periods of time in the future.

A11.8: A swap agreement in which two counterparties agree to exchange a fixed rate of interest for a floating rate of interest over a number of periods of time.

A11.9: A swap agreement in which two counterparties agree to exchange cash flows in distinct currencies over a number of periods of time.

A11.10: A swap agreement in which one of the counterparties agrees to make periodic payments and the second counterparty agrees to make a large payment to the first counterparty should a specified reference asset issued by a specified reference entity experience a credit event.

A11.11: To translate the rates associated with swaps into cash flows.

A11.12: As financial distress on the part of the liability counterparty will force the asset counterparty to write down the value of its asset.

A11.13: Through the use of collateral, netting, and central counterparties.

A11.14: Payment netting where payments are netted out and closeout netting where the gross assets and gross liabilities across all of the agreements are netted out should one of the counterparties to an agreement experience a termination event.

A11.15: A central counterparty clearinghouse that becomes the counterparty to both of the original counterparties to a derivative security.

A11.16: Lower counterparty credit risk and multilateral netting.

A11.17: The private bilateral nature of most OTC derivatives agreements pre-Crisis; limited understanding on the part of regulators of the nature of exposures; the low recovery values associated with insolvent financial institutions; poorly understood and difficult-to-evaluate products and strategies; and the off-balance-sheet nature of exposures.

Chapter 12

A12.1: The actual cashflows associated with an OTC derivative security are typically a small proportion of the notional principal.

A12.2: It fails to take into account closeout netting.

A12.3: It fails to take into account collateral.

A12.4: The Commodities Exchange Act of 1936, the Swap Exemption of 1993, and the Commodities Futures Modernization Act of 2000.

A12.5: A swap refers to OTC derivatives based on broad-based indexes, interest rates, and currencies, among other underlying assets. A security-based swap refers to OTC derivatives based on a single security or a narrowly defined index. A mixed swap has characteristics of both.

A12.6: It makes the clearing of OTC derivatives through a CCP mandatory.

A12.7: It mandates that OTC derivatives trade through formal platforms, such as a designated contract market, a national securities exchange, or an execution facility.

A12.8: It mandates that data related to OTC derivatives agreements be reported to, and maintained by, a registered data repository.

A12.9: The Title VII provision that prohibits the U.S. federal government from bailing out, or providing any other financial assistance to, financial institutions that participate in an OTC derivatives market, effectively forcing financial institutions that wish to participate in OTC derivatives market to push out their OTC derivatives activities to an affiliate.

A12.10: The complexity and the costs associated with complying with its provisions, as well as the concentration of counterparty exposure against CCPs, effectively creating a new type of too-big-to-fail entity.

Chapter 13

A13.1: The BIS's Basel Committee on Banking Supervision.

A13.2: To strengthen the soundness and stability of the international banking system, and to do so in a manner that is both fair and consistent so as to reduce competitive inequality.

A13.3: A bank will become insolvent if its assets drop below its liabilities or if does not have sufficient liquidity to make the payments associated with its obligations.

A13.4: Credit risk, market risk, operational risk, and liquidity risk.

A13.5: The highest quality capital, including permanent shareholders' equity and disclosed reserves.

A13.6: To require a larger capital cushion for riskier assets than for less-risky assets.

A13.7: Minimum capital requirements, supervisory review, and market discipline.

A13.8: The capital conservation buffer and the countercyclical buffer.

A13.9: A ratio of Tier 1 capital to assets where the assets are not risk-weighted.

A13.10: Through introducing two new liquidity ratios, the liquidity coverage ratio and the net stable funding ratio.

Chapter 14

A14.1: The discretionary provision of liquidity to a financial institution (or the market as a whole) by the central bank in reaction to an adverse shock that causes an abnormal increase in demand for liquidity that cannot be met from an alternative source (direct quote from Freixas et al., 1999; see note 1 in Chapter 14).

A14.2: The existence of this safety net enhances the confidence that others have when lending to financial institutions.

A14.3: Emergency lending that occurs when a financial institution is illiquid but solvent, and risk capital support for insolvent financial institutions.

A14.4: As financial institutions will be more willing to engage in risky activities and counterparties will not monitor creditworthiness as carefully.

A14.5: Ambiguity surrounding the willingness of the lender of last resort to provide emergency lending.

A14.6: To protect the money stock, provide support to the entire financial system rather than individual institutions, to behave consistently, and pre-announce policy.

A14.7: Alternative views of the function of the lender of last resort focus exclusively on open market operations; provision of temporary assistance to insolvent banks; and a free banking approach that takes the view that there is no need for a government authority to act as the lender of last resort and instead advocates the removal of legal restrictions.

A14.8: Banking panics.

A14.9: No.

A14.10: The provision of liquidity to financial institutions; provision of liquidity directly to participants in key credit markets; and expansion of open market operations.

Chapter 15

A15.1: The Credit Crisis of 2007–2009 brought to forefront for the first time the topic of *interconnectedness* as losses that originated from individual firms spread across the global financial markets due to the vast number of trading counterparties such firms maintained.

A15.2: Lehman's bankruptcy impacted 8,000 subsidiaries and affiliates worldwide, approximately 1000,000 creditors, and its 26,000 employees worldwide. In addition, Fed Chairman Ben Bernanke justified the Fed's saving of Bear Stearns by citing the beginnings of a "breakdown" in the $2.8 trillion tri-party repo market and their view that Bear " ... was so essentially involved in this critical repo financing market that its failure would have brought down that market, which would have had implications for other firms."

A15.3: Until post–Credit Crisis, risk managers and regulators generally only considered the direct risk that was posed by a distressed firm to other counterparties and did not adequately consider the vast array of interconnections that such firms had, which in some cases caused the spread of additional risk throughout the financial system.

A15.4: Basel Committee on Banking Supervision created a new methodology to determine the systemic risk posed by Globally Systemically Important Banks. This methodology consisted of five equally weighted categories, encompassing 12 distinct factors.

A15.5: The five categories include: (i) size, (ii) interconnectedness, (iii) substitutability, (iv) complexity, and (v) cross-jurisdictional activity.

A15.6: The two most relevant categories from Basel's methodology are *interconnectedness* and *substitutability*; as taken together, these categories cover a majority of the financial and operational types of interconnectedness risk, which are critical to assess.

A15.7: The two broad categories of interconnectedness are: (1) *direct and indirect financial connections:* including (i) lending relationship between two firms, (ii) derivatives contract between two firms, and (iii) trading relationships between firms and financial market infrastructures; and (2) *operational connections:* including (i) vendors and other critical third-party suppliers, (ii) settling banks, and (iii) clearing banks.

A15.8: The OFR applies three measures to its interconnectedness category: (i) intra–financial system liabilities; (ii) intra–financial system assets, and (iii) Market Value of Securities Outstanding.

A15.9: The OFR applies three measures to its substitutability category: (i) assets under custody; (ii) payments cleared and settled through payment systems, and (iii) values of underwritten transactions in debt and equity markets.

A15.10: The first step a firm should take if it decides to undertake an analysis of its interconnectedness risks is to make a comprehensive inventory of external entities on which it relies. Most financial institutions rely on adequate funding and liquidity, credit, access to markets and market infrastructures, as well as the provision of reliable and timely data—among many other processes. External entities that provide or support these services represent external interconnections to your firm. Given that insolvencies occur at a legal entity level, intragroup dependencies between distinct legal entities should also be represented as external interconnections.

Index

Printed and bound by CPI Group (UK) Ltd, Croydon, CR0 4YY

14/02/2023

03191974-0002